Making Niche Marketing Work

How to Grow Bigger by Acting Smaller

Robert E. Linneman, Ph.D.
Professor of Marketing
Saint Joseph's University

John L. Stanton, Jr., Ph.D.
C. J. McNutt Professor of Food Marketing
Saint Joseph's University

McGraw-Hill, Inc.

New York St. Louis San Francisco Auckland Bogotá
Caracas Lisbon London Madrid Mexico Milan
Montreal New Delhi Paris San Juan São Paulo
Singapore Sydney Tokyo Toronto

Library of Congress Cataloging-in-Publication Data

Linneman, Robert E., date.
  Making niche marketing work : how to grow bigger by acting smaller
/ Robert E. Linneman, John L. Stanton, Jr.
     p.   cm.
  Includes bibliographical references (p.) and index.
  ISBN 0-07-037954-8 :   —ISBN 0-07-037971-8 (pbk.) :
  1. Market segmentation.   2. Market research.   I. Stanton, John L.
II. Title.
HF5415.127.L56   1991
658.8'02—dc20   91-2029
                                                                    CIP

 This book is printed on recycled, acid-free paper containing a minimum of 50% recycled de-inked fiber.

First McGraw-Hill paperback edition published, 1992.

  2 3 4 5 6 7 8 9 0 DOC/DOC 9 7 6 5 4 3 2

ISBN 0-07-037954-8 {HC}
ISBN 0-07-037971-8 {PBK}

*The sponsoring editor for this book was Ted Nardin, the editing supervisor was
Marion B. Castellucci, and the production supervisor was Donald F. Schmidt.
This book was set in Baskerville by Carol Woolverton, Lexington, Mass.*

Printed and bound by R. R. Donnelley & Sons Company

To Annabelle and Jan

About the Authors

ROBERT E. LINNEMAN, Ph.D., is a professor of marketing at the College of Business and Administration, Saint Joseph's University, Philadelphia. He is a senior consultant in the fields of marketing and corporate planning and lectures frequently at executive development seminars. He is the author of articles which have appeared in, among others, *Harvard Business Review, Sloan Management Review,* and *Journal of Business Strategy,* and is the author of the books *A Shirt-Sleeve Approach to Long-Range Planning* and *How to Prepare and Use the Annual Marketing Plan.*

JOHN L. STANTON, JR., Ph.D., holds the C. J. McNutt Chair of Food Marketing and is a professor of marketing, Saint Joseph's University, Philadelphia. He has served as a consultant to such firms as Campbell Soup, Procter and Gamble, Frito-Lay, Miles Laboratories, and Kellogg Company, and is also a much sought-after speaker at executive development seminars. His writing frequently appears in such periodicals as *Advertising Age,* the *Journal of Advertising Research,* and the *Journal of Marketing Research.*

Contents

3. Mining for Niches: Where to Look First   26

4. Mining for Niches: Where to Look Next   40

Part 2. Differentiating Your Products and Services

Part 3. Handling Competition

Part 4. Solving Niche-Marketing Problems

Part 5. Putting It All Together

Preface

Markets are splintering. New technology serving these market segments is emerging. Competition is intensifying. No wonder firms are pursuing smaller market segments.

This phenomenon is called many names. Perhaps the most common is *niche marketing*. But don't let terminology obscure a sweeping trend—companies are focusing on smaller target markets. It's becoming—and in some industries it's already become—"niche or be niched."

Many executives are seeking insights on how to sharpen their present niche marketing strategies. Or, in some cases, how to get started in niche marketing. Yet guidelines for making niche marketing work are elusive.

The genesis of this book was to fill this need—to present a comprehensive set of guidelines on how to make niche marketing work. Guidelines that will help managers of firms, large and small, that are moving toward serving smaller and smaller market segments.

To develop these guidelines, we conducted a multistage study between 1988 and 1990. We wanted to learn how experienced companies actually coped with niche marketing problems. How did they solve the problems that arose as they moved from serving relatively few markets with limited products and services to targeting myriads of niche markets with hosts of products and services?

First we undertook a computerized literature search on niche marketing and segmentation strategies. Altogether, we sourced over 1000 articles and books over the course of two years.

Next, we surveyed the *Fortune* 1000 industrial and nonindustrial companies. Two hundred seventeen firms responded. We followed up with personal and telephone interviews with executives of 65 of these firms.

In addition, during our consulting work and executive development seminars, we talked with hundreds of executives.

From these sources we developed 20 guidelines that will help you make niche marketing work. We'll show you how to get started in niche marketing. Or, if you're already in niche marketing, how you can sharpen your techniques. We'll talk about differentiating your product or service. We'll describe how to handle competition and solve common niche marketing problems. Last, we'll explain the importance of putting it all together with a niche marketing strategy.

Of course, 20 guidelines are not inclusive. After all, books could be written on each one of these areas. Rather, these solutions are the ones that have been used for solving some of the most common problems. The guidelines will provide you with general directions, places to begin.

On the other hand, if your problems seem unique, keep this in mind. The guidelines presented here *all* resulted from problems that once seemed unique. Niche marketing is still evolving. And nobody said it's easy. But if others can solve their problems and make niche marketing work, so can you. Although the guidelines presented here may not precisely apply to your situation, they will give you insights to get started.

Acknowledgments

We are deeply indebted to the executives who answered our questionnaires and talked with us.

We also received invaluable help from business and academic colleagues. Specifically, we'd like to thank Rajan Chandran, Joel S. Dubow, Philip du Plessis, Joseph O. Eastlack, Jr., Edward E. Emanuel, Richard J. George, Mark E. Gerson, Ronald P. Gray, Kenneth R. Haldeman, Robert D. Hamilton, Daniel R. Hoffman, Patrick J. Kirschling, Richard H. Kochersperger, Harold E. Klein, Richard A. Lancioni, Johan Murphy, Mike Perry, Michael J. Thomas, Chris Von Veijeren, and James B. Wiley.

Graduate assistants, especially Karen Stevens and Nader Tavassoli, helped as well. And special thanks are due the people who helped us put it all together, Queen Mays, Naomi Elliott, Jane Coyne, Karen Labenz, Hellen White, and Rita Memmo.

The authors also wish to thank Temple University for providing funding for a one-year research leave for one of the authors, Robert Linneman, to work on the book. He was a professor of marketing at Temple University while much of the work was accomplished.

Introduction

Get bigger by acting smaller?

Sound improbable?

But it's not.

That's exactly the strategy that many of the world's largest firms are following.

A Marriott hotel used to be a Marriott hotel: an upscale hotel catering to business, pleasure, international, and group travelers. Today besides the Marriott hotels (the company's major business), there are Marriott Suites, Residence Inns by Marriott, Courtyards by Marriott, and Fairfield Inns. Each serves a smaller, targeted segment of the market.

An American Express card used to be just green. There is still a green card (the firm's major business). But now there is also a gold card. A corporate card. And a platinum card. And an optima card as well. Again, each is targeted toward a unique market.

Campbell Soup decentralized much of its marketing planning. It set up 22 regions in the United States so that it could tailor products and marketing programs to meet the unique demands of these regions.

Some refer to serving these smaller segments as *niche marketing*. Others claim it's *target marketing*. Still others call it *market segmentation*. Or *micromarketing*. In some cases, it's *regional marketing*. But don't let terminology obscure a sweeping trend—firms are focusing on smaller and smaller target markets.

There are no more mass markets. As one advertising executive says, "There will be no market for products that everybody likes a little, only for products that somebody likes a lot."[1]

1

Niche or Be Niched

Perhaps business is going well for you.

You may ask, "Why should I be concerned with niche marketing?"

Because niche marketing is becoming a way of life in most industries. And a market can change at an almost exponential rate where there are big- and small-company nichers. Slippage caused by a mass-marketing strategy may hardly be detectable at first. But by the time it becomes obvious, a good part of your market may be lost.

Perhaps you can't guard against the subtle intrusions of niche marketers into your industry. But you can seek out and hold some of the most lucrative spots in the marketplace.

Riches in Niches

Executives of the 1990s can learn from the primitive people of Africa. They realized there are two ways to cook an elephant. Either you make one pot big enough to hold the entire animal, or you cut it up in little pieces and cook it in a lot of little pots.

Markets, of course, are different from elephants. Cutting up a market into small niches often leads to a sum greater than the original market. By splitting traditional markets into segments and devising separate marketing strategies for each niche, you will be selling products and services that more closely meet customer needs. Overall, your markets will grow. And since people will pay more for products and services that more closely meet their needs, you'll make more money.

Many firms have found riches in niches. A number of years ago the Strategic Planning Institute launched a study called Profit Impact of Marketing Strategy (PIMS), which investigated hundreds of business units from different types of businesses. It reported that the return on investment from larger markets averaged 11 percent. By contrast, the return on investment from smaller markets was 27 percent![2] Smaller markets can mean bigger profits. It's reported that just before the introduction of diet Coke, Tab, with a market share of only 4 percent, contributed more net profit from in-home sales than did the mainstream product, Coke.

Or consider the United Kingdom's machine tool industry. Its success is attributed to the manufacturing of specialty machines for niche markets throughout the world.[3]

Chemical companies, producing resins, have found riches in niches. Serving specialty niches is so common that the manufacture of resins has become more of a specialty than a commodity business.[4] In fact, it's predicted that winning chemical companies will be those that can identify niches and differentiate their products to serve these markets.[5]

Evolution or the Big Bang

The new era of niche marketing has not been marked by a cataclysmic event. After all, serving niche markets has always been a way of life for smaller firms. What's new is that larger companies are also becoming niche players.

We surveyed the 500 largest industrial firms and the 500 largest non-industrial firms in the United States as ranked by *Fortune.* Over 75 percent of them have turned to niche markets for at least some of their products and services because they found that mass marketing just wasn't working anymore.

How did these firms become niche players? Basically, they used one of two approaches—evolution or the big bang.

In some cases a company, starting with one or two products, gradually moved toward smaller market segments. A bank executive from Florida explained how her firm got started:

> We eased into niche marketing gradually. Our mass-marketing approach wasn't working. But it took a real "bomb" for us to try something different.
> We tried a direct mail campaign for equity loans about 5 years ago, sending a "we generation" piece to every home owner in our market area. We got only 25 applications. Our promotion was just too general.
> Then we started looking for a particular niche and matching the offer to that group.
> Success in the initial niching venture lead to a diffusion of a niche-marketing approach throughout the bank. Organizational changes within the firm took place gradually and caused minimal disruption.

On the other hand, some firms used the big bang approach. Campbell Soup, for example, effected its regional marketing strategy overnight. Twenty-two regional marketing divisions were carved from its original nine sales territories and given marketing responsibility.[6] This approach was fraught with problems, at least in the short run. However, when the dust settled, Campbell was successfully able to execute niche strategies.

Making Niche Marketing
Work for You

The principles of niche and mass marketing are the same; their application is different. The accent is on different syllables. In niche marketing:

- *Focusing more closely* on the marketplace is essential.

- *Differentiating among products or services becomes more critical.* And because of the increased number of products and services, cannibalization is a greater threat.

- *Serving a number of different niches takes greater resources* than mass marketing. More plans. More products or services. More channels of distribution. More advertising campaigns. More sales presentations. All of which have to be coordinated and controlled.

- *Developing a marketing strategy is more complex.* A number of niche markets must be strategically linked.

A shift to a more narrowly focused marketing strategy requires changes and disruptions that most people don't like. Serving small markets can create a host of problems in production and operations, logistics, distribution channels, marketing operations, finance, and human resources.

But there is competition out there. Your competitors are ready (if they are not already doing so) to outniche you by customizing their products or services for various niches of your market.

Are You Going to Be Outniched?

If you are in a large company, your mass markets may already be eroded by niche marketers. It's time to reevaluate your marketing strategies.

If you are in a small firm, think about this: now that larger companies are also becoming niche players, you have to look for even smaller market niches. You must become even more adept in your niche strategies.

This book provides guidelines on how to make niche marketing work for you. The rules of thumb are largely derived from the experiences of the leading firms that we surveyed, the top 500 industrial companies and the top 500 nonindustrial companies in the United States. Because these companies have the resources necessary for experimentation, they often are the marketing innovators. Out of their failures and successes, we've extracted guidelines that can help you initiate and sustain a successful niche marketing strategy.

PART 1
Getting Started in Niche Marketing

1

Focus, Focus, Focus

John D. Nichols, CEO of ITW, offered this advice: "Focus, focus, focus."

Pretty good. And a good place to start.

Your markets just aren't what they used to be. They're more splintered. The causes? Consider just some of the changes that have taken place in various segments of the population: single-person households, unrelated people sharing living quarters, working mothers, career women, single-parent families, latchkey kids, senior citizens, a mosaic of ethnic groups and minorities, dinks, and the aging yuppies.

The ability you and your competitors have to serve these markets has also changed. The causes? Such changes as computer-aided design (CAD), computer-aided manufacturing (CAM), flexible manufacturing, just-in-time inventory, offshore sourcing, computer-linked purchasing, more targeted media (such as cable TV and regional magazine editions), point-of-sale information services, single-source data, and more sophisticated methods of data tracking, analysis, storage, and retrieval.

These changes represent both good news and bad news!

The good news is that you can now more narrowly target your products and services.

The bad news? So can your competitors.

So it's a double-edged sword. Or a double-edged opportunity, depending on how you look at it. It's better to look at it as an opportunity, or you won't be looking very long.

Getting Stuck in the Middle

To outniche your competitors, you've got to "focus, focus, focus." There's a story about a first-time quail hunter who kicked up a covey. He thought he didn't need to aim because the sky was so full of quail. Furthermore, with No. 8 shells, he would fill the sky with shot. He began worrying about how he would carry all the quail home. You probably know how many he got.

Zero.

Just because there are a lot of targets and you've got a lot of shot doesn't mean that you don't have to take aim.

Similarly, a broad-focused marketing strategy will often lead you to get stuck in the middle, and you'll wind up with an empty wallet. When you're stuck in the middle, you lack the economy of scale to play the low-cost game or to produce the customized product or service necessary to obviate the need for a low-cost position.

One diversified company, consisting of eleven business units, was experiencing declining sales and a resulting drop in profitability. A consultant was called in. It took the consultant only a short time to realize that all of the business units' products and services were stuck in the middle. The company had been following a broadly focused approach in each of its divisions. This strategy worked, in a limited way, when the economy was good.

Then a recession hit. Buyers could, and did, become more selective. They chose either the lowest cost or the most customized products and services. Because the company was stuck in the middle, it had to merge with another firm to fend off bankruptcy.

What causes a company to become stuck in the middle? Trying to be all things to all people. In reality, you're practicing mass marketing—offering a little bit of something to everybody.

Even if the market you serve consists of a segment that wants the lowest-cost product or service and a segment that wants the highest customization, it doesn't mean that you can't serve both. But it does mean that you can't serve both segments with a single product or service. You've got to have an offering for each segment.

Who sets out explicitly to design a strategy for a product or service that will only marginally appeal to everyone?

Nobody.

Nevertheless, such strategies do exist. How do they come about? They just evolve when not enough thought is given to the price that's being paid for compromises.

Take the case of the food company that originally targeted men, "the hearty eaters," for one of its products. Some executives were concerned about the many women who currently use the product. To exclude them from the strategy would rule out sales to women. Further concern was raised about kids, many of whom eat large portions. They, too, would be excluded.

Because of these concerns, the product was positioned to include men, women, and children. As a result, its promotion did not effectively speak to anyone. Sales were disappointing.

In desperation, the product was repositioned solely for men, "the hearty eaters." Result: it was very successful in the marketplace.

You've Got to Know the Territory

So it's focus, focus, focus, which demands better knowledge about the market. Listen to what two big-company niche marketers had to say. Michael Roach, director, marketing and research at Provident Life and Accident, said:

> Niche marketing is totally different from mass marketing.
>
> If you try to approach niche marketing from a mass-marketing point of view, you're going to fail. Suppose you've been working in a mass-marketing mode. Wipe everything out of your mind that you knew about the market and start fresh.
>
> With mass marketing, you appeal to multiple segments with one offering. But niche marketing requires keener understanding of the market. Let's say you're going to split the mass market into five segments. Now you've got to take a close look at each one of those five segments. It really involves a heavy amount of market research.

Gary Roderick, vice president and director of marketing information and planning at the Society for Savings Bank, pointed out that there is almost a direct relationship between the amount of marketing information and success in niche marketing. "We realized that once we got into niche marketing, we didn't have as much information as we needed. The more information we had, the better we could target market to customers."

You can make all kinds of assumptions when you're doing mass marketing. But when you're after the niches, you've got to have the information.

Marketing research for mass-marketed products tends to search for the lowest common denominator within a large group of people. And even so, think of the megafailures! The New Coke, 7-Up Gold, Sony Betamax, and RCA Selectravision, to name a few.

In niche marketing you're also looking for the lowest common denominator, but for a much smaller number of customers. The tolerance for error is much smaller. The need for information is much greater.

Where to Focus

Research Your Customers

There's no greater source of information than your customers. Although marketers have traditionally delegated to marketing research the responsibility of gathering information from customers, niche marketers must personally get closer to the market.

Look at an incident that happened several years ago. A bank hired an advertising agency to find out what new services treasurers of corporations would like banks to offer. The agency's researcher accordingly went out and asked treasurers what their problems were. He came up with some ideas, but most of these ideas could not be developed into feasible programs. It would have been better if a commercial lender, who was familiar with the industry, did the research. The commercial lender would have been more likely to uncover workable programs to meet the needs of corporate treasurers.

Even if you use professional researchers who have an extensive knowledge of your industry, it's almost like going on a fast diet. You take off a few pounds in a hurry, but then it's back to your old habits and back on come the pounds (plus a few more).

Professional researchers may uncover some significant findings that lead to very profitable new programs. But then they leave. Meanwhile, your markets keep changing. Rapidly. Before you realize it, you're in trouble. (You gained a few more pounds.)

Use researchers when necessary, but don't get hooked on them.

Try this approach. First, listen to what your customers and your distribution channels have to tell you. Then use researchers to verify your observations, not the other way around.

Do you remember the kids' game where someone starts a message and then it's passed on to a number of others one by one? By the time it reaches the end of the chain, the message is completely different from when it started.

When you use professional researchers, you may be playing the same game. Professional researchers frequently use unskilled hourly workers for telephone and mall intercept interviews. And then there's coding, tabulating, analyzing, report writing, and so on, often done by a different person. So by the time the final report is passed on to you, it's traveled through as many as 5 to 10 different people.

Who, in the past decade, has made the most significant advances in automobile engineering, styling, and features? It's the Japanese.

How do they do their research? By sending hoards of engineers to talk to dealers and consumers. In April 1985 Toyota sent 20 design engineers to the United States to research what customers wanted in an upscale car. For 5 months they buttonholed customers and talked with dealers.[1] Imagine—for 5 months! (When we asked American marketers about spending 5 months with customers within a market, they said they were much too busy!)

And sometimes 5 months is just a start. One Japanese company assigned engineers the task of riding around with a bulldozer operator for a year—just to find out how to make the tractor more user-friendly.[2]

That's the Japanese style. Few Japanese companies have market research departments (or anyone with the title of marketer). They look to their engineers and line people to come up with ideas that can be put into action.

Too often U.S. engineers do not get out in the field. No wonder one U.S. manufacturer told us that the most valuable ideas for product improvement came from his customers' engineers (his own engineers never talked directly to the customers).

It's bad enough when engineers do not get out in the field. But what about marketing people not getting out in the field?

Consider these two examples. A market manager from a Bell Telephone regional operating company told us that she could not talk with customers. *There was a policy against it!* Senior management perceived that talking with customers was not a good use of market managers' time. Besides, they were told that that's why there was a market research department.

In a software company, product managers also were not allowed to talk to customers. Nor did the sales force like to have them go along on sales calls. After all, the product managers just got in the way.

The irony is that in both cases these market managers were charged with developing marketing plans!

And upper management! Something has got to be done to get them away from their desks and out into the field. After all, these executives have to approve marketing plans. Sometimes, they initiate them. As the novelist John Le Carré wrote, "A desk is a dangerous place from which to watch the world."

Unfortunately, the closest many U.S. executives ever come to a customer is when they're viewing a videotape of a focus-group interview. It's shocking to note how surprised they often are when they hear what 10 customers have to say about their products or services.

Of course, many upper-level managers do make frequent field trips. But too often everything is orchestrated so that the boss will get to talk only with those employees, channel managers, and customers who espouse the company line.

Too bad. Because it's surprising how many ideas for new products or services can come from actually being in the field. Campbell Soup came up with the idea for cold soups not from marketing-research studies but from a waiter who offered a Campbell marketing manager a choice of hot or cold soup as a first course.

Mitchel Scott, manager, market and customer development, Armstrong World Industries, explained how Armstrong gets management involved in learning about their customers.

> The people who are running the business must have extensive direct contact with their customers. It's not the kind of thing you can assign to a research company and get a report on. You have to have the feel of it if you're going to make a change in the way you manage the business.
>
> We're using the people who run the businesses and key staff supporting people in cross-functional teams. They are actually doing a significant percentage of the research themselves. They're on the phone or face-to-face visiting with end-use consumers. Then, these teams analyze the information. In that way all important managers, both staff and line, have direct access to the information without filtration. We're gaining a lot of value by involving those people directly in the process.

The CEO of a large food company instituted a program that required top management to have dinner periodically with consumers at their homes. It's reported that when one vice president asked the president if he realized this would take them out of the office for 2 days every quarter, the CEO looked at him and responded, "uh huh." Then he went on to say there is nothing more important the vice president could do with his time. Think of the message that this sent to everyone throughout the organization!

Wal-Mart top executives are required to spend most Mondays through Fridays out in the field. Then on Saturdays they discuss what they found out and plan future strategies. Not a bad practice. It won't help your golf game. But it might help you stay in business.

But you don't always have to go out in the field. 3M, for example, regularly invites consumers to come to Minnesota to be part of the company's new development committees.

But since you're serving (or looking for) niches, it's important to do what Ervin Shames, president of Kraft USA, advises: "Talk to consumers individually, not as a homogeneous group."[3]

The Japanese management guru, Kenichi Ohmae, made the same point when he said that he'd rather talk with 3 housewives for 3 hours than examine the results of a 1000-person survey.[4]

Shames and Ohmae point out a crucial fact: you can't find a solution for a total industry or broad classification of consumers. You must find a solution for one user or consumer. Then, it is hoped, this solution will be applicable to a larger group.

We've found this to be a useful way to start niche marketing. Look at the market, one consumer at a time. Find a solution for that consumer. Then determine how many others would be delighted—not just satisfied—with that solution. If that number is large enough, you have a potential niche market. Whether you choose to serve that niche is a strategic question (we talk about it in Guideline 20).

This is a far better approach than the process of breaking down mass markets into smaller segments. Breaking down mass markets implies that you have products and services in search of markets (often turning out to be like a corpse in search of six pallbearers). You need to find out what delights each customer, not what is generally suitable.

Ask yourself this question, "When was the last time I sat and talked with my customers?" And by talked we mean *listened* to them. Not selling them something. Unfortunately, too many executives have to pull out their calendars to figure out the answer to that question—instead of looking at thier watches.

Scrutinize Your Company Files

Some of the most productive time you'll spend (second only to talking to consumers) will be examining company files.

Horace S. Schwerin, former vice president of corporate planning for Campbell Soup, claimed:

> Company files are choked with data documenting the economic, demographic, and lifestyle changes affecting our society. What is rare today (and always has been) is an in-depth analysis of the problems and a search to see whether a careful and creative interpretation of existing data could provide most of the answers before the decision is made to go out and collect new (additional) data.[5]

So see what you have on hand. But make sure you know your sales volumes and profitability. And look at the sales and profit histories of individual products and services.

How far back should you go? Most firms use a 5-year period. Of course, you may have a good reason for using a shorter time frame. Set up your analysis so you can make comparisons from year to year. Then, for each product and service, analyze sales and profits by markets that you're now targeting.

But don't use those data as a substitute for visiting with channels of distribution and customers and for studying what your competitors are up to. Although plumbing your database is a must, that by itself amounts to rearview management. It's putting your head in the past and backing your rear into the future.

Use Secondary Sources, But . . .

Secondary sources aren't substitutes for personal contact. Still, trade associations, government agencies, and industry and business publications can be good sources of information about the market, industry, financial ratios, and competitors. Information from these sources can be found in many libraries.

Don't make the mistake of thinking of libraries as serving only students and retired people. In Japan, for example, when you visit a library such as that of JETRO (Japanese External Trade Organization), you have to fight for a seat. And not with students or retired people—but with junior and middle-level executives who are checking out the markets.

Other good sources of information are available by using your PC. You can access syndicated data banks such as Dow Jones News Retrieval, Dun & Bradstreet, Mead Data Central, CompuServe, Find/SVP, DRI, and Predicast.

Still, we found surprisingly few firms that really used those sources. For example, we once worked with a large manufacturer of building materials who had purchased access to DRI, an on-line service providing economic data, including trend-line/time-series analysis. When we asked to use some of the time-series data, we found that no one knew how to sign onto the system. It had been 3 years since anyone in the firm had used that service!

These secondary sources provide a quick way of gaining information, but they, like analysis of in-house data, can never deliver the same information you can get from direct contact with people in the field.

The A-B-C-D of Successful Niche Marketing

The A-B-C-D of successful niche marketing is to *"Always Be Collecting Data."* If you set aside 2 weeks a year, you'll never get the job done. In the first place, you probably won't get the 2 weeks. But even if you did, 2 weeks would simply not be enough. For example, you might need secondary information, and you'll need time to write for it. Or it might be essential to talk to particular key customers who just happen to be on vacation.

Successful niche marketing requires many bits of information gathered over a period of time. This results in small insights here and there, rather than in a sudden bolt of lightning from a gigantic, once-a-year, last-minute study.

Make customer contact and gathering customer information a way of life.

Recap

Yesterday's mass markets are crumbling. Today's customers look for products and services developed especially for them. Your competitors are scrambling to dominate first one niche and then another. And now you're ready to play this niche market game yourself. How can you win?

1. Aim for a specific target. Otherwise you'll find yourself stuck in the middle, hoping somehow that your product or service will appeal to the "average" consumer. It won't, because there's no such thing.

2. Talk to your customers. One at a time. Find a solution for that customer. Then determine how many others would be delighted with that solution.

3. Hire researchers to verify your findings. Analyze your own files. Use secondary sources like libraries, government reports, and communication services.

4. Let the A-B-C-D of successful niche marketing be your guide: *Always Be Collecting Data*. That's the only way you'll ever become a top niche-market player.

2
Building a Niche-Marketing Database

Always Be Collecting Data. A good rule to follow

But the A-B-C-D rule—by itself—is not enough. Niche marketers we talked with were quick to point out that you've got to have a system for data storage and retrieval. Also, that you've got to be able to retrieve the data in a way that will give information for decision making.

Too bad that many companies' databases just take up space. We asked people in a number of different firms if they had databases that provided information for action. Most responded, "Of course!" with the implication, "What a stupid—even insulting—question." They also claimed they had so much data they didn't know what to do with it all.

Further probing revealed they were right on one point: they had reams of printouts that provided data. But that's as far as it went. They had little information upon which to base action.

In one case involving a service company (one that also had so much data they didn't know what to do with it), we asked to see the most rudimentary information on sales, by product line.

First they explained, "We'll have it shortly. The data isn't in the computer in the form you want it." Two weeks later we heard, "It won't be much longer." And then, a week later, "Couldn't we use some other information?" It turned out that expensive programming was needed to get the very basic data we had requested.

An executive vice president of a large market research company commented to us on this puzzling fact: many of his company's clients lacked

16

well-organized databases. In fact, many did not even have a list of their key customers.

Maybe you're a niching pioneer in your industry, and almost anything works. But competition is out there. You'll never sustain your position as a niche marketer without a database that can help you act.

Vince Gennaro, division marketing vice president, Pepsi-Cola Central, says:

> Information technology has really served to illuminate the conditions and behaviors in the marketplace . . .
> Marketers can answer key questions such as: in each market, what trade and consumer segments are my key competitors strong and weak in? What are the buying patterns of consumers in warehouse stores versus conventional supermarkets? Or, what regional competitor has sourced its volume from my brands' users? . . .
> There is now significant room for a forward-thinking company to gain a competitive edge by making a commitment to information systems.[1]

Lack an action-oriented database?

Then get started on building one.

Profit by the experiences of large-company niche marketers. Follow these nine rules.

1. You Be the Boss

Chances are you don't have the skills to design and program the database. You'll need the help of experts.

For years the experts were either corporate accountants or their clones. They collected data to facilitate financial reporting for annual reports or for taxes. Although these database gatekeepers were willing to share their data, they were not willing to "mess up" their databases. The result: data that did not provide the kind of information needed by marketing managers.

Don't let "experts" take over. During the database planning process, play a key role. Tell the information experts what you do, what information you need, and in what form you need it.

But what if you don't have that kind of clout? Then find other people in the company who also believe in the need for useful marketing data. There's strength in numbers! Look beyond the marketing department. Include people from a variety of functional areas.

And, if you use an outside data collection company, don't use the data it sends you to structure the content of your database. For example, A. C. Nielsen provides data on market size, market share, and so forth.

Nielsen's data is based on markets defined by companies that sell similar products. Such information, though valuable for many uses, is usually too general for niche marketing.

Take Alpo Pet Food Company, for example. Alpo developed a consumer perceptual map to analyze the dog-treat market. This study pointed to a super premium dog snack—a niche that was not broken out in Nielsen data. This niche was small, but these consumers were willing to pay a very high price for the "right" dog treat. If Alpo had relied only on Nielsen data, it would have missed this very profitable market.

2. Build Your Database around the Market

Many companies do not have basic market data. For example, a consumer diet-product company could only account for 50 percent of its product sold at retail, according to one of its executives. They knew which wholesalers and retailers were buying the product from their factory, but after that . . .

Companies are finding major new opportunities by focusing on various points in the channel or by stimulating final demand. For years pharmaceutical firms, selling prescription drugs through pharmacies, never advertised to consumers. It was taboo. Besides, everyone knew that doctors were the only channel point where a marketing effort would pay off. Now pharmaceutical companies engage in consumer advertising for prescription drugs. And it pays off.

But to be able to stimulate demand among channel members and end users, you've got to know who they are.

Anne Klein II, a division of Takihyo Inc., has amassed a database of over 85,000 customers through its "At Your Service" toll-free number. According to Nancy Hegy of Anne Klein II, "From those calls we've gotten good feedback about who our customers are."[2]

We were told by many companies that they couldn't track their sales. Especially at the user level.

"We have millions of customers. It's impossible to keep track of them. We can't do it."

Maybe in the 1960s and 1970s they couldn't.

Or even in the 1980s they couldn't.

But in the 1990s, they can. Just ask Philip Morris. Philip Morris gathered information on about 2 million smokers who responded to a direct-marketing campaign. Philip Morris sees this data as part of its ever-expanding database.[3]

Vons, a West Coast food retailer, uses a customer-activated check-authorization card to collect information on its customers. The retailer utilizes information from its 2 million card users to deliver shopping experiences that respond to specific customer needs.

While some might think 2 million card users is quite a system, Roger E. Strangeland, chairman and CEO of Vons, as with executives at Philip Morris, thinks it's just the beginning. As Strangeland pointed out, "We're still in the embryonic stages of utilizing the program but it holds enormous promise."[4]

No doubt the best source of information on new opportunities is from current customers. But nonusers should also be included.

For example, one manufacturer of industrial products did a good job in tracking its sales. Analysis indicated that the firms's products had high penetration in each segment it served. However, when analysis was expanded to include other segments, the company realized how many opportunities it was missing.

3. Look Beyond the "Convenient Stuff"

Databases are almost always oriented toward pure numbers because it's easy to enter the amount of purchases by your customers. But the why can also be determined and made part of the record. Include reasons *why* specific customers buy your product. Or better yet, *why* and *how* consumers use your products.

Gerber Products' database does just that. Gerber collected and maintained information on questions that mothers asked on its telephone hot line. One problem occurred repeatedly: what to do with the half-full baby-food jars left after feeding an infant. The frequency of this question pointed to a marketing opportunity. Gerber came out with a new product called First Foods—a downsized jar for infants just beginning solid food. First Foods was hailed as a marketing breakthrough.[5]

About the same time Gerber was registering this success, another food company was using its 800 hot line to help customers make better use of its products. The right thing to do. But unfortunately no data was retained. When asked why it wasn't incorporated into the firm's database, the director of consumer services asked, "What would we do with all this data?" This company's hot line gathered valuable information and then, in effect, lost it.

An unusual situation?

Not at all.

One major food company said it had no inexpensive way to identify individuals who use its products. Yet the company never made any attempt to use redeemed coupons, rebate forms, hot lines, and so on, to get this information. The fact was this company was a mass marketer. The firm's marketing personnel didn't want that information because they didn't know (or care to know) what to do with it.

Make sure that every communication with your customers is screened to see if it should be added to your database.

4. Include Profit Analysis in Your Database

Surprisingly few databases have profit information by products and services, distribution channels, and target markets. Without this information, it's tough to be a niche marketer.

For example, one executive told us he primarily bases his decisions on sales figures. Why? Because he has almost no idea what the real profits are.

And that's too bad.

We all can be mesmerized by high sales, even though we're uncertain of profitability. But when that happens, it sounds a death knell for niche marketing. Profit analysis is essential.

Under a mass-marketing approach, relatively few markets are served with relatively few products and services. Although profit figures may be only approximations, one still has some idea (sometimes a very good idea) as to what products and services and markets are the most profitable.

But niche marketing greatly increases the number of products, services, and markets. The profitability of various products, services, and markets becomes less obvious.

Our congratulations go to the retail food industry. It's made great strides toward profit analysis. There's a high level of computerization within the industry. At the store level, there's sophisticated analysis of sales, space, personnel management, and, in some cases, customer analysis. And the payoffs have been high.

The profit-analysis system, called direct product profit (DPP), has had an eye-opening effect on how the industry now looks at food manufacturers. Supermarkets know which products are profitable and which are not. They know this better than manufacturers do, and this gives the stores tremendous leverage in discount and promotion bargaining and, of course, in demanding slotting allowances.

DPP also helps in analysis of department performance within stores. The dairy section was once considered a necessary evil. But DPP has shown that the dairy section is very profitable. On the other hand, some departments with high sales volume (previously considered high-profit centers) have been found to operate at a loss.

DPP has caused many supermarket chains to revise their marketing philosophy. They used to have identical store-merchandise formats. Now each supermarket is stocked to reflect local demand, allowing for sales of high-margin niche products. Vons Pavilions in California, Byerly's in the Midwest, and Macy's Cellar and the Food Emporium in New York tempt "high-touch" shoppers with the sight and aromas of exotic seafoods and freshly baked breads.

Another niche targeted by Vons, owners of Pavilions, is the Hispanic market. Called Tianguis, one-half of this 60,000-sq ft supermarket is for fresh food. Tianguis also offers cookware, such as automatic tortilla makers.

A Florida supermarket chain repositioned its stores—on a store-by-store basis. Each store stocks, promotes, and prices products according to who lives nearby and is likely to drop in.

But in spite of the retail food industry's relative database sophistication, it's still in its embryonic stage. Virtually all of the chains we spoke to claim to use no more than 5 percent of all the data they gather!

5. Collect Data So That Trends Can Be Examined

Unfortunately, constructing a database that permits year-to-year analysis is tough. It requires what most management abhors: planning beyond any budget period. There is also the problem of allocating costs.

Following is an example of what often happens when an attempt is made to construct a database. A large food company proposed collecting data on a very simple issue, "How concerned are you about _____ ? [a specific nutrition interest, such as cholesterol]." Data would be collected on both users and nonusers of the company's products. To identify changes in consumer concerns, surveys would be conducted periodically over a number of years.

The project was turned down strictly over accounting issues. Product managers did not want to pay for data that they didn't currently need. And no one would pay for information on nonusers.

The sequel? Quite frequently these same product managers say, "Although _____ is an issue with consumers today, I wish we could predict how they will feel next year." Consumer opinions could have been better forecasted if the product managers at the food company had authorized the study.

The lesson? A company's cost allocation may have to be revised in order to fund long-term, longitudinal studies.

6. Include Competition in Your Database

Marketers have traditionally been egocentric, paying attention primarily to *their* customers, *their* advertising, and *their* companies. But a good many of the failures in the marketplace come from assuming that competitors are going to roll over and play dead.

Current marketing strategists tell us to keep one eye on the competition. To a niche marketer (or any type of marketer), information on competitors is vital. Guidelines 10 and 11 cover both what information you need and how to use it.

7. Make Sure Your Database Helps You to Better Understand Relationships

It's not just a question of knowing that you have so many customers who purchase so much in a given quarter. Or so many customers in various income brackets. Or certain customers who have particular psychographic characteristics. You have to be able to react to this data. You need a system that will tell you if this niche is like "X," then "Y" should be done.

Being able to react to database information helps in a number of ways. The shipments at Caroline Freight are all coded. This helps the company find prospects for certain niche services, such as unique transportation methods for hazardous materials. Since shipments are coded, it's simple to get a list of all its shippers and receivers of any type of hazardous materials. The company can then use this list for its direct mailings.

At INB Financial, proper use of the database facilitates cross-selling. Warren L. Smith, first vice president, explained to us how it works.

> We know what services our customers use. We know where they live. We look at demographic overlays. Then we can say that the people who live in this neighborhood generally have these characteristics. We can take that down to the block code. We can look at what most people in that geographic area have in the way of services. If a certain unit in that area doesn't have that array, we can market to them directly.

You have an edge any time you can offer specifically to someone something that they most likely would want or should have.

Now a prospect may have his or her major account with a competitor, but if you can offer the prospect a service that he or she really needs, then the relationship between you and the prospect is drawn much closer.

8. Have a Central Collection Place

Information is often lost simply because people don't know where to send it. For example, a company wanted to find out what was happening to information flows. A significant piece of information was planted within its sales force. The company was shocked to find out that none of the salespersons passed it on. When asked why, the salespersons said they had not idea where to send it!

One pharmaceutical company addressed this problem by providing its field staff with an 800 number that is just for reporting any competitive or market information. The person answering the phone then decides where the information should be directed.

American Express also has a system to gather information. Betsy Ludlow, vice president of student marketing, had this to say, "Services [for the platinum-card holders] developed over the past 8 years have been derived from listening to customer service calls at the operations center."[6] Although Ms. Ludlow says "listening" was the source of the ideas, we contend that having a system to receive that information was equally important.

And American Express' experience points out another principle. Although it's important to have systematic data collection, the method of collecting the data should not be so structured that it prevents ad hoc information from getting into the database.

9. To Get Started, First Examine the Data You Have on Hand

Remember how Horace S. Schwerin, formerly of Campbell Soup, advised an in-depth analysis of company data before going out and collecting additional data?

Do what he advised.

And take this from us. When you begin an audit of all the information currently present in your company, you'll have two reactions: first, surprise; then, depression. You'll be surprised because so much information is around. You'll be depressed because it will take so much effort to organize it.

You may have the reverse problem. The president of a small computer software company commented to us about starting the database for his company:

> At first I was discouraged. We just did not have enough information in our files. Furthermore, there was not much published data available either on the target market or our competitors.
>
> But I began to poke around, and I realized that I had more information than I originally thought. For example, although there was not much secondary information on our target markets, still there were data from general industry surveys . . .These data gave us valuable insights regarding key buying motives and other information about our target markets.
>
> Then, although our company records couldn't break out key customers per se, I was able to learn a lot by organizing customers according to billing discounts.
>
> I found that even though I had limited information, I was learning more about my business than ever before.
>
> Furthermore, I've set up procedures to make sure that I'll have the information in the future. For example, for every software package sold, before it goes out the door, I insist that certain information is recorded . . .

He went on to say that analyzing the database, even in its limited stage of development, "has given me new perspectives about our business."

Recap

There you have it. Nine rules to help you build a better niche-marketing database:

1. You be the boss.
2. Build your database around the market.
3. Look beyond the "convenient stuff."
4. Include profit analysis in your database.
5. Collect data so that trends can be examined.
6. Include competition in your database.
7. Make sure your database helps you to better understand relationships.
8. Have a central collection place.
9. To get started, first examine the data you have on hand.

What types of data will you need? Think of the types of decisions you make today. Also think of the kind of information you'll need in the future. After you've read the remaining guidelines in this book, you'll have a better idea of what you'll need.

Sure, it will take time to develop a good database. But you'll get immediate payoffs. As you go through the process, you'll uncover information that will lead to immediate marketing successes.

But start on your database soon. You'll find you have more time in the short run than you think. But less time in the long run than you think.

3
Mining for Niches: Where to Look First

In a speech called "Acres of Diamonds," Russell Conwell told a story about Ali Hafed, a wealthy Persian farmer. One day Ali Hafed heard of the fabulous wealth he could possess if only he owned a diamond mine. That night he went to bed a poor man. Not because he had lost anything, but because he realized he was not as rich as he could be. He knew he must have a diamond mine.

So he sold his fruitful farmlands and began his search. Far and wide he roamed. Youth and wealth dwindled. Ali Hafed, aged, destitute, and brokenhearted, cast himself into the ocean, never to be seen again.

However, not long after Ali Hafed had sold his farm, the most magnificent diamond mines in all of history—the Golconda mines—were discovered on Ali Hafed's old farm.

Of course you're interested in increasing sales and profits. But before you go off into "foreign" lands, focus on your current customer base. Here lie your greatest strengths.

Possibly your present market should be redefined into smaller segments. You can grow bigger by acting smaller. Your customer base is probably *not* homogeneous; wipe out the concept of "our average customer." If 20 percent buy every week and 80 percent just occasionally—say every 3 months—does that mean your "average customer" buys about once every 3 weeks?

Likewise, if 50 percent of your customers are crazy about your product or service and 50 percent just feel so-so about it, does this mean that your "average customer" thinks your product or service is pretty good?

26

(Someone who believes that probably wonders how a person could drown in a lake whose average depth is only 3 inches.)

GTE Service Corporation found that its customers' key buying motives varied. Start-up companies wanted technical assistance, while mature firms wanted technical advances in products and services. The solution: GTE designed packages of servicing options from which individual accounts could choose.

Think in terms of increasing sales—and profits—by looking for niches in your present markets. Then serve each niche's needs better by adapting your present products and services to meet customers' preferences in each niche.

Here are 12 questions to test the appropriateness of your present segmenting strategy for a given product or service. While going through these questions, continually ask yourself, "Have I segmented this market finely enough? Or am I trying to be all things to all people?"

1. Who Are Your Heavy, Heavy Users?

OK. So you know who your heavy users are. And you're concentrating your efforts here. That makes sense. You're spending most of your time (and budget) on the 20 percent of your customers who account for 80 percent of your business. Following the old 80-20 principle.

So far, so good.

But what about your really heavy users? You may have a small percentage of your customers who purchase a very large percentage of your product or service.

For example, the airlines found out that 4.1 percent of adults made 70.4 percent of all airline trips.[1] These were the heavy users. So, to court their favor, frequent flier programs were rolled out.

But among this 4.1 percent—the heavy users—there was a group of really heavy users. Those who took trips to Hong Kong, Calcutta, Marrakech, and the like. Once a month. Or more. To make sure they didn't lose these customers to other airlines—and to gain some heavy, heavy fliers from other airlines—programs like United's Executive Premier (for those who fly 75,000 miles or more a year) were developed.

At Chase Manhattan, once you've arrived (with a heavy, heavy account), you don't have to wait in line. Instead, you'll get your own personal banker. Need a lot of money but the bank is closed? No worry. You can get a cashier's check delivered to your apartment. You'll be invited to special dinner parties at Chase Manhattan's posh Madison Avenue branch. Amid Persian rugs, marble halls, and crystal chandeliers, you'll get to know some of the bank's wealthiest clients. Like yourself.

Casinos know how to take care of their heavy, heavy spenders—the high rollers. If you're a high roller, you not only don't have to wait in line, you're picked up in one of the casino's jets. And then chauffeured to the casino. You'll be given a complimentary suite that would cost the quarter slot players $1000 a night. After checkout the staff will scour your room to find out more about your personal preferences. Like the gum you chew. Or the cigarettes you smoke. And they'll enter this information into their computer. When you return, your favorites will be waiting for you.

If you have heavy, heavy users, no doubt you reward them from time to time. But have you explicitly singled them out? Do you have a marketing program in place for them?

Now we know what managers at consumer products companies would have to say: "Well, we can't keep track of the millions of users of our products just to find the 1 percent or 2 percent who are heavy, heavy users." Those managers should take another look at Guideline 2, "Building a Niche-Marketing Database."

2. Who Are Your Light Users?

Following the 80-20 rule, one national beverage processor targeted the heavy users of milk in an advertising campaign. However, because these heavy users already drank a lot of the beverage, it was difficult to increase their consumption.

At the same time, the other 80 percent of the market was neglected. The many submarkets that have very low per capita consumption were prime material for niche marketing programs.

It makes sense to treat your 20 percent with respect. But it makes no sense to ignore your other 80 percent.

Industry leaders often neglect the minor purchasers who are (or might become) the fastest-growing market segments. Witness what happened to General Motors, Ford, and Chrysler when they ignored the consumers who wanted small cars. Or Xerox when it disregarded the market segments that wanted small copiers.

Sometimes the light users can lead to new and potentially profitable market segments. So check out your light users.

That's what Hillside Coffee did. It found light coffee usage among teens and adults in their early twenties, groups made up of individuals known for having a sweet tooth. The solution was sweet-flavored coffee blends like Vanilla Nut, Swiss Chocolate Almond, and Chocolate Macadamia.

Or sunglasses. Formerly most upscale sunglasses were sold through opticians. To cater also to the younger light-user niche, college students, Sunglass Hut Corporation went to the malls and later to sporting goods stores and campuses. The result? Sanford Ziff, who started Sunglass Hut (now the largest sunglass retailer in the United States, says, "When I started, we sold most of our Ray-Ban Wayfarers to people in their forties. Today, teens and college students can't seem to get enough of them."[2]

Only 4 percent of Thor Industries Inc.'s Airstream travel trailers were sold to people under 45. To bring in younger buyers, Airstream launched the Land Yacht line, which was more affordable than Airstream's Silver Bullet. This strategy was designed to achieve two objectives: (1) to increase immediate sales and (2) to introduce younger buyers to Airstream in the hope that they will become tomorrow's heavy users.[3]

It's true that in many cases your light users may never become tomorrow's 20 percent. Still, you might be able to convince them to spend more. For instance, Forster's ad campaign, "Diet for Two," shows an ice bucket with a 22-oz. bottle of beer. Although Foster is trying to persuade women to drink more beer, it's doubtful they are trying to get women to match quaffing with the steelworkers of Pennsylvania.

You can be sure of one thing. People change. They grow older. They become more sophisticated. They take up new hobbies. They pursue the latest fads. Or they just don't have a reason for buying much of your product or service. But you'll never convince those light users to buy more by ignoring them. Look for the diamonds in your own backyard.

3. Which Customers Are Expanding Their Purchases?

If some customers are suddenly buying more, they may point to new markets.

Joseph McQuade, manager of worldwide business development for Convatec, told us how Convatec noticed its sales for Stomahesive, an adhesive dressing used to attach colostomy devices, were far greater than was expected. Research revealed that doctors and nurses liked the adhesive qualities of Stomahesive. They were cutting up the dressings and using them for other purposes. So Convatec came out with Duoderm. It was essentially the same product, but it was cut into strips that made it easy for doctors and nurses to use. A success? You bet!

In the 1950s and 1960s, skim milk was often available only in boxed powdered form. Then, as customers began to turn away from fat-laden dairy products, milk consumption dropped until savvy marketers detected a rise in skim milk sales. Customers gladly returned to supermarket milk cases to stock up on the latest liquid version of the perfect food. And they bought it in far greater quantities than the powdered form.

So don't just sit back and grin when one of your products or services shows unexpected gains. Find out who's buying and why. The answers may help you turn casual admirers into first-rate suitors.

4. Which Customers Are Decreasing Their Purchases?

Milk companies noticed that as their customers grew older, they drank less milk. One of the reasons? Milk is too hard to digest for many elderly people who have a deficiency of lactase. The solution: put an enzyme in milk so it's more digestible.

Some supermarkets were not happy with their sales growth rates. They knew customers should be spending more in their stores. They discovered that some customers were stopping at delis after visiting their stores to pick up something for their evening meals at home. To cater to this niche, in came salad bars and supermarket delis containing prepared foods. And the food is not cooked by amateurs either. For instance, Kings, a New Jersey supermarket chain, hires experienced chefs.

When good customers begin to spend less, you owe it to yourself, and to them, to find out why. You may not miss them at first, particularly if stable overall sales mask the decline in their spending. But you will miss them eventually. Perhaps a small change in your product or service will bring them back. Perhaps you'll need to make a big change. But think twice before you close your eyes to customers who begin to close their wallets. It costs less to keep a customer than to gain a new one.

5. Where Are Your Customers Located?

Sometimes overlooked are the geographic differences within a country. For instance, in the United States, geographic differences may be greater than you think. Look at what an automobile manufacturer faces. People on the East and West Coasts like small cars. Per capita sales of small cars are twice as high in these regions than they are in the middle states.

In the Southeast, people want compact pickups. But in the Southwest, buyers prefer full-size pickups.

Compare Miami with Houston. Miami households have fewer children, and the city is geographically more compact than Houston. Guess where more station wagons are sold?

Small wonder that automobile manufacturers are splitting up the mass market and trying to grow bigger by acting smaller.

Campbell Soup found out that, on the average, its soups were "just right." But the "just right" was based on averages. The soups were too spicy for Midwesterners and too bland for people in the Southwest. The solution: Campbell adapted their soup recipes to regional tastes.

So take a close look at your customer base. By region. By urban neighborhood versus rural neighborhood. By city. By zip code. Or possibly even by block.

6. Which Customers Can You Serve Most Profitably?

What are two of the most profitable sections in the supermarket?

The salad bar and prepared food.

Astute supermarket managers noticed that many of the noontime customers were shopping at the salad bar and prepared food sections just to buy lunch. In response to this observation, supermarkets developed promotional programs, such as sending fliers to nearby office complexes, to increase sales to this profitable niche.

Wawa, a convenience food chain, noticed that many of its customers were buying sandwich fixings at lunch time. They did the logical thing: in-store sandwich preparation.

Produce growers thrive on consumer pick-your-own programs. They shift the cost of picking, warehousing, and transportation (often the lion's share of costs) to the consumer. Then too, the consumers' quality standards dramatically change. They accept produce in a pick-your-own situation that they would never accept in a retail environment. (Ever try filling up a 5-gal pail with perfect strawberries? After the first pint, anything that's close to red looks good. Mighty good.)

The end results are larger profits for the producers. For the consumer, cheaper produce, besides the thrill of eating it fresh picked! Everybody wins.

7. Do Your Customers Have Different Price Sensitivities?

Quite frequently there's a rather wide range of price sensitivity within a company's customer base. Airlines and hotels found that pleasure travelers were far more price sensitive than people on business.

Credit card companies discovered that some customers wanted all kinds of services regardless of the price. Not so with others.

Banks found that senior citizens watched their finance and bank charges more closely than other patrons did. So at many banks it's free checking for the Gray Panthers.

Office supply companies felt they were insulated from price cutters. After all, they offered their bread-and-butter clients, the corporate accounts, service (and they really did). Furthermore the corporate accounts were believed to be rather price insensitive. But office supply companies were shocked when many of their corporate customers, both large and small, flocked to discount office-supply houses such as Staples. Customers abandoned the extra service in exchange for 50 to 70 percent discounts. As the old saw goes, "Every man has his price."

So look at your customers, and examine their price sensitivities. These might reveal a number of niches.

8. What Do Your Customers Really Value?

Key buying motives will probably vary within your customer base. Examine your customers according to the following eight nonprice dimensions.[4]

- *Performance.* The performance of a product or service involves basic use characteristics. For example, for an airline performance might be defined by the frequency of scheduled trips and duration of flight (that is, nonstop service). For a bank it could mean location (convenience) and the type of services offered. For an automobile, it might be handling comfort, cruising speed, and acceleration.

  It's difficult, however, to develop an overall performance ranking because a product or service might have basic-use characteristics not universally needed or wanted. For example, 0 to 60 mi/h in 6 seconds might cause a teenager's eyes to light up in delight. It probably would also cause a 70-year-old's eyes to light up—in horror.

  Or take Velcro, which is used in both industrial and consumer products. Auto manufacturers use Velcro to hold the interior lining against roof panels. The desired performance characteristic is extreme adhesiveness. Velcro straps are sometimes used instead of laces for kids' shoes. Use the same adhesive quality for those straps as is used for auto interior linings, and kids would sleep with their boots on.

- *Features.* The features of a product or service include characteristics that supplement basic-use characteristics. For an airline, features might include comfortable waiting-area facilities or above standard inflight meals. Since needs vary widely with consumers, many firms customize the features of their products and services for different niches. For example, manufacturing firms, through flexible production, are offering more models and product options.

- *Reliability.* Reliability is the functioning of a product or service within a specific time frame, such as the mean time to first failure, the mean time between failures, and the failure rate per unit of time.

    The repairer was a regular visitor when TV sets bulged with mysterious tubes. Transistors changed all that, and now customers simply won't put up with frequent breakdowns.

- *Conformance.* To what degree does a product's design and operating characteristics meet established standards? For example, do dimensions for parts and purity of materials fall within industry standards? Failures to conform to standards can be measured by the number of defects found through inspection.

    In the area of service, conformance is concerned with accuracy and promptness. When you call your local catering service to provide lunch for a staff meeting, you expect to get exactly what you ordered and while everyone is still in the mood for lunch.

- *Durability.* Durability is a measure of the use a consumer gets before a product breaks down and replacement is considered necessary. To stress durability, some manufacturers of automobile components, such as mufflers, even offer guarantees for the lifetime of the car.

- *Serviceability.* People have different standards of what constitutes acceptable service and differing thresholds of tolerance for breakdowns. For example, many direct-marketing businesses, such as Time-Life books and videos advertised on TV, use their 800 lines for much—or perhaps all—of their revenue-generating activity. Telephone downtime cannot be tolerated.

    AT&T now offers a program to route your incoming calls to another working phone within a very short period of time if your 800 number should go out of service.

- *Aesthetics.* Aesthetics is purely subjective. Stereo sound can be quantified in decibels. But the level that teenagers find pleasing would send adults scurrying for bomb shelters (which, we can assure you, are hard to find nowadays).

- *Perceived Quality.* The consumer's impression of your product or service is particularly important with first-time or infrequent buyers, when buyers cannot measure performance accurately, and when products and services are customized.

    Buyers will pay only for what they believe is quality, but buyers' perceptions of quality may be the result of your signals. In one way or another, the signals your firm sends define value to your customers. Signals include:

Reputation of your firm
Impressiveness of your customer list
Perceived dominance and/or stability of your product or service
Packaging of the product or service
Appearance of the product or service
Advertising and brochures
Sales force
Price (where price is an indicator of a superior product or service)
Size and financial stability of your company
Appropriateness of your facilities

Because signaling is often done unconsciously, you may be sending signals to your customers that are counterproductive. To avoid this, determine the appropriate signals by examining your customers' key buying motives. For example, if the key buying motives are performance and dependability, then signal reputation (testimonials); if the perceived dominance and stability of your product or service are important, then an impressive customer list would be of value.[5]

Now let's assume you've examined your customer base, and you notice wide variances in key buying motives among your customers. You've hit pay dirt. You've found hidden niches.

That's what they did at Du Pont. Its discrete clinical analyzer is a highly sophisticated, automated laboratory instrument used in the health-care industry. The analyzer is expensive, costing tens of thousands of dollars. And that's just for starters. Operating supplies sometimes cost as much as the analyzer.

After 10 years the market was saturated. However, one niche of the target market was largely untapped: small hospitals and clinics. This niche had different key buying motives than the larger hospitals. Besides lower costs, training was needed on how to use the discrete clinical analyzer; reliable servicing was also needed.

To meet this niche's needs, Du Pont put together a special program. First, they came out with a new model for the large hospitals, giving liberal trade-in allowances. Then Du Pont reconditioned the trade-ins. The reconditioned instruments were sold, along with on-site training and service guarantees, to the small hospitals and clinics. Sales to this niche increased threefold.[6]

This successful niche-marketing program was developed because Du Pont noticed wide variations in key buying motives among its customers.

It's helpful to have a system to identify these variations. In the Appendix you will find worksheets to identify key buying motives for industrial products; professional services; and packaged foods, beverages, and drugs. If one of these worksheets doesn't match your product or service, select the one that's the closest fit and make adaptations.

For each one (or line) of your products or services, go through the worksheet and check off key buying motives. If you're marketing a given product or service to more than one target market, then do this separately for each product or service target market. (The *target market* is the segment of the market that you are serving with a given marketing mix—product or service, price, promotion, and place.) We've found it to be particularly helpful if two or three persons go through the worksheet independently and then compare notes.

Focusing on your customers will probably reveal differing key buying motives among your target market. If so, you will have uncovered hidden niches.

9. Do Your Customers Have the Same Frequency of Purchase?

You probably have a group of customers who purchase your product only infrequently. How can you make people who sporadically buy your product or service become frequent purchasers? Let's see how some companies have tackled this problem.

Some have used clubs: the "Book-of-the-Month" Club, record clubs, videotape clubs. You name it, there's a club for it. Clubs make it easy—and cheap—for consumers to get started. And then every month customers can pick from an outstanding collection, converting infrequent purchasers into those who buy once a month. This is especially true for subscribers who must let the company know when they don't want next month's selection.

A variation of the club idea is the Fruit-of-the-Month offered by members of the Florida Gift Fruit Shippers Association. People like to give fancy boxed fruit as gifts, but they only come to Florida once a year. So the gift-fruit retailers sell subscriptions for monthly (or any frequency) shipments. Another win-win situation. The customer gets fancy fruit all year long, and the retailer sells more fruit. Simple but profitable.

There are only just so many birthdays and holidays each year. So with general-card sales growth of only 0.6 percent, greeting card companies turned to untapped niches. People who would just like to send a card of thanks. To thank a child for cleaning his or her room (part of Hallmark's To Kids With Love line). Or to thank a person for a great evening. Or to send a card just to express an emotion, such as missing someone, or love, or joy.[7]

Thanksgiving and Christmas are big holidays for turkeys. But then, after these occasions, sales drop off. After all, who wants to wrestle with a 20-pounder week after week? So many companies, such as Perdue and Louis Rich, came out with all kinds and sizes of turkey parts, from fresh to microwaveable to precooked. Did it work? Just look at turkey sales.

Companies are using the same strategy with chickens. Tyson Foods slices up more than 57 varieties of chicken products, from parts to gourmet dinners, and has had outstanding success. Tyson's value-added sales (versus basic poultry) increased by over $1 billion between 1980 and 1988.[8]

Usually you've got to play a proactive role. For example, in the 1950s and 1960s a summer vacation was the norm. Only a few went to the Caribbean in the winter. And what about now? Do you think millions of Americans coincidentally decided to go to Jamaica, St. Croix, and the British Virgin Islands for a second vacation? Or, could it have been the airlines, the cruise ship companies, and destination marketing at work?

Maybe your product or service is by definition the type that customers need only infrequently. Such as catering for a wedding (let's face it—most people get married only twice). Or tombstones (again let's face it—most people get buried only once). But if you have some frequent purchasers, you usually can find more.

10. What Promotion Best Appeals to Your Various Customers?

Do some of your customers prefer a person-to-person sales approach? Would another method of sales promotion, such as a direct mail sweepstakes, be more effective for others?

When different customers have different key buying motives, you often have to vary your promotional efforts. For example, Du Pont produces Kevlar, a fiber that's stronger yet lighter than steel. Some of the market segments that Du Pont identified were aircraft designers, plant engineers, and commercial fishing-boat owners. Each of these segments had different key buying motives. For aircraft designers, the high strength-to-weight ratio of Kevlar was appealing. Plant engineers were interested in using Kevlar in asbestos-free pumps. For commercial fishing-boat owners, Kevlar could be used in the construction of boats that would carry more fish and travel at increased speed.

So advertising to each of these segments was different, although the product was the same. To the aircraft designers Du Pont said, "The L-1011 is 807 pounds lighter because of Kevlar 49." To the industrial plant managers Du Pont said, "Now, a better answer to your toughest packing problems: asbestos-free Kelvar." To the commercial fishing-boat owners Du Pont said, "The boat hull made of Kevlar saves fuel, gets there faster, and can carry more fish."[9]

11. Who Makes the Purchasing Decisions?

Who makes the purchasing decisions at a supermarket? Only one type of individual? You'd have to be a Rip Van Winkle to say yes to that one. Now, besides homemakers who shop, there are women who work outside the home, husbands, latchkey kids, and so on. Each represents a number of different niches, and each has different key buying motives.

One of the niches Cascade dishwasher detergent has targeted is single men. As a result, some of Cascade's ads speak about the problems of single males.

But sometimes the people who make the purchasing decisions are not the ones who actually buy the products or services: They're the influencers. The kid screaming in the grocery cart. Or the child at home protesting if you don't get the right cereal in the right box.

Kid Cusine, a new, prepared dinner targeted to kids, is a success. It treats kids as if they're the target market even though Kid Cusine dinners are purchased by their parents. What kind of TV shows do you suppose Kid Cusine is advertised on? You got it. On kids' shows, not shows watched by their parents, the purchasers.

Guess who's driving men to drink?

Women.

That's right. But fortunately, they're steering them away from the hard stuff. Women, who are more likely to experiment with different kinds of drinks, have moved toward the lighter, more flavorful ones. They have introduced men to coolers and schnapps. The marketing response? Among others, ads that include women in social-drinking situations. The result? Lightness dominates the alcohol industry.

Check out your customer base. You may not have the information to tell you about influencers, but you better find out about them. It may be a way to find one of those hidden niches.

12. Do All Your Customers Buy Your Whole Line of Products or Services?

Do you have some customers who buy your complete line of products and services? Do you have others who buy only one or two items—real cherry pickers? If so, you've got different niches with differing key buying motives.

In the personal computer industry, some computer buyers want a working system and do not want to worry about putting all the components together. On the other hand, there are the computer techies who prefer to assemble their own computing systems. They select components from various suppliers' product lines.

Bell of Pennsylvania found that the number of special services (call-waiting, call-forwarding, three-way calling, and speed calling) wanted by its customer base varied. So they offered a package of the four services for only $8.03 a month, a savings of 25 percent. Purchased separately, the services would cost $10.70. Some buyers still preferred to purchase only parts of the package at the full cost. By serving both niches, the company comes out ahead.

Recap

To find those hidden niches for a given product or service, answer these 12 questions:

1. Who are your heavy, heavy users?
2. Who are your light users?
3. Which customers are expanding their purchases?
4. Which customers are decreasing their purchases?
5. Where are your customers located?
6. Which customers can you serve most profitably?
7. Do your customers have different price sensitivities?
8. What do your customers really value?
9. Do your customers have the same frequency of purchase?
10. What promotion best appeals to your various customers?
11. Who makes the purchasing decisions?
12. Do all your customers buy your whole line of products and services?

Answer these questions, and you'll know how your present market can be segmented.

As Mitchel Scott of Armstrong World Industries said:

> For us segmentation is used not so much to increase or decrease market targets as to more clearly understand and serve customer expectations within the customer base we currently have. By selling more to these resegmented markets, the end result is the same—increased sales and profits.

The best place to probe for new niches is in your present customer base. But sometimes the grass is greener. . . .

4
Mining for Niches: Where to Look Next

Your best bet for finding those hidden market niches is, of course, in your own backyard—with your familiar product and service target markets.

But your best bet can't be your *only* bet. If you don't look beyond your well-studied customer base, you can forget about new customers. And without new customers, no business can survive.

Consider the fate of the American big city department store. Throughout the prosperous 1980s, one after another succumbed to financial decline and bankruptcy. Did they fail to meet their old customer's needs? Not really. By and large that segment remained steadfast. Rather, the department stores' troubles arose from ignoring all those other customers in the market, such as the prosperous and savvy two-earner families, shopping together in the evening and demanding top value and service. Without these (and other) new customers, the department stores' customer base was bound to shrink.

Ahead are seven potential veins of new niche markets along with examples of how they've been mined by imaginative firms. Use these as a starting point, but don't let them limit your imagination.

1. Look at Those Who Use the Product or Service Category but Not Your Brand

There are people out there who use your competitors' products or services but not yours.

Why?

One possibility is that the competition has already read this book and implemented niche-marketing strategies. If this is the case, your task will be very difficult.

But it's more likely that they're serving the heart of the market and there's room for niche players. We recommend targeting a market niche rather than taking the leaders head-on. (We talk more about this in Guidelines 10 and 11.)

This is true in almost every market.

Consider toothpaste. Who would ever think there was room in the market for more toothpaste? After all, how many ways can you brush your teeth? You might believe that all the market niches have been covered. Not so!

For example, as kids become a more important part of household decision making, they offer new marketing opportunities. Oral-B, a new toothpaste on the market, is strictly for kids. Does it taste like adult toothpaste? No.

Did you ever hear 7-year-olds ask for spearmint? No. They ask for bubble gum. And that's what the toothpaste tastes like.

Will adults buy it for their own use? Not likely. But are kids buying it (or are parents buying it for the kids)? You bet.

Now we know what you're thinking: "That's an exception. There's no other room for successful niche products in the toothpaste market. It's saturated." But it's not.

How about a toothpaste formulated to reduce plaque? Tooth decay has almost been wiped out, so other dental concerns, such as plaque, have become more important. Savvy marketers were quick to capitalize on this lucrative niche.

Of course, before these niche products came out, kids and baby boomers were buying toothpaste already on the market. But only because they lacked a better alternative. Bubble gum-flavored and plaque-removing toothpaste became successful niche products because insightful marketers discovered there were needs not being met by existing brands.

Notice that we're not talking about share building's increasing your share of a mass-marketed product or service from 22 percent to 24 percent. Rather we're talking about developing new niche products and services for people who already use the same type of product or service. We're talking about finding the weak points in the mass market and then positioning products and services for these niches.

Look again at your product or service category (or categories). Are there customers buying your competitor's products or services simply because there are no alternatives? Because no one has recognized their unique needs?

If so, you're halfway there. You already know the territory.

2. Look at Those Who Don't Use the Product or Service Category but Could

Perhaps there are a number of potential customers who could be buying your competitors' or your product or service but don't.

Find out why.

Look at what happened with snacks for dogs. For many years the primary dog snack was a grain-based biscuit such as Milk-Bone. This category occupied a couple of shelf facings in the supermarket. But a good percentage of dog owners didn't buy these dog treats.

To get greater penetration, the grain-based dog-treat manufacturers lowered prices. But many dog owners still walked right by the displays. They wanted treats for their dogs, and they didn't think that grain was a treat. After all, when was the last time you saw your dog attacking a wheat field?

But when more expensive dog snacks, such as jerky or beef, were put on the market, the nonusers flocked to buy them. So at a time when dog ownership is going down, revenue from premium snacks is going up. Today one aisle at the supermarket is usually devoted to pet food, and a large percentage of it to premium dog snacks.

There may be potential customers out there that you've never seen, and, what's more, neither have your competitors. Find them. The present products and services may just not be—or be perceived to be—tasty enough. Or healthy enough. Or easy enough to use. Solve these problems, and both you and the customers win.

3. Look at Creating New Products or Services in an Old Category

While some businesses are trying to make improvements in existing products and services, others are taking a new look. They're trying to find new solutions to old problems. These marketers believe there is no such thing as a mature market, only tired products and services.

For example, for years people have been running off athletic fields with incredible thirsts. Some companies offered new flavors, new sizes, and new packages for the same old drinks. The result: the same old sales. Then Gatorade offered a new choice—not only a refreshing drink but one that replenishes body electrolytes lost during exercise.

When the product was created by scientists at the University of Florida, none of the big companies would touch it. Why? Because it was targeted to a small niche market. But eventually Stokely-Van Camp (later acquired by Quaker Oats) realized the potential and bought Gatorade.

Now Quaker Oats dominates the market (it turned out to be a very big niche) and everyone is trying to enter. Small wonder. Gatorade is Quaker Oats' largest profit contributor.

How long have people been using cloth diapers? So long that no one thought there was much of an opportunity here. That is, until Procter & Gamble noticed that it wasn't easy to use cloth diapers when traveling. Or, for that matter, anywhere away from home. So, Pampers was targeted for this niche market.

Notice how sometimes you get a nice surprise when you create a new product in an old category? Who would have thought that Gatorade would have garnered such a share of the market? Or that disposable diapers would almost replace cloth diapers?

Today there are categories of me-too products and services that have been around for years. But someone, sometime, is going to make a breakthrough.

How? By recognizing some need that the category is not satisfying.

Make this person be you.

4. Look at Technology within Your Company

You probably already have the technology to serve new niche markets, but you may not recognize it. Not so at 3M.

3M is well known for its use of technology to develop new products. While most of us think of Post-it notes, that's only one product out of a multitude. For example, 3M has highly developed technology in films, adhesives, and plastics. The company used this technology to make decals to replace paint used on airplanes, thereby creating a new market niche. The product was a natural because airlines wanted to do everything possible to keep weight and fuel costs down.

The use of plastic decals, which are much lighter than paint, is an excellent example of using a firm's technology to satisfy a niche market's key buying motives.

Who is the largest producer of unbranded photography film sold by K Mart and other mass merchandisers under their private labels? Again 3M, using its technology to serve a niche neglected (intentionally) by Kodak.

Or take Reflectone, a producer of flight simulators targeted primarily at the government. Reflectone realized that parts of this technology, such as interactive video and computer-aided instruction, could be used in other situations. Why not, they thought, devise a totally electronic center for film deposits and pickups?

Using the technology developed for flight simulators, they produced a fully automated kiosk for film deposits and pick-ups. Drive up and, by means of interactive video and automation, you'll be greeted and given instructions, have your questions answered, and get a receipt and delivery date.

A warning.

Although you will be very familiar with your new products or services (after all, they are part of your existing technology), you probably won't be as knowledgeable about your new target market. While we have urged you to focus on your present customers, it's equally essential (more so, if that's possible) to focus on your potential customers.

Misunderstanding your target market spells failure.

For example, have you ever seen a Reflectone film kiosk? Probably not. They're no longer produced. Why?

Reflectone's management was oriented toward selling to the military. Marketing activity was primarily directed toward top generals and toward fulfilling the government's extensive contract requirements. Government contracts have well-specified minimum standards. If you meet these, you have a good chance of getting the contract. Uncovering consumers' key buying motives, so vital to consumer marketing, were skills never mastered by Reflectone's management. And so the automated kiosks became just another good idea.

Make sure that your technology is used so that it will respond to users' key buying motives.

5. Look at Marketing Skills within Your Company

Perhaps one of your company's strengths is marketing. If it is, then you should utilize these skills to serve new niche markets. Let's see how some companies are following this principle.

For years Midas very successfully specialized in mufflers. But, with its well-known name, why not offer other services? And so today you can pull into a Midas center and get new brakes, shock absorbers, springs, a front-end alignment—as well as a muffler.

At Sears, not only can you buy kitchen cabinets, storm windows, roofs, and gutters, but you can also have Sears install them. Of course, the installations are not done by Sears. Sears doesn't have the expertise. Installation is done by independent subcontractors hired by Sears. But by utilizing its skill in marketing, Sears provides a valuable service to its customers while taking some off the top from installers.

Hallmark Cards, having a well-recognized and respected trade name plus a distribution system of 6000 independent dealers, capitalized on these market strengths. Hallmark expanded its product line into non-card items that could be sold through its distribution system. New products included crystal, pewter, and jewelry.

But a word of caution. Just because customers value your name for one product does not necessarily mean they will hold your other products in high regard. Years ago, Sears had sold appliances to the middle and upper-middle classes. It decided it could sell clothes to these clienteles as well. The customers were already in the store, after all, and had demonstrated considerable loyalty to the brand name.

Sears consequently upgraded the quality and price of its clothing, only to find that the better-heeled customers continued to pass through these departments (en route to the appliances) without buying anything. They still purchased their refrigerators from Sears, but they bought their clothes from department stores and specialty shops. The Sears name on a man's suit was simply not the same, at least in the minds of customers, as the Sears label on a washing machine. It was a costly mistake in strategy, and the direct result of Sears' failure to gauge the attitudes and values of its customers. After all, the customer determines the market, not the seller.

6. Look at Conglomerate Diversification

Do you see attractive markets but lack the technology *and* marketing skills to capitalize on them? Then think about diversification.

But we really urge you to think twice—in fact, ten times—about it.

Be careful!

The list of those who have tried and failed at conglomerate diversification is miles longer than the list of those who have reaped big profits. You don't have to look far to find failures.

For example, take food manufacturing companies. It's no news that about 50 percent of all food dollars is spent in restaurants, fast food outlets, and other similar businesses. So what do you suppose many of the big food manufacturers did? Why, they went out and bought restaurants. How are they doing? Just ask Campbell Soup. After several years of floundering with Hanover Trail Steak House, they sold it!

Company after company has found that the niche markets that will realize the most profits and growth are those product and service markets that they know best. And so they're shedding unrelated businesses. "Back to basics" and "stick to your knitting" are today's watch words.

Just as the Sirens lured Ulysses to the rocky coast, the siren call of conglomerate diversification can lead you into rocky times. Often it's better to stuff cotton in your ears.

7. Look at Emerging Markets

Do you want another place to look? Look at emerging markets.

The possibilities are almost limitless.

How about the home-services niche? More and more women are finding they have less and less time for housework. Errand-running, house-cleaning, child-care, food-shopping, clothes-shopping, and food-preparation services are all undeveloped. But not for long!

Or take a look at the freshly prepared food take-home-and-eat market. National manufacturers have not yet figured out how to enter this market. They can freeze, freeze-dry, vacuum-pack, or can food, but they still haven't worked out how to deliver it fresh. Most restaurants have not tapped this market because they want people to come to them to be served.

Some entrepreneurs have developed localized niche markets in freshly prepared, high-quality food that is delivered at home, but there's still a vast untapped market.

Or flip on the TV. There's a rock video from the U.S.S.R. signaling a whole new nation of kids and young adults clamoring for blue jeans, guitars, Reeboks, cosmetics, hair products, magazines, and tape players. What other niche markets will open up because of that changing environment?

But you don't have to go that far from home to find emerging niches. Talk to your own kids, or listen to kids you know. They're different from us. They know the brands they like, and substitutes just won't do. They know and insist on quality. They read labels. They plan to make a lot of money—and spend it. And they probably will. What does that tell you?

Read a lot of newspapers. Forget the sports and business sections for the moment and look elsewhere. There are waste-disposal problems. Road deterioration. Floods of foreign visitors. All potential markets that didn't exist yesterday.

And listen to the marketplace. To your family. To your friends. And even to your enemies. And read. Be aware of what's happening out there, and you'll uncover those hidden niches.

Look at the niches—the growth markets of the 1990s—*American Demographics* came up with after they examined the marketplace.[1]

Parents. There were more than 4 million births in [1989], the highest number since 1964. About 90 percent of Americans have children at some time during their lives. For a huge segment of society, that time is now.

Children. The baby boomlet started in 1977, but it's peaking right now—making children a hot [niche] market for the 1990s.

Teenagers. The oldest members of the baby boomlet became teenagers in 1990 when they celebrated their 13th birthdays. After a decade of steep decline, the teenage population will grow again.

Fathers. As the baby boomlet begins to walk, talk, and do homework, fathers will become more important.

Empty Nesters. The family nest is most likely to empty when people are in their fifties. The baby boomers will begin to turn 50 in 1996. You can bank on healthy growth in the number of empty nesters towards the end of the decade.

Grandparents. In just 10 years, one-third of all grandparents with grandchildren under the age of 18 will be baby boomers.

The Very Old. The number of people aged 85 and older will continue to grow rapidly in the 1990s, making it the only growth segment among the elderly population.

Individuals. In the 1980s we moved from the family to the household as the primary unit of consumption. In the 1990s, we'll move from the household to the individual.

Stepfamilies. Families are not a hot market for the 1990s, but stepfamilies are. They now account for 20 percent of married couples with children.

The Fit. Millions of baby boomers will join in a passionate battle against time, doing everything from running marathons to plastic surgery.

The Unfit. Beyond age 40, serious health problems become much more common. The number of people with chronic diseases should increase sharply with the aging of the baby boomers in the 1990s.

Asians. Asians are the fastest growing minority group in America today, a [niche] market over 8 million strong.

Hispanics. Hispanics will become this country's largest minority group by 2010, when the U. S. Census Bureau projects that they will outnumber blacks.

Activists. As the baby boomers become middle-aged, the nation's activists will take center stage. If your business is not prepared for attack, the activists could severely damage your company's image.

Savers. As college costs loom on the horizon, the baby boomers will try desperately to save money. This makes the boomers hot prospects for savings instruments in the 1990s.

Downscale. The pendulum of public concern is swinging back in favor of helping poor and near poor people. We may even see a redefinition of poverty which increases—not decreases—the size of the downscale segment.

Upscale. With the baby boom generation entering its peak earning years, the number of affluent households will grow.

The Middle Class. Americans continue to identify themselves as middle-class, no matter how upscale their income. To get your message across, don't talk to the elite or you'll miss your market.

Women in Charge. As career-minded baby boom women gain in job experience, the number of women who control the bottom line will grow rapidly.

Workers. The share of the population in the paid labor force is greater today, at 66 percent, than ever before in our history.

Students. During this decade, the number of students aged 18 or older will approach, and might even pass, the number of students under age 18 for the first time in history.

Entrepreneurs. There are too many boomers for the few top spots in America's businesses. The consequence will be a lot of new businesses started by frustrated employees.

Vacation-Home Owners. The baby boom generation is about to become prime customers for vacation homes. Look for vacation-home ownership to take off in the next few years.

Fun Seekers. Americans now spend more money on entertainment than on clothing. Expect the fun-seeking to continue in the 1990s, especially for entertainment experiences like Disney World.

Housewives. Markets may have fragmented, but traditional markets still exist—they've become [niche] markets just like all the rest. We've come full circle: from housewives as the mass market of the 1950s to housewives as an important [niche] market of the 1990s.

What products and services could you offer to these emerging markets? Of course, the *American Demographics* list is just a beginning.

Recap

Niches can be found outside your present customer base. To find them, consider each of the following:

1. Those who use the product or service category but not your brand.
2. Those who don't use the product or service category but could.

3. New products or services in an old category.
4. Technology within your company.
5. Marketing skills within your company.
6. Conglomerate diversification.
7. Emerging markets.

PART 2

Differentiating Your Products and Services

5
The Basic Differentiation Strategies

Perhaps your customers have changed. You no longer have a mass market, just a number of niches. Working women. Latchkey kids. Graying Americans. . . .

And your competition is out there picking off—or getting ready to pick off—these niches by catering to their specialized needs.

Here is what you should do.

First, your product or service may still fill the bill for at least one niche of this now fragmented market. Finely tune your product or service a little more for this niche. Preempt or halt competition that could nibble away at your market share.

Next, decide how you can delight other customers by differentiating your product or service for other niches. Differentiation means satisfying customers *better* than anyone else. Differentiation gives people a reason to choose your product or service over any other competitive choice.

But how do you make your product or service stand out from all the others clamoring for attention? Highly creative people amass extensive fact files. They know a little bit about a lot of things. Then, when they need an innovative solution or idea, they draw on bits and pieces from their fact files and combine that information in various ways. The result: brand new solutions.

Expand your fact file by taking a look at how some big-company niche marketers have differentiated their products and services. They've used one—or a combination—of five strategies.

1. Differentiation with a product or service strategy
2. Differentiation with a customer-service strategy
3. Differentiation with a channel-of-distribution strategy
4. Differentiation with a communication strategy
5. Differentiation with a price strategy.

Most of the examples are probably not drawn from your own industry. But don't think you have nothing in common with Georgia-Pacific or Waldenbooks. You can often learn more from other industries than you can from your own. And, in the process, you may figure out how to leap-frog over your competitors.

When seeking solutions for your customers' problems, expand your thinking. Ask whether, concerning my product or service and *my customers'* needs, I can:

- Put it to other uses (as is or with modifications).
- Adapt (to other ideas, developments).
- Modify (change color, motion, sound, odor, form, shape).
- Magnify (stronger, longer, thicker, extra value).
- Minify (smaller, shorter, lighter).
- Substitute (other patterns, layout, sequence, components).
- Rearrange (components, patterns, sequence, layout).
- Reverse (inside out).
- Combine (blend, alloy, assortment, ensemble; combine units, purposes, appeals, ideas).[1]

1. Differentiate through a Product or Service Strategy

"Let them have any color they want as long as it's black," said Henry Ford. That made sense (and a lot of money) for a while. Then along came an upstart by the name of General Motors. GM outniched Ford and, in the process, almost bankrupted the one-color company.

For most businesses, marketing a single product or service to a mass market doesn't make sense. The market's too diverse. There are too many niches. And competition is there ready to serve customers' specialized needs.

Many large-scale companies have differentiated through product and service strategies to serve a number of niches.

Watches

Timex, a traditional mass marketer, was a very successful producer of durable, inexpensive watches until the early 1980s. Then changes took place. There was new competition and a new emphasis on design and fashion. Swatch for the teens. Luxury styles for adults. And so on.

So Timex switched gears and developed specific products for specific niches. The Watercolors line ($24.95) for teens. Big, Bold and Beautiful ($35 to $55) and Doubles ($45 to $55) for women. Carriage ($40 to $60) for men. In the sports niches, Skiathlom for skiers, Victory for sailboat racers, and Aerobix for exercisers.

But Timex didn't stop there. How about a watch/computer for bicyclists? The Velo-Track, besides telling time and date, times laps for racers and offers a 24-hour countdown timer and an alarm. Or Timex Hooks for fishermen. It's equipped with a built-in water thermometer, compass, and tide moment detector.

Timex's product line increased from 200 watch designs in 1972 to 500 varieties by 1989. And so have profits.[2]

Photography Film

Advanced amateur photographers used to have two choices when it came to buying film: general purpose film or ultra expensive professional film.

So Kodak came out with a premium line of color-print film (Kodak Ektar) targeted at advanced amateur photographers. "Most consumers will continue to find their best value in Kodacolor Gold," said Wilbur Prezzano, general manager of Kodak's photographic-products group. Yet, if only the advanced amateurs currently buying Kodacolor Gold switch to Ektar, it's estimated that, because of Ektar's higher margins, Kodak's profits could increase by 10 to 15 cents a share.[3]

Kodak is still in the film business just as Timex is still in the watch business. But each has expanded its markets through creative niche-product differentiation strategies.

Apparel

Levi Strauss differentiated its traditional denim jeans, which just didn't fit men over 45—a segment that accounts for about 25 percent of America's male population. They introduced Levi's Action Slacks, with expandable waistlines and more flexible material. Action slacks were just what this niche wanted.

The shoe industry has become expert at differentiation. How about shoes for windsurfing, skateboarding, aerobics, sky-diving, and bicycling? And now, from Converse, the martial-arts shoe (the fact that martial-arts competition is performed barefoot is immaterial).

Food

Kellogg, in a slow growth industry, zeroed in on a segment that didn't eat much cereal—the baby boomers, ages 25 to 49. Kellogg came out with differentiated products such as Mueslix. Convenience and nutrition, two key buying motives, were pitched. Cereal use by this age group increased by 26 percent, helping the "no-growth" ready-to-eat cereal market to expand three times faster than the grocery-category average.[4] Kellogg, with only a handful of cereals a few years ago, now has over 46 varieties, each targeted to a specific niche.

Tropicana, languishing in the relatively static orange-juice market, went after the gourmet niche with its Pure Premium.

Autos

Auto companies are also discovering riches in niches by coming out with products for small market segments.

Lee Iacocca went after a niche—the families with small children who wanted more passenger space. The Chrysler minivan became a big success.

Chrysler also brought back the convertible. Dropped in the early 1980s because demand was considered too limited, convertibles accounted for 2 percent of sales in the new car market in 1988. Convertible trucks soon followed.[5]

Hotels

Years ago, not only was a Marriott a Marriott, but a Hyatt was a Hyatt. But times have changed. To better serve the needs of the market, Hyatt has also become a champion of differentiation.

Hyatt serves a number of niches, all in the upscale segment: Hyatt Regency (business and pleasure); Grand Hyatt (larger than the Hyatt Regency, catering to conventions, business, and pleasure); Park Hyatt (European style for business and pleasure travelers who are looking for a quiet, sedate hotel); and the Hyatt 300 (all suite hotels, located in suburbs for business travelers who want luxury and space). The Hyatt Hotels—the original hotels—are older, usually slightly lower priced but still cater to upscale travelers.

Lifestyle research pointed to a niche that wanted fantasy vacations. So, at the Hyatt Waikoloa (Hawaii), if you're a car-racing fanatic, you can wheel around a Ferrari at the Hyatt's private track. Or perhaps you've always wanted to swim with a dolphin. The Hyatt Waikoloa will provide you with a trained dolphin, and together you can explore coral reefs.

Club Med, Inc., once the Mecca for the adults-only crowd, was fast losing much of its youthful clientele as they grew older and had kids. So, the company opened a resort (Sandpiper Bay, Stuart, Florida) targeting parents with infants.

Marriott and Hyatt still offer hotel rooms. Club Med is still a resort. But all three have differentiated their product to appeal to specific clientele clusters.

Lumber

No one can differentiate lumber. Right?

Well, don't tell that to Georgia-Pacific. They began to shrink-wrap two-by-fours in plastic for the burgeoning do-it-yourself yuppie market (to avoid the damage of splinters in their BMW upholstery).

Or how about other lumber companies that have developed complete packages for specific construction purposes, like an 8- by 10-ft deck?

Credit Cards

American Express started out just with its green card in 1958. But the needs of some of its card holders changed (much of the change had to do with the growing familiarity with charge cards). And then there were new competitive card offerings like Visa and MasterCard. So American Express, over a period of time, came out with "different strokes for different folks": the gold card, the corporate card, the platinum card, and the optima card. Each has different cardholder enhancements.

In addition, American Express targets college students, prime cardholder prospects. Students get all the benefits of other green card members, but are given certain service enhancements that are uniquely relevant to them. As Betsy Ludlow, vice president, student marketing, put it:

> The green card . . . [is like] a big Hoover vacuum cleaner designed to sweep all our mainstream prospects; however, what is needed for the edges are a couple of Dustbusters designed to penetrate those harder to reach places. The point is, different products are needed for different purposes—but both, in the case of the Hoover and Dustbuster, are needed to complete the entire job.[6]

Book Stores

Waldenbooks, which has grown from 524 stores selling 20 million books to 1319 outlets selling over 100 million books, is not stopping with cookie-cutter expansion. It's opening a number of different types of outlets for different niches: for children—Waldenkids; for upscales—Brentano's; for book and gift buyers—Waldenbooks and More; for computer users—Walden Software.[7]

Magazines

It's hard to think of an industry that differentiates its product more than the magazine industry.

Take a look at *Imagen/Northeast.* Covering Connecticut, Massachusetts, New Jersey, New York, and Pennsylvania, it focuses on upscale U.S. Hispanics, by region and by income levels.

For patients in doctors' waiting rooms, Whittle Communications' *Special Reports* contain articles on topics such as health, sports, and personalities—the kind of material people like to read while waiting to see their doctors.

Many magazines are using (or are considering using) selective binding to achieve ink-jet imaging. Through a computer process, hundreds of versions of a magazine can be printed in a single run. R. H. Donnelley used selective binding for *American Baby* to provide 1.1 million readers with special versions of the magazine, according to whether they are prenatal or postnatal.[8]

How about targeted subscriptions? Time-Life Inc. (in cooperation with Targeted Communications) offers customized subscriptions of Time-Life publications. Complete with a gatefold outer wrap with a two-page spread (designed to your specifications), it's targeted specifically toward your customers. Kodak is a frequent user, sending out Time-Life targeted publications at regular intervals to 2500 photojournalists.[9]

Newspapers

What can we learn about differentiation from the newspaper business? Most large cities have only one major paper, a virtual monopoly. Still, small local newspapers put up stiff competition, so the major newspapers fight back with sectionalized and regionalized editions. The *Philadelphia Inquirer, Washington Post, Chicago Tribune,* and *Los Angeles Times,* among others, offer various news and feature sections to appeal to different segments of readers in their circulation areas. Geographically zoned editions help them compete with suburban papers.

Television

Cable companies serve specialized niches, offering more choices for viewers. No wonder the big three—ABC, NBC, and CBS—are concerned that the national networks' share of TV viewers dropped from 90 percent in the 1970s to 68 percent in 1988. (In the summer rerun season, it was about 60 percent.)[10] So it's no surprise that NBC now owns CNBC, Consumer News Business Channel, a cable station that targets more focused segments.

Or, that ABC is a part owner of Life-Time (Estonia) and ESPN (Connecticut) cable stations.

Enough. But still we've only given you a sampling of niche product and service differentiation strategies already in place. These companies are believers. They *know* what product and service differentiation did for them, and they're already dreaming up new strategies. How about you?

2. Differentiate through a Customer-Service Strategy

Differentiation may seem easy for some products and services. Just modify the product or service. Like Timex did. Or Hallmark. Or Levi Strauss.

But many products and services are almost commodities. Or, in fact, may be commodities. If you're faced with this dilemma, think in terms of varying the services that surround your product or service. Here's how some companies have done this.

Hotels

The kiddie niche is in. Club Med decided to make room for children at six of its resorts, offering baby-sitting and day camps for children aged 2 to 11. Hyatt has started a Camp Hyatt program. Activities include kite flying and sand-castle building. Lake Arrowhead Hilton Lodge's elaborate children's day-camp program has activities such as mining for gold and fishing.

How about the reunion niche? The Radisson Hotel in Wilmington, Delaware, offers a weekend package for them.

Or the vacationer? Marriott customized its 18 resorts to allow guests to experience ideal vacations. The various packages are for different profile groups, such as sun-and-fun devotees, golfers, and adventure seekers. Whatever the package, it's geared to the specific resort's theme.

The list goes on and on, but differentiation spells profits for these major hostelers.

Courtesy of Sidney Harris.

Computers

Apple Computer has not made its biggest gain in sales to businesses from head-to-head competition with IBM. Rather, Apple's success comes from offering solutions through narrowly focused industry-specific software products.

Even IBM pushed its personal computer dealers to pursue a niche strategy by specializing in serving one—or several—segments such as banks, retailers, or hospitals. Why? Because IBM believed that the way to expand the market is to create new customers. As David Thomas, head of IBM's national distribution said, "There are people in this business who do well, and they do well because they have focus. That's the way to grow a market."

IBM believed that if a dealership is going to sell an expensive personal computer system, it has to understand the customer's business. And how can the dealer do that selling to 40 different niches?

So IBM's recommendation: select a few niches. Cater to them with specialized service.[11]

Affinity Marketing

The Dewar's Highlander Clan is an exclusive family of individuals sharing a set of common values, including a respect for tradition, a devotion to authenticity, and a conviction that quality never varies.

If you're a member of the clan, you can get discounts on crystal glassware, Scottish kilts, and other selected merchandise. You may even get a free trip to Scotland!

Like to be a member? No big deal. If your name is on Schenley Industries, Inc.'s, mailing list of 2 million scotch drinkers, you'll get your invitation.[12]

Or how about being inducted into the LightStyle Club? Sponsored by General Foods' Crystal Light soft drink mixes, a membership will get you a newsletter and a brochure offering bargains on beach towels, T-shirts, and other items, each having the Crystal Light logo.

Look for ways to differentiate by varying the services that surround your products and services.

It's simple yet effective. Remember what Club Med did. Grew right along with their initial consumers. And Apple. Sold solutions. Not just the hardware. And user-friendly. Or Dewar's. Made it a family deal. Appealed to tradition.

Once again, turn to your data. Who are your consumers—both heavy and light users? What are their key buying motives? One might be fast service. Another might be free parking. Another, doing business at irregular hours. If you can make it easier for your customers to buy, you'll make it harder for your competition to compete.

3. Differentiate through a Distribution-Channel Strategy

Think of varying your channels of distribution. How can you make your product more accessible to the consumer? Take a look at what some companies have done.

Supermarkets

Supermarkets are making home deliveries—not just in New York City but in places that you might not suspect. Like in Dallas (Minyard Food Stores); San Antonio, Austin, Corpus Christi, and Laredo (H-E-B Food Stores); and Atlanta (Kroger). It's a real time-saver for people just starting professional careers, for senior citizens, and for working mothers with young children—all rapidly growing segments.

Mass Merchandisers

Some mass merchandisers offer interactive home-shopping services. There are hybrid cable and phone systems, such as GTE's Mainstreet; J. C. Penney's Telaction; and PC-based systems, such as CompuServe and Prodigy. Your niche market can shop at midnight.

Financial Services

Sell financial services through electronic media? That's what Compu-Serve does. And it works.

CompuServe found that people who subscribe to electronic media services are numbers-oriented. They are accustomed to analyzing figures, tables, graphs, and the like. And they aren't intimidated by computers. In fact, they're more likely to trust what they see on the screen than the word of a financial advisor.

Prescription Drugs

Taking a page from the American Association of Retired Persons (AARP), Walgreens and J. C. Penney have begun mail-order services for prescription drugs. For Penney the distribution channel was in place. It was simply a matter of utilizing it for another product. For Walgreens the product was in place, but they recognized mail order was a more accessible distribution channel, at least for certain groups of customers.

If you can find a faster, more convenient way to deliver your product or service to your customers, you've found the secret to another differentiation strategy: differentiation with a channel-of-distribution strategy. In a way, varying your distribution channel to make your product or service more easily accessible is a natural extension to the strategy of differentiation through customer service. Make it easy. Make it convenient. And make it fast. Beat a path to your customers' doors instead of waiting for them to come to you.

4. Differentiate through Communication Strategy

Even though markets are becoming more fragmented, one of your products or services may still be suitable for a number of niches. Yet each niche may have different key buying motives.

You can't show all the product or service benefits in one ad. Key buying motives—for each niche—would become obscured, and the advertising campaign would be a disaster. But you can have different promotions for each niche to which the product or service appeals.

Lipton Tea, in the United States, shows Chris Evert drinking iced tea out of a can; in the United Kingdom, matrons sipping tea from elegant cups; in the Middle East, men gathered around tiny cups.

Or take Procter & Gamble. They have six different promotions for Crest. Among the six targets are blacks, Hispanics, and kids.

Or Johnson & Johnson. It created a new market for its baby shampoo by tempting adults to use it.

Some companies promote according to lifestyles. Audi of America sponsored 10 sailing events in 1988. Audi also provided postrace entertainment, caps for crews, and rugby shirts for skippers. Local Audi dealers were encouraged to become involved by providing test drives for crews and friends. Audi also plans to build long-term relationships with select upscale sports-enthusiast niches such as rowers, skiers, and equestriens—likely prospects for their cars. Hilary Mark, vice president of Audi's advertising agency, DelWilber & Associates, says: "Lifestyle marketing can reach out to the people where they live. It can create an emotional bond at the lifestyle level."[13]

Courtesy of John Jonik.

Your products and services that work across niches deserve special examination. Do they appeal to each group for different reasons? If so, you have to respond to a whole series of key buying motives. You can develop more than one image as Johnson & Johnson did, or you can associate the product or service with the target market's lifestyle as Audi did.

5. Differentiate with a Price Strategy

Here are some more examples for your fact file, cases of how some firms have differentiated with a price strategy. Turn them to your own advantage. Remember, you're probably familiar with examples from your own industry. Look at other industries, and see if they have something to offer you.

But a caution: Although many marketers think of price first, we recommend that you think of it last. Of the five differentiation strategies, price is the easiest for competitors to duplicate.

Still, price can be an effective differentiation strategy. Sometimes just changing your pricing structure—implementing variable pricing—will expand your markets. You'll be able to meet the needs of more customers. Serve more niches. The result: you'll grow bigger by acting smaller.

Consider variable pricing for segments that have different price sensitivities. A one-price policy means that in some cases the price is too high. A price too high scares some potential customers, and it results in lost sales. On the other hand, a price too low (for some segments) means that you've left too much on the table. This is money no longer available to invest in making your company more competitive. It could be used for funding research and development. Or providing additional features or services. Or improving your plant. Or training employees. Or it could also be used for increasing dividends.

Let's see how some companies have put variable pricing to use.

Airlines and Cruise Lines

Airlines targeted budget-conscious travelers, who might not otherwise use airlines, with their super-saver fares requiring advance purchase and/or weekend stays, often with no cancellation stipulations. This strategy opened up a whole new niche, filling otherwise empty seats.

Fortunately (for the airlines), super-saver restrictions, though suitable for many pleasure travelers, are prohibitive for most business travelers—the airlines' bread and butter.

Cruise lines have found that deeply discounted fares for people who book just before departure appeal to the economy-minded, highly flexible-traveler niche.

Hotels

Hotels found a way to fill up rooms over the weekends. They offer package deals for price-conscious people who'd just like to get away for a minivacation.

But a number of these same hotels also cater to a nonprice-sensitive niche. Besides suites, they offer the exclusivity of an executive floor with more posh rooms and better service. Of course, at much higher prices.

Restaurants

Many restaurants, plagued with empty seats early in the evening, especially on weekday nights, use early bird dinner specials.

Some spots, just seeking more volume, go after the price-sensitive senior citizen niche. Like McDonald's with its Golden Arches Club (where the second cup of coffee is free if you're over 60).

Autos

Auto leasing attracts a certain market segment by offering monthly payments that can be 20 percent to 30 percent less than an outright purchase and no down payments. Using this price strategy, auto manufacturers encourage the cash-strapped segment to make frequent trade-ins and to trade up from time to time. The manufacturers theorize that getting drivers behind the wheel will also help to build customer loyalty.

Utilities

You even can offer cash discounts for purchasing certain merchandise. Some utilities, faced with load shortages, offer customers discounts for purchasing energy-efficient appliances through retailers.

Frequent-User Clubs

Frequent-travelers programs have spawned a group of look-alikes.

Many hotels, including Holiday Corp., Marriott, Hyatt, and Hilton, reward frequent stayers (but with mixed results). Or, how about frequent-eater clubs. At the American Harvest restaurant in New York City, five tables in a month (with a minimum bill of $20 per person), entitles you to $100 in free meals.

When you sign up for a Citibank Preferred credit card, you earn two CitiDollars for every $10 you charge. You can cash the CitiDollars for discount merchandise from Citibank's catalogs and brochures.

If scotch is your thing, then you may strike it rich with the Connoisseur Club by Cutty Sark. Proof-of-purchase seals earn points toward catalog merchandise.

The idea, of couse, is to encourage brand loyalty among that highly desired niche: the heavy, heavy user.

Selective Couponing

And then there is selective couponing.

Who buys anchovies? Why, people who eat sardines, of course. Well, you can directly reach this niche with Catalina Marketing's (Anaheim, California) Checkout Coupon program. When a shopper purchases sardines, the checkout scanner transmits this information to the register which then produces appropriate coupons promoting anchovies.

Why not zero in on users of your competitors' products and services? That's what some casinos in Atlantic City do. They use selective couponing to coax gamblers from competing casinos. Stop and Shop followed the same strategy to win customers from competing grocery stores. So did L'Oreal Visuelle when it stole customers from Revlon and Cover Girl Cosmetics.

Tie-In Offers

You don't have to go it alone—find a compatible partner. That's what many big-company niche marketers are doing. For example, consumers can earn points with Northwest's Worldperks and get discounts at Hyatt, Marriott, and Radisson hotels and upgrade their rentals at Avis, National, and Thrifty.

Or they can accumulate points with Hyatt's Gold Passport; upgrade their purchases with Northwest, Avis, and Budget; and get discounts on the Royal Caribbean. If you stay enough nights, you get free airline tickets and car rentals.

Or how about a "Frequent Smileage Program"? Offered jointly by Pan Am and Polaroid, participants earn points by using Polaroid products. These are redeemable for free companion tickets on Pan Am.

Or affinity credit cards. Like United's Mileage Plus, First Card, a gold MasterCard sponsored by FCC National Bank, builds an expanded customer base for the bank. United gets a cut on card charges. And users benefit because they earn one mile of credit on United's Mileage Plus for each dollar they charge.

Or, perhaps you can tie in with a product club. There are product clubs like these:

Club	Participating brands include
The Great Payback (Sears)	Post Cereals, Ore-Ida Potatoes, Weight Watchers Entrees and Desserts
Frequent Shopper Advantage Club (Frequent Shoppers Advantage Inc.)	Nabisco, Oscar Mayer, Coca-Cola, Clairol
Giftlink Shoppers Reward (Procter & Gamble)	Ralston Purina, Kraft, Campbell Soup, Ocean Spray

Factory-Outlet Malls

Many name-brand manufacturers, such as Izod, Vanity Fair, Liz Claiborne, Jordache, Bass, Van Heusen, and Ralph Lauren move surplus merchandise (sometimes seconds) through factory-outlet malls, without destroying their market positions.

Assuming your price is competitive in the first place, can you afford to use price as a differentiation strategy? Maybe. Some airlines and restaurants profit from reduced prices for otherwise empty seats. Outlet malls have become big business.

But think about this. For a price strategy to work, it must be well publicized. And once it's out there, your competition is in on the game plan. So don't get stuck with a permanent fire sale.

Our advice (once again!): Consider everything else before lowering the price.

Combining the Differentiation Strategies

Practically all the big-company niche marketers we talked to used a combination of differentiation strategies. For example, Russ Browne, first vice president of marketing for the NBD, N. A., explained how his bank is planning its delivery system, as well as its products, for various target markets:

> We're trying to match our delivery system with different segments. For example, at the low end we're giving minimal assistance—it's almost self-service. And obviously at the high end, where you've got the significant balances, that's where we give extensive and personalized private banking treatment. Then we have a range of alternatives in

between. We're trying to do a better job of matching our delivery-system resources with profit opportunities.

L'eggs is another example. Hanes Corporation, a leading manufacturer of women's hosiery, had been selling its hosiery exclusively through traditional outlets (specialty and department stores). To combat private labels sold at supermarkets (offering low cost and shopping convenience), Hanes came out with L'eggs.

With L'eggs, Hanes did it all. They offered a product of higher quality than was normally sold at supermarkets yet of lower quality than was marketed as Hanes' top of the line. They used a new (for Hanes) channel of distribution. They developed unique packaging and display. And they priced L'eggs lower than Hanes' hosiery sold in department stores.

Customization—The Ultimate Differentiation Strategy

So far, our examples have shown how to differentiate products and services for niches. But perhaps you can tailor your product or service toward individuals (like the village cobbler did in preindustrial local markets)—yet still serve the same number of customers as you could using a mass-marketing approach.

How about customizing suits without using tailors? Some men's stores in Japan do just that. First, the customer "tries on" various suits by looking into an electronic mirror that superimposes suits of different styles, colors, and materials on the customer's body. The customer makes a selection. Then the customer is electronically measured. This information is fed to laser equipment that controls the cutting and sewing. The suit is ready the next day.

Or, mass-producing homes, each one designed by the home buyer? In Japan (again) the buyer can sit at a computer terminal and, with the aid of a sales representative, design his or her home. Using over 20,000 standardized parts, the buyer can select style, room size, and layouts. If the designed house costs too much, no problem. With a few touches on the computer keyboard, the house can be scaled down to the customer's budget.

The customer's specifications are then sent electronically to the factory where parts are assembled on a production line. Within 30 days the prefabricated modular parts are delivered to the buyer's homesite.

How about cosmetics?

Growing numbers of women are finding they can get—and are getting—comparable cosmetics at drugstores for less than half the price of those at department stores. To help arrest this trend, Laura Lupton,

Inc., developed a system for in-store analysis of a woman's hair, skin, and eye color. Counter salespersons then customize the blend of cosmetics according to each customer's characteristics. Another example of differentiation by producing unique, individualized products.

Uncertain as to how your favorite photo should be enlarged? And, aside from that, you're in a hurry? Well, Kodak's Create-A-Print lets you compose your photo on a color monitor. You can experiment with a variety of croppings and sizes. When you like what you see, print as many copies as you want—all in less than 5 minutes.

Of course, there are less exotic methods of mass customization where the customer also participates in the assembly. Salad bars and ice cream shops where customers can make their own sundaes are common examples.

Less familiar are the soft drink fountains in some supermarkets. They permit consumers to develop a customized blend of over 25 different sodas. How do they work? The bank of fountains contains cherry, orange, grape, cream, cola, piña colada, and a host of other sodas. A customer takes an empty bottle and fills it with any combination desired, such as 50 percent cola, 25 percent orange soda, 25 percent cream soda. During the 20 minutes we watched, virtually no one took exactly the same combination. Some put as many as five different flavors in their bottles.

But does it cost more? No. Since customers can refill their own bottles, it can cost less than bottled soda.

Of course, in some industries customizing is not easy. Production costs are often too high. But sometimes cost is not the problem—delivery time is. Detroit has been able to customize automobiles for years. Yet most people buy a car off the showroom floor. Production costs are not the problem. Most customers just don't want to wait the 4 to 6 weeks for delivery. And, though car purchases are usually planned, the actual buying may be done rather impulsively.

However, consumers' desires for customization may change with faster delivery systems. In Tokyo (where else?), you can "design" your own car, and Toyota will have it ready in a week.

But how small can the target market get before you stop customizing? How about one ad for each potential customer?

Impossible?

Not at all.

Dreyfus Corporation, using ink-jet printing, took the first major step in customizing ads in *Money* magazine by replicating each mailing address within the body of a full-page ad. Advertising its tax-exempt mutual funds, Dreyfus slotted the top part of the Internal Revenue Service's Form 1040 individual tax return with the subscriber's name and address between the lines, "The IRS knows your address," and "It's only fair that you know ours."[14]

While this customizing was primarily to get the subscriber's attention, the next step is to use other information (besides name and address) to change the copy to meet the specific needs of the subscriber.

The copy could read "Now that both of you are working, you have more income. All the more reason why you should think in terms of tax exempts." Or, "Protect your two children, Tom and Ann, by maximizing your savings."

Your ability to accomplish this rests solely on the quality of your database; the technology is available.

Regardless of present difficulties, customization is the wave of the future. Who wouldn't want a product or service that exactly met his or her desired specifications?

Ask yourself, "What can my company do to move closer to customization?"

Recap

And there you have it. Five strategies that companies have used to differentiate their products and services.

1. Product and service modifications
2. Customer-service variations
3. Different distribution channels
4. Targeted communications
5. Variable pricing

Mull over these solutions for a minute. Were they dreamed up in the boardroom? Not likely. You've got to be pretty close to your customers to think of shrink-wrapping two-by-fours in plastic. Differentiation doesn't always entail big and dramatic changes, but it *does* require close attention to your customers and to the marketplace.

Don't make the mistake of modifying your product or service *before* checking to see if there's a market for it.

Study your customers first. Individually. Then ask yourself, "How can I differentiate my product or service to delight *my* customer?" Once you've found a way, then is the time to find out if your innovation will appeal to others, perhaps *many* others.

6

Six Commonsense
Rules for
Differentiation

Let's say you're already turning the basic strategies for differentiating your product or service over in your mind. You recognize that you can go in any number of directions, but, basically, differentiation hinges upon modifications of some kind in the following areas:

- Product or service
- Customer services
- Distribution channels
- Communications
- Price

OK. You've embraced the theory. But how do you make sure you're on the right track?

Follow these six commonsense rules.

Rule 1. Remember that
Small Can Be Beautiful

Wipe out the thought that bigger is always better.

As we saw in Guideline 5, Timex, Georgia-Pacific, Waldenbooks, and a host of other companies have found this out. They're getting bigger by acting smaller.

Rule 2. Be Differentiated,
Not Just Different

Make sure you have a product or service that offers a significant benefit to the target market.

Always ask, "What do customers really value?" And then appeal to those values better than anyone else. That's what differentiation implies.

Niche strategies often fail because the products and services are not sufficiently differentiated from other products and services serving broader market segments.

It's not enough just to be different. Everyone wants to be a Frank Perdue (the "chicken differentiator"). And there's nothing wrong with that. But face the fact that, try as you will—at least for now—you may have a product or service that you can't figure out how to differentiate.

Let's take a look at how some companies came out with products and services that were different but not differentiated. And the unfortunate results.

Courtesy of Punch Publications.

Unwanted Luxury Differences

Hassled by air travel?

Sure. Who isn't?

In 1983 Regent Air was formed to provide luxury cross-country flights. Planes were equipped with such niceties as telephones, copiers, and meeting facilities. To make doing business even easier while in-flight, a well-qualified secretary was on each flight. If you wanted to look your best upon arrival, a manicurist-hairstylist was aboard. You even got limousine service to avoid the chaos of getting to and from the airport. All for $3240 per round trip (versus, at that time, about $1400 for conventional first-class seats).

But the number of people who wanted this service was extremely limited. The luxury features did not offer enough value to the market. The company shut down after only a few months in operation.

Unwanted Bargain Differences

People Express was the exact opposite of Regent Air. People Express offered no-frills service at bargain rates. Part of the reason People Express could offer low fares was its labor costs. These were kept down partly because employees had stock options.

Now for stock options to be worthwhile, People Express had to grow. But the market for no-frill seats was limited and usually avoided (with good reason!) by airlines' bread-and-butter customers, the business travelers.

Although there were a number of reasons for People Express' demise, its faulty strategy (low salaried employees counting on making a killing through stock options) would have, by itself, eventually brought it down.

Differences Needed but Not Wanted

Don't become overzealous about consumer needs. You may have identified a product or service that consumers should want. Still, make sure that they *do* want this feature.

While searching for ways to differentiate its orange juice, Proctor & Gamble discovered that teenage girls and young women needed more calcium in their diets. So Citrus Hill with calcium orange juice was born.

Did it live up to Procter & Gamble's expectations?

No. Even though all the data showed that the market segment needed calcium, it didn't want calcium in orange juice.

The same thing happened to Ford. In the late 1950s, Ford's models were equipped with a safety package that included seat belts and padded visors and dashboards. This was equipment needed to keep drivers and passengers from getting clobbered in accidents.

Guess who got clobbered? Sure. It was Ford (along with thousands of drivers and passengers who didn't have Ford's safety package).

Technology Ahead of Consumers

Some products and services lacked acceptance because they were too far ahead of their time. For example, the first automated teller machines (ATMs) in the United States were financial disasters. It took more than a decade before ATMs caught on.

There are countless examples of other products and services that didn't make it (yet). Nimslo International Ltd.'s 35-mm range finder camera, which takes three-dimensional photographs, just didn't take off with amateur photographers. Coupled with high processing costs, it was technology the consumers just didn't want.

Would you like to have a "smart house"? Would you like to have lights and appliances scheduled, controlled, and monitored automatically? Would you like other advanced features, such as those that electronically watch for fires and burglars?

Well, the technology is available. Yet, consumer acceptance is not. Part of the reason is that people fear the loss of privacy.

R. J. Reynolds decided against a national rollout of its smokeless Premier cigarette after its long-term test marketing in Phoenix, St. Louis, and Tucson. There were many reasons for the product's failure to live up to expectations. But perhaps central was that consumers just didn't want to smoke a cigarette that heated instead of burned the tobacco. And that shouldn't have surprised anyone. After all, most people expect smoke when they smoke.

Banking on Subtle Tastes

The classic case is, of course, the New Coke.

Blind taste tests showed that people had a conclusive preference for a reformulated, slightly sweeter cola. So Coca-Cola came out with the New Coke.

A disaster. Coca-Cola realized, somewhat belatedly, that consumers' brand loyalties are complex, often emotional. Taste, by itself, is not the sole determinant.

Campbell Soup taste-tested its dry chicken soup against that of Lipton's, the leading manufacturer of dry chicken soup. Campbell's dry soup had significantly more chicken than Lipton's. In fact, in the original Lipton recipe (the one Campbell was taste-tested against), Lipton's soup had almost zero chicken content. Yet, people tasted the two, side by side, and said that Lipton's had more chicken flavor. People were confusing the flavor of sage and onion with the taste of chicken.

Misguided Attempts to Change Users' Buying Patterns

Why swim upstream?

A milk producers association, the United Dairy Industries Association, pushed whole milk to the public. And why shouldn't they? After all, the association's members, dairy farmers, got paid by the percentage of butter fat in the milk. The higher the percentage, the greater the payment. So dairy farmers love fat in milk.

But consumers are looking for low-fat products.

Now here's a question for you. Are sales of whole milk increasing or decreasing?

Of course, they are decreasing.

And what about low fat milk? Sales are increasing.

But the United Dairy Industries Association avoids any mention of low-fat milk. Apparently it believes that if salmon can swim upstream, so can cows.

Questions to Ask Yourself

To offer products and services that match your target market's buying behavior, ask yourself these questions:

- If you have a luxury—or a bargain—product or service, is the niche large enough, both in the short run and long run, to make it profitable?

- Do your customers really want your product or service, even if they need it?

- If you have the newest state-of-the-art product or service, are you "too far in front of the troops"?

- Are you counting on subtle taste differences?

- Are you asking customers to change their buying patterns when there is little reason for them to do so?

If the answer is yes to any of these questions, your product or service may be different, but it is not differentiated. Double-check—no, triple-check—your assumptions.

We're not trying to scare you out of trying to differentiate your product and services. You should. But for now, if the best you can do is to make your products and services only different, you should rethink your marketing plans.

Rule 3. Borrow from the Competition—Then Go One Better

Closely monitor your competitors. If they come up with a good idea, don't let the NIH (not-invented-here) syndrome keep you from adopting it.

But if you only mimic the competition, you'll be forever in a catch-up mode. Therefore, you must try to outniche them.

You can pick up ideas by taking a close look at companies in the same business you're in but who do not compete directly with you (parallel companies). For example, a regional bank might examine banking practices in other regions.

Of course these companies may also be latent competitors, looming as threats in the future. For example, a parallel company in another country may be tomorrow's *bête noire*. Detroit's automakers realized this—somewhat belatedly—about the Japanese auto companies.

Even if you don't uncover suitable niching strategies by looking at parallel companies, this activity is not a total loss. At the minimum, you'll learn their modus operandi. This is invaluable information should they decide to penetrate your markets or should you decide to try to gain entry into theirs.

But remember that the best ideas of all may come from outside your industry. For example, frequent-flier clubs spawned frequent-user clubs, such as The Great Payback, Frequent Shoppers Advantage Club, and Giftlink Shoppers Reward. These companies overcame the NIH syndrome. Therefore, you should copy where you can—but only borrow the best.

Rule 4. Position by Differentiation and Segmentation

Your product or service can't be all things to all people. Yet you can, by a number of customizations, appeal to a host of well-defined niches. To succeed, however, your offerings must be well positioned.

Positioning is the outcome of two components: product or service differentiation and segmentation. Although we suggest starting with differentiation and then going on to segmentation, it's often a back-and-forth process.

The first step in positioning is to decide how you can differentiate your product or service. Remember to look at customers as individuals. What are their key buying motives? Although customers may have a number of purchasing motives, only a few are key. Concentrate on these.

The next step is segmentation. Put customers into groups (or segments) according to key buying motives. Then decide whether each segment is worthy for you to target. (We talk about that in Guideline 20.)

Think of niche marketing as a value-added situation. By differentiating and segmenting, you're adding specific values for a specific group of people.

Kellogg's Mueslix succeeded because it appealed to the niche's key buying motives: convenience and nutrition. Hallmark's To Kids With Love cards were a much needed way for upscale, working parents to communicate with their kids. Apple Computer's industry-solutions approach served those customers whose key buying motive was problem solution.

Key buying motives also can be satisfied by going upscale. That's what Tropicana did when it came out with a not-from-concentrate orange juice, Pure Premium. Or Kodak with its top drawer amateur film, Ektar. Or downscale. Marriott introduced Fairfield Inns.

Rule 5. Develop a Clear Image for Each Niche

If members of the niche identify your product or service as being specifically for them—and it's something they want—you'll be successful. It's as simple as that.

Be sure you have a clear image of the people in your target market. Don't make the mistake of trying to speak to those outside of your niche as well. Communicate how your product or service helps them fulfill their key buying motives. But don't try to tell them everything. Concentrate on one or two of your niche's key buying motives.

And to avoid blurred images, use a new name. Like Ektar (Kodak) and Pure Premium (Tropicana).

Why Line Extensions Fail

So many companies violate this very simple rule and do exactly the opposite. They want to give their new products or services free rides to success by using the brand names of existing successful products or services. In other words, line extensions.[1]

In most cases this just doesn't work.

Look at Clorox, which introduced a detergent under the Clorox brand name, a name totally associated with bleach. Since the clear image for Clorox was to make things white, consumers were concerned about using Clorox detergent. As Dennis Ferguson, a buyer for a regional supermarket said, "[consumers of Clorox detergent] . . . don't want all their clothes to turn white."

Even those consumers who realized Clorox detergent was color-safe were given no basis to differentiate it from, for example, Tide with bleach. Leveraging the brand name was not enough to give Clorox a smooth ride into the detergent market.[2]

The clear image created by Seven-Up for its main product was the uncola. It even advertised, "Never had it, never will" for cola color and caffeine. The image was unique. Great. But greed set in. Seven-Up wanted an inexpensive entry into the cola market and came up with the line extension, 7-Up Gold.

Backed by a $10 million advertising compaign, 7-Up Gold was introduced as the soft drink that "had it," cola color and caffeine. But as Roger Casley, president of Seven-Up Bottling Company of San Francisco, said, "The product was misunderstood . . . People have a clear view of what 7-Up products should be—clear and crisp and clean and no caffeine. 7-Up Gold is darker and it does have caffeine, so it doesn't fit the 7-Up image." Even John Alhers, the CEO of Seven-Up, said, "I'll be honest. It's a failure."[3]

When Line Extensions Can Work

There are certain instances in which line extensions can work.

Shared Image. When Fisher-Price introduced a new line of children's furniture, it marketed it under the house brand name, Fisher-Price. In the area of toys, the Fisher-Price image is safety and durability. That same appeal was used to market its children's furniture, a very successful case of image sharing in a line extension.

Barbasol decided that its base product, shaving cream, might have more appeal to some customers as a scented product. So out came Barbasol Lemon Lime Beard Buster. The company made another line extension when it added lanolin (Barbasol Sensitive Skin Beard Buster) for sensitive skin. And Barbasol Musk Beard Buster. And Barbasol Menthol Beard Buster. These line extensions represented consistent images with different target markets. They wouldn't benefit from a new brand name, nor would they hurt the existing one.

Service Is Key. Another situation favoring line extension is one in which service is the key ingredient or key success factor. This is especially true for services such as insurance. It makes sense, for example, that CIGNA Insurance would use the CIGNA name on all its insurance products.

Market research companies count on experience and trust as a key success factor. Thus, A. C. Nielsen Company uses the Nielsen name for all of its products such as Nielsen Retail Audits, Nielsen Media Research, and Nielsen ScanTrack.

Limited Budget. If you absolutely don't have the funds to create an image for new products and services, you might be forced, as a last resort, to share image with existing ones. But be sure you use consistent images between products and services. Otherwise, what appears to be the less expensive solution may be the most expensive, as Clorox and Seven-Up found out.

Rule 6. Constantly Watch for Shifts in the Marketplace

Your customers and competitors have changed. And they will continue to do so. Just as you will. You'll change jobs. You'll make more money (hopefully). You'll change eating habits (you'd better). And so on.

So its "focus, focus, focus" all the time. We're back to Guideline 1. But the point is central: You need to know your markets as you never did before.

Timing is everything. As Alvin Toffler says in *The Third Wave*, "Capitalizing on *the wave* is like surf-boarding. If you ride the crest, you'll succeed. Too early, you'll get wiped out. Too late, you'll slowly sink."

Recap

Differentiation will help you grow bigger by acting smaller. To make differentiation work, follow these six rules:

1. Remember that small can be beautiful. Wipe out the thought that bigger is always better.

2. Be differentiated, not just different. Always ask, "What do customers really value?" Then appeal to those values better than anyone else.

3. Borrow from the competition—then go one better. Learn from your competitors, but don't stop there. Leapfrog over them by picking up ideas outside your industry.

4. Position by differentiation and segmentation. Look at your customers as individuals. Then segment by putting customers into groups according to key buying motives.

5. Develop a clear image for each niche. Communicate how your product or service helps a specific niche. Don't try to speak to those outside this niche as well.

6. Constantly watch for shifts in the marketplace. Changes are taking place, and timing is everything.

7

Avoiding Cannibalization

*The only thing worse than eating your own
lunch is to have someone else eat it.*

Serving more markets with new (or slightly modified) products and services can lead to cannibalization. In fact, our work with big-company niche marketers pointed out that cannibalization was a major problem for about 1 in 10 of them. Of course, having your new products eat away at your established markets is something you'd like to avoid. And perhaps you can.

The Fundamental Rule: Market Different Products and Services for Different Niches

It's as simple (but note—we didn't say "easy") as this: Market different products and services to different well-defined, distinct niches. And the more narrowly defined the niche, the easier it is to differentiate a product or service and avoid cannibalization.

American Express believes that its different card offerings (green, gold, corporate, platinum, and optima) suffer only minimum effects from cannibalization. Betsy Ludlow, vice president, student marketing, claimed that this is because each of American Express' target markets is well defined. Furthermore, each product offering has unique enhancements that are exclusive to that segment. Says Ludlow:

> I suppose our personal [green] card would be at greatest risk of cannibalization . . . But I don't think the risk is significant. The features of the green card . . . still have the broadest appeal amongst the largest number of people. This product is our work horse and every year we introduce new enhancements that continue to strengthen our core product.[1]

There is little cannibalization here. Why? Because American Express has targeted different products for different niches.

Campbell Soup also found that using new names for new products that were aimed at different segments helped avoid cannibalization. Prego, Casera, and Pepperidge Farm are all Campbell brands.

Or, take Coca-Cola. The company came out with a new product, Diet Coke, that was in direct competition with its former diet drink, Tab. Placing all their bets on Diet Coke, they ignored Tab.

But now they revived Tab and repositioned it with an upscale image instead of going after the hard-core dieters. They targeted those areas where Tab did the best, and they are marketing Tab only in those areas that are low consumers of cola.[2]

Still, even though you have different products for different niches, there will always be some cannibalization. However, your present customers are less likely to switch to differentiated products or services that are more expensive than the original product or service. For example, when Kodak introduced a more expensive film, Ektar, which was targeted toward the advanced amateur photographer, they suffered little cannibalization. Richard Larbach, director of worldwide business planning for Kodak's consumer film products, claimed, "You don't worry about [cannibalization] as much when you're moving [consumer] upward."[3]

The Bark May Be Worse than the Bite

But what if you've got a new, improved product or service that will be in direct competition with your existing products and services? It's possible that there are more niches than you think and that the market will accept both.

Examine Kodak's experience with a technological product improvement. John A. Lacy, general manager of marketing and vice president, business imaging systems division, said:

... electronics was viewed as a potential threat to many of our traditional film products. We had a difficult decision to make: should we stay with traditional products, or switch to the new technologies? We did both ... and we let our customers decide. From them, we learned that there was a clear need for both traditional and new technologies ...[4]

Did Kodak's strategy pay off? You bet.

A savings bank came out with a money market investment fund indexed to Donoghue's 7-day money fund average. The bank thought it would have a cannibalization problem since it also offered a money market investment fund whose rate was not indexed. They worried that the nonindexed accounts would be lost and that the only thing the money market investment fund would do, in the short run, would be to increase its cost of funds.

But they decided they would live with that because the purpose of the product was gap management—to maintain the spread in the changing interest-rate environment with a variable-rate product. As it turned out, they didn't have a lot of cannibalization.

The same thing happened at Alpo Pet Food Company. At a staff meeting, the brand manager of its super premium dog treats (a niche market) reported soaring sales. The brand manager of the regular dog biscuits reported the opposite. His sales were declining, and he claimed that the niche product was taking away sales from the regular dog biscuits.

This started a not-too-friendly interchange.

"I don't think this is what's happening. We're serving two distinct markets," claimed the manager of the super premium product. "Can you prove that my product is taking sales away from yours?"

"No, I can't afford the study."

"Well, I can." So she sponsored a research project to identify the source of the increased volume of super premium dog treat sales. The study showed she was right: her product's success was not at the expense of regular dog biscuit sales.

A final point.

When two or three niches are being treated as a single market, no one is getting the product or service he or she wants. Offering a better choice for each niche may lead to more brand loyalty, greater frequency of use, and/or greater use per frequency.

This is not cannibalization.

It's good niche marketing.

When Kleenex first offered the small purse-sized package of tissues, some thought it would cannibalize the traditional box of tissues. Many women already took layers of tissues from the boxes and carried them in their purses. Sure, some people used fewer boxed tissues because they used the purse-sized packet instead. But overall, people carried more. Total tissue use was up, and the purse-sized tissues brought in higher profit margins.

Cannibalization? Hardly.

When the Dog Bites

Of course, severe cannibalization will occur sometimes. Your new product or service may be quite superior to the old. In addition, it may be aimed at the same niche. Furthermore, your customers may have a good reason to switch. Then the new product or service will probably take business away from the old.

But what if you stick to the old product or service because of the threat of cannibalism?

Look what happened to Gillette. It was reluctant to introduce a stainless steel razor blade because it would cannibalize its bread-and-butter product, the Super Blue Blade. Of course, this didn't stop the competition. Just because Gillette didn't want stainless steel didn't mean that consumers didn't.

Consider the secondary effects of Gillette's failure to sell stainless steel blades. It gave Wilkinson Sword an entry into retail stores. Wilkinson could never have gotten shelf space if Gillette had already been there with stainless steel.

Finally, after Wilkinson (and others) had shaved off 15 percent of Gillette's market share, Gillette introduced its stainless steel blade. And since then, Gillette has profitably continued to attack itself with new and improved products.

Suppose you develop a new product or service. Sure you can keep your new product or service under wraps until a competitor makes its launch. Just be sure that you weigh the cost of giving your competitor a head start against possible cannibalization.

CPC International recognized that its new cholesterol-free mayonnaise would probably take business away from its existing light-mayonnaise business—possibly by as much as 60 percent. Still, CPC believed that it would increase its overall market share. Besides, what if Kraft beat them to the marketplace with a cholesterol-free mayonnaise? CPC's light-mayonnaise business might still lose 60 percent of sales, only not to another CPC product but to Kraft's instead.[5]

Sir Alexander Maxwell, chairman, Philip Morris, offers this advice. "Every new product you ever bring out takes business away [from an old product]. The issue is, if you have a good idea, do it yourself. Because if you don't and somebody else does, you're a total loser."[6]

The Fatal Mistake

But what about all the horror stories we've heard about cannibalization? Don't blame the results on niche marketing. Blame them on product churning.

There is a difference between niche marketing and product churning. Product churning is coming out with new products and services to expand sales. Period. It's not coming out with clearly differentiated products or services for clearly defined niches.

For example, during a 5-year period, one major consumer products company introduced over 600 products. Some were new brands. Most were line extensions. But only a few were truly successful. Some were just marginally successful, and many were outright failures. In fact, the situation caused David Oligvy (who had advised the company 6 years previously to come out with more new products) to yell words to this effect at a meeting of the firms' executives: "Stop it! Stop it I say. Never in my wildest imagination did I believe you'd carry out my advice to this extreme!"

Recap

Once you start coming out with more products and services for smaller market segments, cannibalization is always a threat.

But you can keep cannibalization at a minimum by making sure your products and services offer real, discernible differences for well-defined, distinct niches.

But what if you come up with a better product or service for the same target market? It's better to eat your own lunch than to have someone else eat it. Besides, the effects of cannibalization may not be as great as you think.

But what about all the horror stories we've heard about cannibalization? Usually they're not the result of niche marketing. They're the outcome of product churning. Which you want to avoid like the plague.

8
Making Regional Marketing Work

Don't confuse regional marketing with selling spicier soup in Texas. Or reorganizing the sales force by regions to gain more control. Or spending heavy-up dollars in a local market.

Regional marketing is a niche-marketing approach. First, you divide the country into regions, such as the Southeast, Midwest, or whatever, depending upon regional preferences. Then—and this is crucial—you shift responsibility for many marketing activities from the national product or service manager at headquarters to the regional marketing manager in the field. Finally, you localize marketing mixes to capitalize on unique sales opportunities in each of those regions.

Regional marketing represents a major philosophic change. It's a niche-marketing solution to fragmented national markets.

Why Regional Marketing?

The Many Regions of the United States

International marketers have long recognized the need to tailor their marketing strategies to various regions with differing governments, levels of economic development, languages, cultures, religions, and the like. On the other hand, domestic marketers have seen the United States as one big, homogeneous country. In fact, the United States has more regional dissimilarities than many people believe.

If you're selling construction equipment, where is your market? When certain regions, such as Nevada, were experiencing growth, others, like the Wheat Belt, were fighting to keep communities alive.

How about if you're a manufacturer of specialty metals selling to defense contractors? Some regions, such as California and Texas, have a greater concentration of defense contractors than others.

The market for agricultural sprinkler systems is far flung. But you won't find it in Manhattan.

Or look at some demographic figures. About the same number of people live in New England as do in the Mountain Region. Yet the Mountain Region is growing at a much faster rate, and the population's median age is lower.

- The South gained almost 20 million jobs while another region was christened the Rust Belt.

- The Northeast, not known for rapid population growth, still leads the nation in household income growth.

- Portland, Maine, is almost totally white. Washington, D.C., is predominantly black.

No wonder Olgivy and Mather now provides its clients with detailed consumer profiles on eight United States regions in addition to the traditional national data!

Beyond Regional Differences

There's more driving companies to switch to regional marketing than just regional differences. There are disparities within regions; more localized media; and better, more specific data.

Local Differences.   Localities within regions often have unique characteristics. Take a look at Miami. Fifty-six percent of the population is Hispanic. But in neighboring Fort Lauderdale, only 4 percent is Hispanic. And the differences are not just demographic. For example, price wars among supermarkets occasionally heat up in some cities. Meanwhile, nearby communities are unaffected.

Local News Media.   But it's not just the differences among regions and localities. Regional marketing can work because there are regional and local media. Regional magazines such as *Sunset*, state magazines such as *New Jersey* and city magazines such as *Philadelphia Magazine* make targeting local markets possible. In addition, there are regional editions of national publications, local television, cable, radio stations, and so on.

Better Data.   It's tough to address smaller segments unless you've got the data. And we're light years ahead in data collection than we were just a decade ago. Scanners in supermarkets, ATMs in banks, and hand-held computers, to name just a few technological advances, provide more data at the regional and local levels.

More Regional and Local Promotion Programs

More regional and local media and specific data help make regional marketing work. No wonder there's more trade promotion geared to regional customers. And more promotion of events, causes, and issues for local customers.

When Regional Needs Aren't Met

If you have regional differences but still cling to mass-marketing approaches, you're asking for trouble. Look what happened at a frozen-dairy product company. At a regional sales managers' meeting, the Northeast sales manager, who was in charge of sales only, said he was afraid that new local legislation would have a negative impact on his sales. The national brand manager said that, as far as he was concerned, this was not a problem; it was a local situation. So no special support for the Northeast would be forthcoming from national headquarters.

The national brand manager's response was followed by two further events. First, the regional sales manager left the company. It was clear to him that his local situation was not considered important by the company. Second, the local problem was a harbinger. It quickly became a national problem.

In another case, a company defined a serious competitor as one that took away at least $5 million of sales from the national brand. That wasn't happening. Yet the regional markets were getting clobbered by regional competitors. However, by the company's definition, not one of the regional competitors met the $5 million trigger point (although cumulatively they did). Besides, the national brand manager could not develop a single campaign to defend against the many regional competitors.

Ignore regional differences, and you pay the piper.

The Myth of Being Number One

You can be number one in the nation but only number three or number four in most regional markets. Strong regional competitors might own the regional markets. But because these competitors only market within their regions, they might have only a small national market share. Consequently, you could be number one nationally by default. All the while, you could be losing market share and sales in the regions. Not much of a leadership position!

If your product or service is in such a "leadership" position, save your praise for the sales meetings. Not for board meetings where they're interested in profits.

The trend is clear. Brand leadership in the future will often be defined in terms of regional and local markets, not a national one.

The Shift to Regional Markets

No wonder so many companies are shifting to regional marketing. Consider the following sampling:

McDonald's, a significant player in the regional marketing game, spends about 50 percent of its total advertising budget regionally.

The major portion of American Airlines' total marketing budget is dedicated to regional marketing. Each region has separate marketing plans. For example, Chicago has a plan and the Southwest has a plan. The reason? In January, Chicago residents have very different travel needs than residents in the Southwest. Lots of people from Chicago would like to go to the Southwest in January. But in January how many people from Phoenix would like to casually stroll down Chicago's Michigan Avenue and window-shop? The travel needs of each of these markets must be addressed separately.

But regional differences aren't the only cause for the switch to regional marketing. Often the unique characteristics of local markets within regions can be handled better at the regional level than at the national level. For instance, Anheuser-Busch subdivided its regional markets into ethnic and demographic segments. Then it came out with different advertising campaigns for each segment. One result: the conquest of the Hispanic market. In California, Anheuser-Busch's share of this niche is estimated to be between 60 percent and 70 percent.[1]

Yet regional marketing managers can handle only so much disparity, or they will wind up handcuffed like so many national product or service managers who try to develop marketing programs for the nation. So the number of variations in the local markets should be a determining factor in deciding the size of the regions.

Is Regional Marketing for You?

Regional marketing is *not* for every firm or for every product or service. So before you turn to regional marketing, resolve the following nine questions for each of your product and service lines.

1. Can Your Management Think Profits—Not Costs?

Regional marketing causes a big change in the cost of doing business. In almost every area costs are higher.

For example, there are shorter production runs and more frequent changeovers than when a single product is produced to national specifications. Expect an increase in cost of goods sold for products produced for regional markets.

Costs are also higher because of a loss of advertising efficiency. Regional spot-TV rates (as measured by reach) are higher than the national rates—an average of 30 percent higher. Advertising production charges are higher since a number of regional ads are run instead of one national ad.

There are additional costs for coupon insertions in lower circulation newspapers and magazines. Small wonder that General Foods reported that it cost 2 to 3 times as much to run numerous regional events than one national event![2]

So regional marketing will cost more.

If it costs more to make more, so be it.

But that view is not always accepted. We've found that in a number of companies, senior management doesn't see it that way. Executives with a marketing orientation focus on profits. But executives with a sales orientation focus on sales volume. They think profits will come—if not now, later—with sales.

If you've got a lot of salespersons dressed up like marketers, you've got some selling to do before you can think about implementing regional marketing in your company.

2. Do Your Target Markets' Needs Vary from Region to Region?

Selling insurance to people in Florida, with its higher-than-average age but higher-than-average income, is very different from selling insurance to big families of the Midwest.

Lens Crafters (eyewear) tailors its product mix to each of its stores. The most popular styles in New England are almost preppy: simple, classic, and unisex. In South Florida, people like brighter colors and a little bit more of the Christian Dior look.

If your customers' needs vary by region, it's a strong case for regional marketing.

3. Do Your Trade Outlets and Practices Vary among Regions?

Do you have regional differences in retail outlets? For example, Des Moines is dominated by conventional supermarket-store layouts. Yet warehouse stores prevail in Minneapolis.

Do members of your distribution channels, from region to region, sell, advertise, or run their businesses differently?

One major automobile manufacturer found that in some parts of the country its dealers were very aggressive in getting people into the showrooms. In these markets they could spend less on spot TV and more on price deals. In other regions the dealers relied on the automobile manufacturer to get people into the showrooms. Here the manufacturer had to spend more on TV, leaving less money for price deals.

Differences in trade outlets and trade practices are a strong indicator of the need for regional marketing.

4. Do Your Available Media Differ among Regions?

Ringling Brothers found that it has to pitch the big top differently in the 90 markets it serves. One of the major reasons is that its available media vary from region to region. In New York it's pretty basic. There are half a dozen television stations, three major newspapers, and, of course, subways and buses. But how different it is in Hershey, Pennsylvania. Since there is no principal newspaper, Ringling advertises in as many as 30 local newspapers. Outdoor billboards are rare in New York City but numerous in the Southwest. And so on. It's small wonder that Ringling has a staff of about 40 people charged with being regional authorities.[3]

Faced with similar media differences? Then one approach to all may not be your best choice.

5. Are There Local Variations in Legislation That Affect You?

Many products and services are affected by local laws. Insurance. Labeling. Warranties. Selling practices (two states do not allow self-service gas stations). Direct mail programs. Adverstising (remember when Florida was going to tax all national advertising shown in that state?).

If your products and services are closely regulated—and these regulations vary from region to region—localizing marketing programs may be advisable.

6. Do You Have Strong
Local Competitors?

If you're operating nationally and you have strong local competitors in some—or all—regions, you can count on this: They will all have different price strategies, different service strategies, different distribution strategies, and so on.

You'll need lots of luck if you try to develop a national program that will effectively and efficiently handle that competitive mishmash.

7. Do Marketing Practices of
Your National Competitors Vary
by Region?

Coca-Cola and PepsiCo have battled in the national arena for years. But the real hand-and-fist marketing still takes place at the local level. They work with bottlers. They sponsor almost any local activity. They advertise in school papers. They provide local restaurants with place mats. And so on. Coke does this because Pepsi does. Pepsi does this because Coke does.

The more your competition practices regional marketing, the more likely you should also.

8. How Good Is
Your Database?

Regional marketing requires a more extensive database than national marketing. For example, if you use consumer demographic or psychographic tracking information to make marketing decisions, then you'll need it for each region. When doing research, instead of a national sample size of say 1000 to give statistical validity and reliability, you'll need a sample of 1000 from each region. When you track competitors, instead of monitoring just a few national firms, you also must keep watch on scores of regional and local competitors.

Think about what kind of data you now have and what regional data you can get. Remember, successful niche marketing requires information, not intuition.

9. Do You Have a Good
Reporting System?

With regional marketing you'll be dealing with a number of decentralized units. Without information there's no control. It's as plain as that.

If your present information channels leave much to be desired, listen to our plea: Don't start regional marketing until you get your reporting system in order.

Data requirements will pyramid. One executive told us that today each of his company's regional offices has nearly as much data as the company had nationally in the mid-1980s.

Making Regional Marketing Work

The experiences of regional marketers point to six important rules. You'll find these rules quite similar to the rules of general niche marketing. Only the accent is on slightly different syllables.

Rule 1. Analyze the Market

Start off by making sure you really understand the market (it's back to Guideline 1, "Focus, Focus, Focus"). You've got to have a thorough understanding of your customers, the trade, competitors, and other external forces, such as local legislation.

Make sure that regional marketing is necessary. As a check, try to find as much commonality among regions as possible. It won't be wasted time. These findings will also serve as a basis for a national strategy. And, you'll need a national strategy regardless of what you decide to do about regional marketing.

Rule 2. Use an Evolutionary Approach

Pick products and services that have the most to gain from a regional strategy. Focus your attention on those first. Make sure they become company success stories.

Have your regional marketing managers waiting, yes, even crying, for the next products and services to be given the regional treatment. That's much better than having them complain that too much has been thrown at them all at once.

Rule 3. Develop a National Strategy

You still need to develop a national strategy for each product or service that has been designated for regional marketing. The regional plan must be within the context of a national plan. Otherwise expect chaos.

Rule 4. Decentralize

The national brand manager's job is to determine the national strategy for the product or service. He or she should find an umbrella of core benefits that will clearly and consistently position the product or service in the customers' minds in all regions.

The rest is up to the regional managers, who have to comply with the national strategy while at the same time develop localized marketing programs including advertising, sales promotions, and trade allowances. Their job requires a hands-on, tactical approach.

The national brand manager's job is to develop and implement strategy. The regional manager's job is to devise and execute tactics. It's as simple as that.

Well, maybe it's not quite that simple.

First, sometimes the national brand manager tries to develop tactics. Then the regional managers spend time trying to outguess the national brand manager. Or perhaps they try to "get" the national brand manager. Or the regional managers try to protect their own turf. All this activity is at the expense of thinking about how best to serve customers.

To avoid this kind of backbiting, give regional marketing managers clear responsibility and authority to make certain decisions in their own regions. Don't let them evolve into just another layer of management. Don't permit the national brand manager to veto regional decisions.

Another complicating factor is that it's a rare national brand manager who welcomes decentralization, especially since a significant portion of his or her budget is "given" to the regional marketing managers. In some of the companies we talked to, as much as 60 percent of the total marketing budget is dispersed to the field.

Besides reduced budgets, national brand managers stand to lose partial control of information. No longer will they be first to "take a cut" at the data before action plans are formulated. With information available at the local level, regional managers will often act on a real-time basis with first-hand information.

So decentralization adds up to less money and less control of information for the national brand manager.

And what aggressive national brand manager wants to give up power, especially to regional managers? After all, there traditionally has been a clear distinction in status between corporate staff and field staff. And, in almost every case we encountered, the regional marketing managers were undertrained and ill prepared for their new responsibilities. On the other hand, the national brand managers were much more knowledgeable in strategic and tactical planning.

Yet the transition of power must take place.

Some of your national brand managers may have to be fired. But allow them time for adjustment because regional marketing will be different.

Rule 5. Make Sure You Have
the Right Regional Managers

Start by defining the responsibilities of regional managers. This will demonstrate what the regional managers must know and be able to do. Usually they must be on top of market conditions, such as customers, competition, the trade, and local laws. The regional managers must also be attuned to local media, events, and personalities, besides being able to put it all together and develop a marketing plan.

Next, find the right people for the job. Make experienced senior marketers regional marketing managers. But if you're like most companies, you don't have many—or any—such people on tap. So you'll do as most companies do. You'll choose your best sales managers to be regional marketing managers.

Now this approach is fraught with problems. These individuals' bonuses and promotions have come from the sales volumes they've generated from the trade. Then, one day they become regional marketing managers. Guess what? They continue to act like salespersons (or sales managers) to the trade. So they spend most of their marketing dollars on the trade. And with gusto.

One company's first step in implementing regional marketing was to place trade spending in the regions. What do you think happened? They *overspent* their budget by $85 million in their first (and last) year.

To make matters worse, usually these sales managers-regional marketing managers neglect other elements of the marketing mix. Like consumer advertising.

So, since many of your regional marketing managers will probably come from the field, education and training will be a must.

We've found that in most cases experienced salespersons aren't short on creativity. But they lack understanding of basic concepts of marketing. Like consumer promotions. And concepts of marketing management. Like the difference between strategy and tactics. (How successful will they be in integrating their local tactical programs into the overall national strategy?) Salespersons are also short on planning skills. For instance, how to execute and evaluate a promotion plan.

Besides formal training, think about some form of job rotation. One company we talked with found that cross training prior to formal training was very helpful. Brand managers were sent to the field, and the designated regional marketing managers were brought to headquarters.

A good practice. Field personnel can better comprehend the need and value of training and can better understand the brand managers' role and problems. Then, brand managers will be in a better position to appreciate the problems faced by the newly appointed regional managers. All of which will help the new organization function more smoothly.

But regardless of how much you train, your regional marketing managers are still going to experience difficulties. For instance, they will have a hard time locating a good advertising agency. Big national advertising agencies are not equipped to deal with regional issues. With the exception of a few, they're still mass-market oriented.

Once you've found the right people, it will probably be some time before you are able to provide regional managers with information similar to that which you have at the national level. And it will be an even longer time before they are effective with its use.

Rule 6. Have Your Communication Network in Order

You're decentralized. Now you need real-time communications. Unless everyone is working from the same page, you can expect loss of control. Establish information-reporting systems. And, make sure everyone knows reporting relationships.

If your plans call for the use of specialized equipment, such as hand-held or lap-top computers, see that they're available and usable. In most cases, this calls for specialized training to build users' confidence in the systems.

Establishing a good communication system is a nitty-gritty, time-consuming part of regional marketing. But mess up here, and you can plan on spending the next year digging yourself out of a hole. If you're still around.

After Implementation: What to Expect

Our work with regional marketers indicates that you'll probably go through six stages in implementing regional marketing. The time you spend in each stage will vary *inversely* with the extent to which you've followed the advice given in this guideline.[4]

Stage 1. Shock at the Corporate Level

National brand managers immediately feel the impact of changed reporting relationships. For example, suppose data shows that a product's sales are slipping. How can the brand manager get more information?

Before decentralization, the national brand manager would only have to contact the national sales manager. Now the brand manager has to get in touch with every regional manager. In one case national brand managers had to contact 22 different regional marketing managers!

It's 6.4 on the Richter scale at headquarters!

Stage 2. Shock at the Regional Level

The Richter scale is also registering 6.4 in the regions.

The newly appointed regional marketing managers are not quite sure of what they should do. Or, how they should go about doing whatever it is that they're supposed to be doing.

The regional marketing managers ask a bunch of questions, such as, "What can I do in advertising?" "What ad themes can I use?" "Which agencies can I use?" "Who approves the budget?" "How do I develop a marketing plan?" "And by the way, what exactly is *marketing*?"

Stage 3. Euphoria in the Field

The shock waves subside. Regional marketing groups now realize they're in charge of their own destiny.

And, what a deal! They have a budget with discretionary expenditures for trade discounts, advertising, local promotions, and the like.

No more bureaucracy. No more trying to convince headquarters to "see it our way." No longer being slow to react to changing market conditions while waiting for headquarters to make up its mind.

Many regional marketing groups feel like they've died and gone to heaven.

Stage 4. Dialing for Dollars

The regional marketing managers have years of backlogged ideas that they always wanted to try. Now they can.

But their budgets don't last.

So they call up the national brand managers and ask for more money. Sometimes they get it. But too often the money received is not well spent. Why? Inexperience in the field.

Stage 5. Mutual Respect

The national brand managers have now watched both their money and power shift to the regions. Much to their chagrin, some regional programs have been highly successful. Regional managers begin to realize that the national umbrella program is important.

Both groups recognize that they need each other.

Then too, there are new standards and new controls in place. But most important, there is a new level of understanding.

Stage 6. Improved Profits— and Growth

Respect leads to confidence. And confidence fosters teamwork.

Each group focuses on its own objectives, does its own job, and is not overly concerned with its counterparts.

As in sports or the military, teamwork leads to success. And in business, success spells profits and growth.

Regional marketing: Finally it's working!

Recap

Regional marketing is a niche-marketing approach to fragmented national markets.

But is regional marketing for you? Ask these nine questions:

1. Can your management think profits—not costs?
2. Do your target markets' needs vary from region to region?
3. Do your trade outlets and practices vary among regions?
4. Do your available media differ among regions?
5. Are there local variations in legislation that affect you?
6. Do you have strong, local competitors?
7. Do marketing practices of your national competitors vary by region?
8. How good is your database?
9. Do you have a good reporting system?

If you decide that regional marketing is for you, expect problems. But these problems can be minimized by following these six rules:

1. Analyze the market.
2. Use an evolutionary approach.
3. Develop regional plans within the context of a national strategy.
4. Decentralize.
5. Make sure you have the right regional managers.
6. Have your communication network in order.

9
Test, Test, Test

Some things are easier gotten into than out of. That's the first thing that will cross your mind when your new product or service fails.

Launching a new product or service is simple compared to dropping one. You've got lots going for you during a launch, especially optimism and enthusiasm.

Dropping a product or service, on the other hand, is like working with a leper—no one wants anything to do with it. There's the problem of your wholesalers' and retailers' inventories. And how do you handle customers who have already invested in your product or service? What about repairs and continuing services? Will the failure of your niche product or service alienate prospects for your other products and services?

These are not the kind of questions you're likely to dwell upon in the heat of persuading top management to give the go-ahead for a new product or service. They're too negative.

Marketers plead, beg, and beseech top management to launch new products and services. And well over one-half of these products and services fail. Why? Either the products and services weren't tested or they were poorly tested.

If you're in niche marketing, you've got to be an expert at market testing. Testing is even more important in niche marketing than it is in traditional mass marketing because you're working with more specialized needs.

Suppose your entire marketing program is centered on satisfying a specific key buying motive for a narrowly defined target market. Further, suppose that the target market fails to see your product or service offering as meeting its key buying motive. It's over. There will be few—if any—fringe markets that will be interested in your product or service.

100

No matter how well you think you know the niche market, you've got to test your offering. Then test it again. And again.

Of course, testing niche markets can be a catch-22 situation. You've got to do a better job of testing than you would in mass marketing. Yet because the niche is relatively small, you don't have the budget or time that you might for a mass market.

So forget about the esoteric textbook approaches. Instead, follow the methods suggested in these 10 rules.

Rule 1. Start Testing Early

Don't delay testing until you think all the bugs are out of your product or service and it's ready for market. Engage in concept or other diagnostic testing to gain insights on how to change your product or service while it's in the development stage.

With a niche product or service there's a great temptation to delay testing. The rationale goes something like this, "After all, we're talking low volume, small-scale stuff."

Sound logical?

We hope not.

Because it isn't.

Waiting to test until you think your product or service is ready for the market usually puts you in a go or no-go situation.

Here's why. If you wait, the costs of modifying the product or service are usually high. And, perhaps of equal importance (to you), you stand to lose face if the test shows that costly changes have to be made after so much has already been invested. So, at this point, there's a great temptation to enter the market even if the test shows only a very low chance for success.

Rule 2. Work Closely with Your Target Niche

Chances are you're serving highly specialized needs. So why take a chance? Involve your customer directly in the product or service development. Make sure the product or service satisfies the desired core benefits and that it's user-friendly.

At Black & Decker, products are tested on the customers' sites. Black & Decker's engineers and marketers work one-on-one with end users. (As a bonus, Black & Decker often receives feedback on competitors' products.)

It happens much the same way at National-Standard Company's specialty products division. Customers tell them which products are not meeting their expectations. The division may get this information from questionnaires, its sales engineers, or through some other form of feedback.

Then the specialty products division design team, including representatives from the technical, manufacturing, and marketing groups, goes into action. The team meets with the customers. The team observes, usually at the customers' plants, how the product is used and determines what improvements are necessary.

Prototypes are made with appropriate modifications. The design team again visits the customers' plants to test the new design to see if it meets specifications. If it does, then it's rollout time.[1]

3M goes a step further. It even includes consumers in new-product development teams.

Would you like more opinions? Then besides one-to-one questioning, test further, for example, by using the mall-intercept white-card concept testing. Ask consumers to judge ideas for your proposed product or service before the physical product or service is actually developed. If you're in industrial marketing, do the same thing at trade shows, conventions, and association meetings. Or you can use focus groups. Both consumer and industrial marketers have found this method to pay off.

But when you use these techniques, don't fall into the trap of thinking that just because you ask the question you need answered you'll get the response you want.

The general rule of thumb is to ask about the problems or frustrations that consumers face when dealing with a specified situation. Then go back to the lab to come up with a product or service solution.

Too many times the researcher says, "Tell me how to solve your problems." Or, "Would you buy this new product?" If consumers knew the solutions, they would probably already have solved their problems.

For example, if 20 years ago you had asked golfers what their problems and frustrations were, they probably would have said, "Can't hit the ball far enough," or, "Slice (or hook) too much." Very few—if any—would have said, "I need a metal-headed driver."

The same thing holds for metal bats. If you had asked Little League coaches, "Would you like to have metal bats?" the answer would have been, "No." But if you had asked them what some of their problems were, they would probably have said, "Bat expense."

Working closely with your target market helps avoid wishful thinking research. It's easy to get snared in that trap, even if you do extensive research. For example, Levi Strauss was considering entering a new market (for them): men's wool-blend suits.

Levi used a textbook approach for researching the market. Except for one thing: they ignored the findings. At almost every step the researchers predicted the concept wouldn't work. And at almost every step the marketers paid no attention. (If they had also been working with the target market, they would have known the researchers were on track.)

The result?

Do you see any Levi suits around?

Rule 3. Pretest Your
Finished Product or Service

Give your product or service to selected prospects. After they've had a chance to try it, offer it again. Only this time try to sell it to them. Even if it's at a low cost. This is a good indication of your product's or service's acceptance. Nobody pays even $1 for something he or she doesn't want.

Or, if purchasing cycles are long, call the prospect after he or she has had time to use it. A few honest answers can provide good insights into the viability of your product or service.

Exhibit your product or service at trade shows. Hand out brochures. But also find out if prospects are real prospects or just tire kickers. Try to get orders on the spot. Or ask for their names, addresses, and telephone numbers and when it would be convenient for a salesperson to call on them.

Rule 4. Pretest Your
Advertising

You don't necessarily have to use expensive advertising copy services. We never cease to be amazed at how executives will say they want to do an extensive copy test on new ads. But when the executives find out *how* expensive it will be, they do *no* testing.

Seek out inexpensive ways to test. They *may not* be as accurate. But then again, these less expensive testing methods may provide you with enough information to let you know whether you're on the right track or not. For example, follow, in principle, the practice of the former great advertising manager of Gimbel's, Bernice FitzGibbon. She had her writers take their copy into the store and read it to customers. That's a quick way to find out, among other things, if your ad is talking target-market talk.

If you've a photo in your ad, consider pretesting it by showing it to a sample of your prospects. You might be surprised at what they'll see.

One company we worked with produced an ad intending to show how safe it was for people to visit its place of business at night. The photo in the ad showed people coming out and milling about the front entrance at night. What did the prospects see? Sample responses included: "Peo-

ple coming out into a dark, unsafe place . . ." "It looks like someone's
getting mugged over there in the corner . . ." "Eerie."

Are you using direct mail? If so, before you make your big drop, try
several versions with small mailings. Vary your copy. Vary your offer. And
so on.

Rule 5. Pretest at All Levels of Your Distribution Channel

Make sure the distribution channel is ready for your niche product or
service. At least two issues need to be researched. First, is the channel
right for the product or service? For example, Avon was a company that
sold exclusively door-to-door. Avon was a big success—in fact, it became
one of the largest retailers of custom jewelry. Any channel would be
right for Avon. Right?

Of course not. Avon bought Tiffany, made a mess out of it, and sold it.
Avon discovered that what sells door-to-door doesn't sell at Tiffany. One
short visit with a Tiffany store manager should have tipped Avon off to
that.

Your second area for research is to find out whether the distribution
channel will support your new product or service.

Many distribution channels aren't attuned to niche marketing. Traditionally, channel members profit from high volume, not from value-
added activities. So some channel members will be evaluating your new
product on generated sales volume. Your niche product might well be
relegated to the back shelf.

If you have a multilevel channel, make sure you know what will happen at each level, not just the channel stage you sell to directly. There
might be a difference.

And, don't forget to check out your product or service with your own
salespersons. After all, they're your first customers!

You gain another benefit from testing your product or service at all
levels of the channel. Besides providing you with valuable and often vital
insights, it also helps you gain acceptance. Since channel members have
been involved in the development process, they feel ownership in the
marketing approach.

Rule 6. Start Small

You're serving a small market segment with specialized needs. Therefore, your margin of error is small—smaller than would be tolerated in
mass marketing. Our advice: Test-market the product or service.

We found that many niche marketers have a tendency to roll out to their whole target market on day one.

Resist this temptation.

Test your product or service in a small geographic area with one salesperson. With a small number of wholesalers. Or retailers. Or users. If it proves to be successful, then, and only then, roll out to your entire target market.

While some argue that small-scale rollouts can be more expensive, there's a side benefit from starting with a few people and a limited market. Since you will have to make some adjustments in your product or service, target market, price, or promotion, it's far easier—and less expensive—to make the necessary adaptations on a small scale.

Rule 7. Avoid Analysis Paralysis

Avoiding the paralysis that results from too much analysis is good advice for anyone, but it is especially useful to niche marketers.

Niche marketers must be quick. They serve specialized needs. And, in many cases, the first product or service in the market will be the winner.

If there is a chance your product or service will fail unless you act quickly, then act quickly!

Test to find out if the proposed product or service will succeed in the marketplace. But when conditions demand speed, be fast. Speed up your testing by making it simpler. Test in a smaller region. Test with a smaller group of customers.

Rule 8. Posttest

Make sure you can measure sales. Sounds simple, doesn't it? Well, sometimes it's not so easy.

You're interested not only in sales volume but also in who is buying your product or service. Are the purchasers actually those that you've targeted? Or are they of a different composition? Key to successful niche marketing is focus, focus, focus. And that's pretty hard to do unless you know who your customers are.

Companies' accounting methods can capture sales. But we've found that most firms fall short in being able to match sales with end purchasers of the product or service, especially when they're selling through intermediaries. So, part of your prelaunch planning is to establish how to track end purchasers (back to Guideline 2).

Also, make sure you can evaluate your promotion. Because you're working with a small budget, you've got to make sure every dollar counts.

Of course, there are some elements of your program that you're going to have to accept on faith. But don't let that stop you from measuring those aspects that can be measured. For example, when advertising, use a coupon to find out which publications generate the highest interest. Also, when sales are called in, always ask, "How did you hear of us?"

Don't be satisfied with just testing initial or trial sales. Keep your eye on those customers who bought your product or service. Do they—or will they—buy again?

Many executives have popped open the champagne bottles as the first-time customers lined up to buy their new products and services only to find it was the last they saw of them. Marketing hoopla can force initial sales, but unless the product or service lives up to its promise, the party's over.

One niche marketer we talked with began by doing the right thing. He decided to start small with one salesperson in one sales territory. But then he did the wrong thing. He picked his best salesperson and territory. Of course, this salesperson felt it was a personal challenge to sell the product. His customers bought it (but only because he was well liked and respected). Sales exceeded targets.

So, the marketer proceeded to a national rollout.

Meanwhile, back in the test territory, the product didn't live up to expectations. There were very few repeat purchases. The salesperson's personality and ability could force first-time sales. But that's all.

So don't let your research stop the day of the rollout. Follow up with users as soon as you can. Do they like your product or service? Does it live up to your promises? Will they buy more?

Niche marketers should make customer-satisfaction follow-up mandatory to determine whether the product or service lives up to its promise.

How can you reach those first-time purchasers? Visit them. Or call them. Or use warranty or rebate cards. Or use high tech methods, such as Catalina's checkout system. If necessary, use your sales force. But if you do use it, don't expect your salespersons to do all the work. They're looking to sell, not to do research.

Rule 9. Learn from Testing

Let your tests educate you. If your tests reveal that your product or service doesn't stand a chance with your targeted niche market, don't dump your test results along with the product or service.

Find out why it failed. Was it because the product or service didn't meet the niche's key buying motives? If so, where did it fall short? Did it lack the right features? Was it not user-friendly? Was the price too high? Or was it unbelievably low? Did the product or service fail because of faulty promotion? Did the target market know about your product or service *and* its key benefits? Was the product or service conveniently accessible?

Use the data as a learning opportunity. We think you can learn just as much from failure as you can from success. In fact, failure often can be an indicator of what you need to do in those markets to succeed.

Rule 10. Continue to Test

Take a lesson from direct marketers. They test, test, test. One of their standard approaches is to look for the method that brings about the best conversion (sales) rate from a direct mail program. They keep testing other methods until they find one that beats the conversion rate of the existing program. Then they start testing against this new winner.

Direct marketers define the success of a program in terms of the number of tests tried before a higher conversion rate is discovered.

We attended one meeting where the guest of honor was introduced as the person whose program had withstood the tests of over 150 challenge programs before it was displaced. That's the way to determine the direct marketer's mark of excellence: the number of tests it takes to dispace a marketing program.

Direct marketers also accept the inevitability of finding a better way. They expect and accept change.

So should you.

Conditions change. Users often find new ways to use your product or service, and you may be able to satisfy even more focused needs. When competition enters the niche, test their product or service against your own. What is their competitive advantage? You must continually respond to changes.

Recap

Don't fool yourself into believing that just because you're coming out with a niche product or service you don't need to test the marketplace. Even though the volume of your product or service may be small, you'll still find yourself in a quagmire if it fails.

Don't set your niche product or service up for failure by skipping the test marketing just because you think you'll be saving money.

Start early while the product or service is still in the development stage. Get your customers involved. But don't stop there. Once the product or service is developed, pretest it. You may not be able to afford expensive methods. But there are simple, inexpensive methods that will shed light.

Pretest your advertising too.

And don't just test the end users. Is your distribution channel right for your new product or service? Test it. Test it at all levels, starting with your own salespeople.

Once your product or service is on the market, focus on the posttest phase. Measure your sales. And who is actually buying.

Don't let up. Keep on testing. Build testing into your niche-marketing procedure.

PART 3

Handling Competition

10

Competing in a Favorable Weight Class

A cover story in *Business Week* advised, "Stop worrying about your competitors . . . The companies that are succeeding now put their customers first."[1]

Putting your customers first—we like that. That's why Guideline 1 of this book is called "Focus, Focus, Focus."

But "stop worrying about your competitors"? Well, *Business Week* is right, if—and it's a very, very big *if*—you don't have any competition.

Believe us, it will do you little good to put your customers first if, at the same time, there are already a number of competitors serving the same customers and serving them better than you can.

AMC's problem with marketing its cars wasn't a lack of putting the customer first. Its problem was General Motors, Ford, and Chrysler—not to mention Toyota, Nissan, Honda, Mazda, and other foreign manufacturers.[2]

What if your competitors have you outclassed? Suppose they've got better manufacturing plants, better customer loyalty, better distribution facilities, better economies of scale, and so on? You can't compete with them. You're out of your weight class.

You don't think so? Well then, be prepared to share the same humbling—and costly—experiences of General Electric and Xerox in computers and of Exxon in office automation. These are big-market examples, but the same principle holds for niche markets as well.

But you might say, "Well, GE, Xerox, and Exxon shouldn't have taken IBM head on. They should have found a niche." But even if GE, Xerox, and Exxon had targeted a niche, could they have stopped worrying about the competition? Of course not.

Neither can you. Ever. And this holds true whether you're entering a new niche, already serving a niche, or trying to become number one in a niche.

Failure to assess the competition is a major fault of most marketing plans. That was the conclusion of a consulting company that studied a number of marketing plans. Many of these plans assumed that their competitors were going to roll over and play dead. Or, at best, that they were going to continue doing the same thing they had done in the past.

Accept that you'll always have competition. In fact, if niche marketing is in your future, you'll find yourself in one of four scenarios:

1. You enter a niche, and your competition is there waiting for you.

2. You establish yourself in a comfortable little niche, and a competitor tries to take it over.

3. You and your competitor both are established in a niche and find yourselves in head-to-head combat for the number one position.

4. You enter a niche that is free of competition, but you know the threat of competition is not far off. (We'll cover this one in the next guideline.)

So you can't get away from competition. But you can follow some rules of thumb to make sure that you're competing in a weight class where you have an advantage. That's the best you can expect. And if you've done everything else right, that's good enough.

Rule 1. Do Competitive Benchmarking

Wipe out the concept of "our competitors." The reason? Simply because your customers do not buy from your competitors as a group. They buy from Competitor A, Competitor B, and so on.

Sounds like we're quibbling, doesn't it? Well, we were. But we wanted to make a point. A point that's often overlooked.

Take the case of a convenience food-store chain. It decided to do a competitive price analysis of all its competitors. The survey results showed that, in general, the chain was about mid-priced. About average.

But some store managers complained that something was wrong with the survey results. They were being clobbered by the competition on price.

So the results were analyzed in a different way. Since prices that are charged in the next county really don't matter to the customer, an examination was made on a store-by-store basis. An analysis was made of specific competitors near each of the chain's stores, and competitors' prices were not averaged.

Now the structure of this analysis made sense. After all, customers don't average the prices of various competing stores. A customer chooses one store among readily accessible alternatives.

The new analysis revealed that price competition varied widely among its stores and, for a given store, from competitor to competitor. The chain then set prices for each store according to the competition (usually to the most aggressive competitor) the store faced.

Prices now varied among the chain's stores, but they were no longer being trounced by competitors' low prices.

Too many businesses develop competitive strategies based on all competitors as a group—the competition. But each competitor has unique strengths and weaknesses and different strategies. Take the competition on one at a time. In your planning, take advantage of your competitors' differences. The water buffalo wishes it could (see page 114).

The first step is to determine how you stack up against each of your competitors. Here's how you do it for each product or service in your target market. (To help you with this competitive analysis, use the Competitive Benchmarking Chart in the Appendix.)

1. Identify your competitors. This is easy in some cases. But what if you have so many competitors that it's impractical (if not impossible) to list them all—let alone benchmark your company against them?

If you're faced with this situation, place your competitors into strategic groups. For example, an executive of an advertising agency claimed to have hundreds of competitors. The dilemma was resolved by placing these competitors into several strategic groups: industry specialists (full service), industry specialists (limited line), generalists, and boutiques. If you do group your competitors, be sure they are listed in such a way that you'll be comparing your firm against best-in-class competitors.

2. Determine the key buying motives of your target market (see Guideline 3).

3. Determine the key success factors. Although there are many things you must do to successfully serve your customers, there are only a few critical tasks (key success factors) that will determine your success or failure in a given target market. Ask "What is it that I must excel at in order to serve these needs?" For example, a firm selling ready-mixed cement to large builders on a bid basis usually will find that superior service and above-bid product specifications mean very little unless the firm also turns in the lowest bid. In this case the key success factors would be low-cost procurement of raw materials, production, and delivery.

Companies tend to behave as if their competitors were a homogeneous entity. As a result, their strategies and tactics are undifferentiated. Any company with less than a 50 percent share of market that behaves this way puts itself in the position of a defender and sacrifices enormous latitude. In the animal world a pack of hyena, perhaps 20 strong, will overcome a water buffalo many times the size of each hyena. They do it instinctively by surrounding the water buffalo and making repeated half-attacks, causing it to whirl about constantly using up its defensive energy. The hyena's behavior is a form of social order which allows them, as a group, to confront on equal terms the more massive water buffalo. If this ordering did not exist the water buffalo could take on its attackers in sequence overcoming each one, and ultimately the pack, with ease. Companies, by behaving as if competition were a homogeneous entity, put themselves at a disadvantage. There is no such social order among participants in a business. In fact it is expressly illegal. Companies of all sizes are missing the opportunity to exploit the differences and lack of alliances among competition. The water buffalo would not.

Reprinted with permission, Cresap, A Towers Perrin Company.

Identification of specific key success factors has two main advantages: (a) it helps you identify sources of competitive advantage and gives you insights for competitive strategies, and (b) it helps you concentrate your marketing efforts on those few tasks that really matter.

Of course, you cannot disregard other required functions of your business. A firm must do an acceptable job on all marketing tasks. But it must be superior on the one, two, or several critical elements—the key success factors.

Key success factors must be factors you can measure against your competitors. For example, although low price may be a key success factor, it's too broad. It does not pinpoint sources of competitive advantage. Low price could be the result of a number of factors, such as volume purchasing, favorable supplier location, long production runs, low-cost labor, and cost-efficient promotion.

4. Rate your company's strengths on key success factors in relation to each of your competitors (or strategic grouping of competitors).

5. Rank how the target market perceives, relatively, your firm's and your competitors' augmented product or service. *Augmented* refers to the whole bundle of amenities surrounding the product or service as well as to the product or service itself. Customers do not merely buy the product or service (with the exception of "pure" commodity goods, such as corn, oats, and soybeans that are traded on the Chicago Board of Trade). Rather, they also purchase the amenities that accompany the product or service, such as the reputation of the vendor, image of the product or service, credit terms, and delivery times.

Don't underestimate the importance of knowing your target market's perception of your augmented product or service compared to those of competitors. Your target market's perception is the only one that counts.

6. Estimate the relative financial strength of your firm in relation to other competitors. Do your competitors have the financial resources necessary to carry out aggressive or even maintenance-level marketing programs?

7. Rate your company's and your competitors' relative commitment to the product or service. Are they willing to be aggressive, do they just want to maintain their position, or are they ready to divest themselves of the product or service?

Now you've figured out what it takes to be successful, who you compete against, and how you stack up against individual competitors in those critical areas (key success factors) that really count. Furthermore, you understand your individual competitors' resources and commitment to the niche.

Now let's see if you're actually in a favorable weight class.

Rule 2. Don't Underestimate the Strength of the Defender

It sometimes happens on the battlefield that one side has a major advantage. For example, when the English defeated the French at Crécy in 1346, they had a better weapon. The English longbow could fire 6 times faster than the crossbow. Armies that have a major comparative advantage should use it. And they don't have to worry about competing in their own weight class.

So should companies.

But the word *major* is the key. The advantage must be something more than a slightly better product or service, manufacturing process or operations, or sales force. The advantage must be of major significance.

In the business world, however, cases of major comparative advantage are rare. How often do companies come up with products like Du Pont's nylon, Xerography, or Land's polaroid camera?

Unless you've just developed nylon or a Xerox copier or a Polaroid, you had better take a page from a book by the Prussian general, Carl von Clausewitz. He studied hundreds of battles in which neither side had a comparative advantage. In doing so, he arrived at a number of principles of warfare, which were published in *Vom Krieg (On War)* in 1832.

One of these was the principle of defense. The defending army has an inherent advantage. It's protected in some manner: trenches, bunkers, foxholes, or the like. Because of this protection, the attacking force is at a disadvantage. Clausewitz found that, as a rule of thumb, the attacking force should have a resource advantage at the point of attack of at least 3 to 1.

This principle also holds in business (although the required resource advantage depends on the situation).

Suppose that you've located a niche. It's got good growth potential. And it fits in nicely with your business. But, unfortunately, there are firms already serving this niche.

Can you outgun them? Think about this.

Don't believe that just because your product or service is slightly better it's going to turn the odds in your favor.

Only the customer says which is the better product or service. You don't enter the market with a "guaranteed" better product or service. You enter the market with a product or service, and you hope the market will say it's better.

Take the Sony Betamax. Although its market failure is attributed to a variety of errors, it basically stemmed from an arrogance associated with having a product that outperformed competition in the laboratory. Sony found out that while engineers may measure performance, customers determine which product is better—they choose the augmented product.

Remember, your competitors are established. They're entrenched and have the greatest defense of all; customer loyalty. In addition, they probably have a host of other advantages. Distributor loyalty. Experience in manufacturing. Marketing. And so on.

And you're charging over the hill. Exposed.

You may represent a billion-dollar firm. And so you automatically tend to think that you hold numerical superiority. But that's strictly big-firm mentality at its worst.

Here's an axiom you should cut out and place on your desk—where you can see it every day: It's not how many resources your firm has, but how many resources your firm will commit at the point of attack.

Unfortunately, too many companies are willing to take on a market leader but lack, or are unwilling to commit, the necessary resources. Look at GE's move into computers and Exxon's foray into office automation. At the time of attack, both companies were larger than IBM. But at the point of attack, both companies' resources were only a fraction of IBM's.

The lesson seems obvious.

Still, companies with numerically inferior forces keep going on the attack. After watching all the others flounder, AT&T still entered the computer market. At first AT&T floundered. And years later AT&T was still floundering.

Even if you've got better manufacturing facilities, more salespersons, and better advertising coverage, it still may not be enough. What are the key success factors for serving the competitor's niche? Are any of these factors related to service? Will you have to make quick product or service adaptations for unique situations? Or meet demands for impromptu delivery? Can your organization match the nimbleness of the professional nichers who may be in this market? Big companies are noted for not being too swift in some of these areas.

Make sure that you've got the required resources—at the point of attack. Keep in mind the inherent superiority of the defense.

Rule 3. Don't Underestimate the Strength of the Attacker

Now let's suppose you're playing defense. You may have a very profitable niche. But it may attract a big competitor who will commit a lot of resources at the point of attack.

A by-product of success is complacency. You're currently raking in profits. Why change? Why fix something that isn't broken? You say, "Who do these guys think they are? Moving into *our* market? We own it." Even though you may now own the market, you still must defend it.

Your first step should be competitive benchmarking. How do you match up with your attacking competitor vis-á-vis key success factors? What about the resources of the competitor? Its commitment?

Given the results of this analysis, can you defend your position? Or will you need some sort of strategic alliance? Or should you exit from the niche?

Look what happened to Johnson Products Company. The founder, George E. Johnson, recognized an opportunity—there weren't any hair products on the market specially formulated for blacks. By cultivating this niche over a period of time, Johnson Products became a very successful company. In fact, it was one of the most highly touted black entrepreneurial firms.

However, when the market reached a certain size, it attracted the major players, such as Revlon and Avon. They developed products for the black hair-care market. With promotion funds (of a size not available to Johnson Products Company) plus well-known trade names (also not available to Johnson Products), they soon took over.

Johnson Products has been losing ever since.

Don't forget the axiom: It's not how many resources your firm has, but how many resources your firm will commit at the point of attack.

Rule 4. Be Careful Going Head-to-Head Unless You Have an Overwhelming Resource Advantage

Now suppose you're going head-to-head with another competitor to become the market leader of a particular niche. Let's take another lesson from Clausewitz.

Clausewitz studied open-field battles, where neither side had a comparative weapon or defensive advantage. He found only two instances in which the numerically inferior force (as defined by having one-half or fewer troops than the opponent) defeated the numerically superior force. The obvious lesson: If you're outnumbered, stay away from the battlefield.

Suppose you've decided it's time to become number one in the niche. First, go through the process of competitive benchmarking. If your competitor has larger resources, forget about the attack.

But let's suppose you do have a resource advantage over your competitors. To have a good chance of winning, make sure your resource advantage is overwhelming.

And don't let bravado get in the way of reason.

A newly appointed president of one of the burger chains (going head-to-head with McDonald's) made the statement, "I don't know the meaning of the word *fear.*"

Fine and good. But we sure hope he knew the meaning of the word *death.*

Rule 5. Look for the Leader's Achilles' Heel

There are times when you can take on Mr. Big (when Mike Tyson's hands are tied). And this is when the strategist earns his or her salary. If you are outnumbered, figuring out how to succeed in that marketplace means using more brains than brawn.

Watch for indications of leader weakness.

Signals of tied hands include blindness to market shifts, changes in technology, rigid game plans, changes in financial objectives, high reaction costs, portfolio restraints, and governmental regulatory pressure.[3]

Blind Spots

In the 1960s there used to be a joke heard around Detroit.

> QUESTION: "Do you know what the three most overrated things in America are?"
>
> ANSWER: "Home cooking. Sex. And Japanese cars."

"Invincible" leaders have a tendency to see themselves that way—invincible. And it happens all the time in a number of ways.

Some overlook consumer demand (Xerox ignored—or underestimated—the demand for small copiers). Some don't respond to changes in technology (Zenith stayed with handcrafted TV sets while great changes were taking place in design and automated production). Some don't take account of changes in channels of distribution (Sears stayed pat, but people went to specialty stores and discounters like the Price Club).

Changes in Technology

The leaders' strength may be in technology, but new advances can wipe out this advantage. Electromechanical cash registers were replaced by electronic cash registers. Typewriters by dedicated word processors. Dedicated word processors by microcomputers. And so on.

Of course, if you're Mr. Big in the market, you should view these examples as symbols of your own vulnerability. If you rise above others by developing better technology, you're probably in an industry in which your competition can easily surpass you with even better technology. Present technology is never a protection for market position. Sometimes your competitors may even develop a technology impossible for you to match. Then it might be best to throw in the towel and look for another arena.

Rigid Game Plans

A competitor might be reluctant to meet an attack if it has to change the strategy that has served it so well in the past. McDonald's didn't want to change its finely tuned assembly line method of making hamburgers to meet Burger King's "Have It Your Way" campaign. This was a successful battle (but not a victory) for Burger King.

Crippling Financial Objectives

A leader might be after short-term profits and, therefore, choose not to come out with niche products and services to meet the competition. Like General Motors and small cars and the Japanese.

If one of your competitors becomes a leveraged buyout, watch for shifts in financial priorities. For example, the buyout of one service company caused the firm to focus on very short-term profits. As a result, the company eliminated a number of services that didn't have immediate payoffs. It became vulnerable—and lost business—to a number of competing firms that were not subject to such short-term pressures.

The same thing happened to RJR. Mired in debt, it lost market share while Philip Morris jabbed away.

Even the threat of a corporate buyout can be a sign of vulnerability. When top management is trying to deal with corporate raiders, attention to the marketplace often wanes. For instance, while trying to decide who should own the company, United Air Lines lost significant market share.

High Reaction Costs

A leader may resist cutting prices to meet the competition's invasion of the fringes of its market because the leader might have to make across-the-board price cuts, thereby making this defensive strategy unacceptable. Such price cuts might spell lower profits for the leader. Or lower dividends. Or lower share prices. Or it might mean that the leader might have to use another channel of distribution, thus disrupting its present channel relationships.

GTE Sprint had only a small percentage of total land lines for long-distance calling in the United States. But its lines were 100 percent optical fiber. They knew that AT&T could never match their advertising claim ("100 percent optical fiber"). For AT&T to replace all its land lines with optical fiber would cost billions of dollars! This made Sprint's attack very effective since AT&T's response costs were too high.

Portfolio Restraints

The leader might be a division charged with generating cash. Or it might be a weak performer. In either case, this division might find it impossible—or imprudent—to ask for funds to engage in a marketing war.

Regulatory Pressures

Firms can lose their competitive edge if they are subject to unusual regulatory pressures from the federal or local government. A company might be under government surveillance because of an antitrust suit. Or predatory pricing. Or other infringements of regulations that might restrict aggressive retaliation.

The leader may even be reluctant to retaliate in the marketplace because of false beliefs about regulatory pressures. New marketing employees of the Bell regional operating companies frequently were miffed by old-timers who insisted that certain marketing activities were ruled out by regulations. Yet nowhere could these regulations be found!

Or perhaps the leader is used to acting in a certain way. AT&T had many accountants accustomed to reducing price to please regulators rather than focusing on customers' needs. When first deregulated, AT&T was a lamb ready for slaughter by competitors with finely honed marketing skills. In fact, its market share slid from 100 percent to 65 percent in 7 years.

Recap

You have more than your fair share of energy, enthusiasm, and training. Good. But before you lead your forces into battle, study your competition. Look for their weaknesses. Their strengths. Determine your chances for coming out on top.

We'll say it again: Avoid the big-firm mentality.

How much funding will you be able to get for a particular niche? How will that compare with your competitors' resources? And, how entrenched are you—and your competitors—in the market?

It's not how many resources your firm has, but how many resources your firm will commit at the point of attack. That's what counts. Not how much money is in the corporate till.

Not enough resources for defense? Get out. Salvage what you can. (Retreat is one of the most difficult strategies for businesspeople to follow. They seem more bent on kamikaze marketing than on living to fight again on a different battlefield.)

Not enough resources for offense? Call off the attack. There's no sense in squandering your resources (and careers of executives) on the charge of the light brigade.

Don't make your marketing strategy an ego issue. Save the bravado for sales meetings. Not for the marketplace.

11

How to Keep from Being Outniched

Large-company niche marketers were quick to point out to us that the extent of their commitment to niche marketing varies from one product and service to another and from market to market.

Makes sense. The more your competitors nip off smaller and smaller market segments, the more likely it is that you'll have to follow suit. In some businesses you've got to fight to keep from being outniched.

Consider a vodka battle played out several years ago. Wolfschmidt, a new brand of vodka, attacked Smirnoff on price, charging one dollar less while claiming the same quality.

Heublin (Smirnoff) decided against matching Wolfschmidt's price. Instead they raised the price of Smirnoff by one dollar and came out with a fighting brand, Reskla, priced the same as Wolfschmidt. Heublin also came out with another brand, Popov, selling lower than Wolfschmidt.

Heublin outmaneuvered Wolfschmidt by encirclement. They had a premium brand (Smirnoff), a fighting brand (Reskla), and a cheaper brand (Popov).[1]

For years Campbell Soup stuck with the red and white label on its canned condensed soups. But competitors came out with new products specially designed for more narrowly segmented markets. Progresso for the ethnic market. Ramen noodle for those who favor cheap, quick, and filling soups. Lite Line dry soup for the dieters.

These competitors' products were not hitting Campbell head-on but attacking the flanks where there was minimum defense. This was easy to do, since Campbell was following a Maginot Line defense. But like the Maginot Line defense against the Germans, Campbell's defense was not

effective. Competitors were outflanking them. They had more differentiated products for the fringe markets than did Campbell.

When Campbell realized the need to protect its flanks, it came out
with a number of new products for various niches.

Then there's the candy war. Hershey replaced Mars as the industry's
sales leader.

How?

By offering customers more choice. And choice is important to hard-
core candy munchers, who usually switch from bar to bar. Hershey and
its subsidiaries offered Hershey Kisses, Reese's peanut butter cups,
Reese's Pieces, Golden Almond chocolate bars, Hershey Miniatures, Big
Block chocolate bars, Marabou milk chocolate rolls. And so on. Would
you like some more? OK. Peter Paul Mounds, Peter Paul Almond Joy,
Bar None, Kit Kat, Mr. Goodbar, Whatchamacallit. Would you like some
more? Just the number? OK. Fifteen or so more.

But Mars banked on a handful of products and shunned small niches.
For example, Mars killed its Summit bar even though sales reportedly
were at $40 million. Eventually, however, Mars woke up. It started to act
smaller to grow bigger. It began to offer more variety on the shelves.[2]

In these three cases—Heublin, Campbell Soup, and Mars—market
leaders scrambled to take—or keep—charge of their markets. All became niche players or intensified their niche strategies.

What will your competitors do? Of course, we don't know. But small
firms are always there chipping away at your markets. And we do know
that many of the largest firms have started to market to smaller segments
and are planning to segment their markets even further, perhaps not
across the board, but at least for some products and services. So it's likely
you've got to take action to keep from being outniched. Here are some
key rules to follow (assuming that the numbers are on your side).

Rule 1. Attack Yourself

Attack yourself as Gillette did in the wet shaving market. Its own Trac II
attacked its own Super Blue Blade. Its own Good News! attacked its
Super Blue. Its own Atra attacked Good News!, the Super Blue, and
Trac II. And then its Sensor attacked its Atra, Good News!, Trac II, and
the Super Blue. (There were also a number of line extensions, such as
Trac II Plus and Good News! Micro Trac. We left them out because the
example was getting complicated—besides, you still get the point.) All
the while Gillette increased market share in a competitive market.

The best defense is a good offense. It's an old cliché, but it's still good
advice.

And while we're on clichés, forget this one: If it isn't broken, don't fix it. Someday your product or service may be "broken," thanks to your competitors' new products or services. And then it may be very costly— or perhaps too late—to fix it. Start a crusade now for constant improvement.

Rule 2. Make the Game Too Tough to Play

Sun Tsu said, "The supreme excellence of war is not to win a hundred victories in a hundred battles, but to subdue the armies of your enemies without even having to fight them."

Deterrence is the ultimate business strategy. You win without costly battles with competitors. Raise barriers to make it difficult for competitors to invade your markets.[3]

Cover All Bases

In Brazil, when continual farming had depleted a plot of land, the adjacent area was slashed and burned. And then farmed. This had been going on for generations. There was always more land. But then they reached the sea.

Many companies unwittingly are following a slash-and-burn strategy. Of course it's not called "slash and burn"; the euphemism is usually "restructuring" or "downsizing."

Firms that follow such a strategy cut out low-end products and services—the so-called junk segments—and concentrate on the higher end. They specialize in servicing segments that want more expensive— perhaps even customized—products and services, segments that offer high margins. They leave the low end to competitors—often the unknowns or companies with less status in the industry.

This may work fine at first, but it could spell disaster in the long run. Look at what might happen.

The low-end producers improve their R&D, production processes, distribution facilities, and market acceptance. Their next step: in addition to serving the low-end markets, they inch upward to the next higher market segment, making this segment a highly competitive business.

The high-end producers are now unhappy with their less-than-targeted returns from this segment. So they leave this new junk segment to the low-end producers. The high-end producers now concentrate on the segments demanding even more expensive products or services that still offer acceptable margins.

But the low-end producers keep inching upward. Furthermore, these low-end producers now have scale. This enables them to outspend the high-end producers on, among other things, manufacturing and operations technology, product or service R&D, distribution facilities, and promotion.

Eventually, the high-end producers have no place to go. They have reached the sea.

Of course, there is a great temptation to focus only on the most profitable segments and leave the junk for the competitors. And in some cases this may be the right approach. But serving too few segments may allow competitive inroads.

We all know how the Japanese came into the U.S. automobile market via the low end. However, once they got a foothold and established trade names, marketing know-how, distribution, and servicing facilities, flexible production facilities enabled them to move into the middle market. Which, of course, they did, thus eating into the higher-margin segments—Detroit's bread and butter—formerly dominated by General Motors, Ford, and Chrysler.

Their next step? The luxury markets. Nissan's Infinity. The Toyota Lexus. The Toyota Supra. Even Honda, with its successful Acura line, was not content just to be there. Its sports car competes with the Mercedes-Benz 500 SL and the Cadillac Allante.

The auto industry is not an isolated example. GE became number one in jet aircraft engines by filling a gaping hole in Pratt & Whitney's product line.

Xerox practiced skimming the market and left the small-copier market to the Japanese, who filled the gap and now are giving Xerox a run for their money in large copiers.

PepsiCo was able to penetrate Coca-Cola's market share by, among other things, concentrating on the take-home market, a segment at that time neglected by Coca-Cola.

Model proliferation helped Komatsu eat away at Caterpillar's market share.

If you follow the practice of segment retreat, make sure that you're aware of the possible competitive consequences. To avoid these, consider covering all bases. Besides being a defensive play, covering all the bases can lead to market broadening. Armstrong World changed its mission from floor coverings to decorative room coverings, thus expanding its domain to include walls and ceilings. In this way Armstrong has moved closer to providing one-stop shopping—a place where customers can coordinate room interiors. Besides growth, Armstrong also gained benefits in production and marketing, enabling the company to be better poised for defense.

Seiko, with worldwide marketing of 2300 models of watches, left very little uncovered territory—and thus fewer opportunities for competitors.[4]

Thomson Medical, maker of Slim-Fast, the dietary powdered drink, developed a new product, Ultra Slim-Fast. But the company continued to market Slim-Fast at a very low retail price, almost at break-even. Slim-Fast was aimed at a very price-sensitive niche. The main purpose for keeping Slim-Fast was to raise the cost of market entry for a potential low-price competitor.

Clog Channels

Make it tough for your competitors as Lipton Soup did.

Lipton's largest sales volume came from its chicken noodle and onion soups. Still, its more exotic lines, such as Trim Line for the calorie counter and Hearty Instant Soups, fulfilled an important strategic role. Besides providing some sales and profits, they prevented other soup manufacturers from attacking Lipton's flanks. The volumes on these other soups were so small that a grocer couldn't afford to stock two brands. And Lipton was already there.

So, if a competitor wished to attack Lipton, it had to attack Lipton's strength: the chicken noodle and onion soups. Lipton was almost impregnable.

But not quite.

Nissin Foods was the first major Japanese food company to enter the dry-soup market. Nissin Foods did it as most Japanese companies do: on the low end with ramen noodle soup, six to eight packages for $1. Other producers soon followed. Lipton ignored them until ramen noodle soup's share of the market climbed to 18 percent. While Lipton concentrated on blocking channel access for its traditional products, they overlooked covering all bases.

Make the Cost of Entry Prohibitive

By increasing capital requirements, you can make it difficult for competitors to enter the market on a low-cost, experimental basis. Or you can finance your buyers. Or you can offer liberal return and warranty policies.

How about increasing the cost of switching? If you train buyers in the use of your products and services, they'll find it more difficult to switch to unfamiliar ones offered by your competitors. A strategy that IBM has followed for years.

Or you can make your customers captives by giving them a price discount on their next purchase. Taster's Choice coffee does this with in-pack coupons. Or you can increase customer inventories—and assure long-term usage—by offering quantity discounts, such as four bars of soap for the price of three.

Or you can just lower the price. In price-volume industries, a low-price policy sometimes acts as a deterrent to would-be competing nichers. Low cost might offset the advantages of a more differentiated product or service. (But remember our caution in Guideline 5.)

Rule 3. Always Block Competitive Moves

In 1878 a young missionary, bent on making conversions, arrived in the heart of Africa. He set up his camp just outside the clearly marked terri-torial boundaries of a tribe.

Carefully keeping his distance, he observed the tribe in their daily ac-tivities. Within weeks he knew many of them by sight, if not by name, and ventured to wave friendly greetings to them. They returned his greet-ings.

He waited for almost a year before he felt sure it was safe to make his move. Smiling and waving as he had done so often in the past, he stepped into the tribe's territory. Three spears whizzed from the bush. WHAP. WHAP. WHAP. The missionary fell dead.

Unfortunately for him, he didn't know the tribe's history. Long ago their forebears had permitted a member of another tribe to enter their territory. That newcomer was soon joined by others, and, since they caused no bother, they were allowed to remain.

But on one villainous day the newcomers attacked the village, slaugh-tering everyone there. Only a small hunting party that had left the vil-lage early that morning survived.

Since that time, the tribe's unwritten law was: Should a person enter the territory of our tribe, then that person must die. If we only drive the person away, then many more will come.

In business today the usual way to respond to a new market entrant is to wait and see. Will the competitor be able to gain a toehold? Will it withdraw? Or will the new entrant slaughter you? Most outcomes of a wait-and-see policy are bad!

The best defense is to take no chances. What if your competitor's product or service succeeds? Then you'll have a costly battle on your hands. Stop your competitor's attack before it gains a beachhead, while it's still in the water with its back to the sea.

But what if you already have competitors? If they make threatening moves, stop them.

Honda stoppped Yamaha. Yamaha made a public announcement that it was going to replace Honda as the number one manufacturer of motorcycles in Japan.

The president of Honda issued a battle cry: "Yamaha has not only stepped on the tail of a tiger, it has ground it into the earth! Yamaha wo tsubusu!" This has a number of meanings, including "we will crush (break, smash, squash, butcher, slaughter, or destroy) Yamaha."

And that's exactly what Honda did.

Honda used product variety and pricing to defeat Yamaha. In a year and a half Honda brought out 81 new models to Yamaha's 34. Both firms cut prices drastically. Yet Honda's price to dealers was still lower than Yamaha's. Dealers were able to realize 10 percent larger profits from handling Honda motorcycles than from handling Yamaha's.

As a result of this war, Honda's share of the domestic market increased from 38 percent to 43 percent, while Yamaha's declined from 37 percent to 23 percent.[5]

What about little wars? You might not even notice the loss of a subniche to a competitor. Often attacks at the fringes of your markets come from products or services based on new technology, developed and marketed by firms that you don't even think of as being competitors. Or possibly you might choose to ignore the attack. After all, one little niche may account for only a small volume of sales and profits. However, such losses can spread like a cancer, and, like a cancer, they can be deadly. You are better off stopping them.

And this principle applies to smaller firms as well as to corporate giants.

A friend of ours used to run a fishing boat on the East Coast. But then he switched from taking out anglers to taking out sightseers, a new service for that particular locality. He built this business up to where he was taking out about 100 sightseers a day.

Then one day a fishing boat captain, known to our friend, docked next to his boat and told him that he thought that he, too, would get into the sight-seeing business. Only he wouldn't compete with our friend. He said he would continue to take out fishing parties, but only 4 days a week. Then he would take out sightseers on the other 3 days, but only in the early evening when our friend was not running his trips.

Now our friend had been a student of marketing warfare for several years. He said that at one time he would have told the fishing boat captain that it would be OK and would even have given him some tips on getting started. But our friend's new knowledge made him aware of what might happen.

So he put his arm on the fishing boat captain's shoulder and told him, "Now I don't want you to take this personally, but quite frankly I'll put us both out of business before I'll let you in. Taking out fishing parties is your business. Taking out sightseers is mine. And I'm going to defend my business with everything I have."

The next day the fishing boat captain said that he had changed his mind!

But before you take such actions, better check with your attorney.

Rule 4. Try to Minimize "Quarteritis"

Everyone agrees that the best defense is a good offense and that making the game too tough to play are good strategies. Except when it comes time to pay. Then far too frequently that ubiquitous American disease, "quarteritis" (the need to please Wall Street by showing quarterly gains in sales and profits), sets in. The list of afflicted companies is too long to include here.

One reason for the reluctance to fund defensive strategies is that benefits are difficult to measure. How can you prove, for example, that the costly strategy of continually coming out with new models is cost effective?

Or how can you prove that erecting barriers, which can also be costly, is keeping competition out of your markets?

Claiming such benefits sometimes reduces your arguments to "George Gobelian logic." The comedian George Gobels used to claim that he played a vital role during World War II: he was stationed in Oklahoma, and prevented the Japanese from invading that state. He'd say, "The Japanese didn't invade Oklahoma, did they?"

So investment in defense is often neglected. Like the American automobile manufacturers' experience with small cars. Xerox's experience with small computers. And so on. No doubt their strategies paid off in the short run. If F. G. Donner, CEO of General Motors in 1960, had crushed the German and Japanese nichers, what probably would have happened? Quarterly sales (small cars sell for less than large cars) and profits (small cars are less profitable than large cars) would have dropped.

And the price of GM's shares would have dropped.

And possibly even Donner right along with them.

Investing in defense is a tough road to take. But to convince others, you've got one thing on your side: there are plenty of examples of what happened to companies who didn't.

Recap

Keep in mind the axiom: The more your competitors nip off smaller and smaller market segments, the more likely it is that you'll have to follow suit.

To avoid being outniched:

1. Attack yourself.
2. Make the game too tough to play.
3. Always block competitive moves.
4. Try to minimize "quarteritis."

Sit back passively and you'll be niched right out of the market.

PART 4

Solving Niche-Marketing Problems

12
Don't Go a Niche Too Far

In a small cemetery on the outskirts of the eastern Dutch hamlet of Oosterbeek are buried hundreds of members of Britain's First Airborne Division.

In September 1944 the Allies launched operation Market-Garden. They successfully secured four bridges along the Rhine. Then, the British First Airborne Division attempted to secure a more forward position by capturing the fifth bridge, located at Arnhem.

Because of logistical problems, promised Allied reinforcements failed to arrive. As a result, German tanks and armored vehicles crushed the assault. The battle later was chronicled in the book and movie, *A Bridge Too Far.*

We've been urging you to consider niche marketing. But you can go a niche too far.

It's nice to talk about developing products or services and marketing programs for market niches. But once you begin to put this talk into action, you may find yourself juggling too many balls. There is that tendency. Usually when you find 1 niche, you'll find 10 more.

A niching strategy increases complexity and taxes your resources. Exceed your company's capabilities and you fail. It's as simple—and painful—as that.

Avoid Robbing Peter to Pay Paul

Make sure that your niching strategy doesn't sap vital resources from your base business.

135

For example, let's assume competitors are nibbling away at the fringe of your market with specialized products. So you start a niching strategy to protect your base business.

So far, so good.

But further suppose that to fund the niching strategy, you divert funds from your base business. Now you might have gone a niche too far.

Translate this situation into a marketing warfare analogy. Imagine a general looking out onto a battlefield. He sees that a flank is exposed, and he commands a colonel to lead his regiment out to cover this flank. When the colonel reaches his position, he surveys the situation and finds that his flank, too, is exposed. He orders a major to take a company out to protect it. This continues until a corporal sends a private out to protect the last of the flanks.

All the flanks are protected. Yet in securing them, the troops have become so diffused that the center line is weak and vulnerable to attack.

The logic of protecting the flank seems valid. Still, there will always be a flank. Be sure to evaluate whether the benefits of protected flanks, with your niche products or services, exceed the cost of a weakened center line, your base business.

In marketing warfare the first rule is the principle of force. As Napoleon, almost echoing the words of Clausewitz, said, "The art of war consists of having larger forces than the enemy at the point which is to be attacked or defended."

Even if you've committed a huge army (translation, big bucks) to ward off competition, it's the spending on each product or service that counts.

Yet, many marketers spend too many resources protecting the flanks. Since "new troops" for the new flanking products or services are often not available, funding comes from the base business. The consequence: the base business is less protected.

Look what happened at Campbell Soup. Campbell entered the jarred spaghetti sauce market in 1981 with its brand, Prego. By November 1983, Prego had about one-fourth of the market.

But Prego was in a battle with a number of Ragu jarred spaghetti sauces: the traditional Ragu and three of its flankers—Extra Thick and Zesty Ragu, Ragu Homestyle, and Ragu Gardenstyle.

Fearing that Prego was losing market share to Ragu's flankers, Campbell introduced a line extension called Prego Plus. Prego Plus achieved a few share points, although it never gained a significant percent of the market.

Meanwhile, the original Prego's market share declined. Although overall total advertising dollars were increased, the advertising budget for Prego was cut to help support Prego Plus. Sales force attention and trade attention were also split between the two varieties.

Then Campbell introduced a third item to the line, Al Fresco. Al

Fresco's marketing effort was supported, in part, by funding that came from the budgets of Prego and Prego Plus.

From 1983 to 1988 Campbell's market share of jarred spaghetti sauce remained unchanged. The effect of the new brand, Al Fresco, was to take sales away from Prego as well as from the already poorly selling Prego Plus.

Belatedly, Campbell postulated that had it spent all its efforts on Prego's base business, Prego's market share would have increased to about a third of the market. Campbell, in protecting its flanks, had almost abandoned its center. It had gone a niche too far. After a major reevaluation Cambell publicly announced it was getting back to the basics in this market.

Always ask, "Will this niching strategy rob resources from our base business?" If so, it might be wise to delay or even abandon launching those niche products or services.

Niche Marketing Can Be Hazardous

Most of the niche marketers we've worked with, along with hundreds of the company executives we've questioned, agree that niche marketing pays off. Yet not without difficulties.

As might be expected, those who started with the big bang approach had headaches. But even those who took the evolutionary path were not home free.

What are the most common problems? Robbing Peter to pay Paul is one. But we found others that cropped up again and again.

Potential problem area	Example
Production and operations	Difficulty in maintaining quality assurance across larger product offerings
Logistics	Ballooning warehouse costs with increased number of products
	High shipping costs for small quantities
Distribution channels	Disruption of existing channel relationships
Organizational structure and planning	Proliferating bureaucracy
Personnel	Management resistance and the lack of people with niche-marketing experience
Media and sales promotion	Hard-to-reach niche markets
Sales force	Inability to effectively handle more than one product or service

Guidelines 13 through 19 focus on each of the above potential problem areas in niche marketing and provide practical tips on how to avoid them or, if necessary, how to overcome them. Maybe this is all you'll need.

But the solutions we suggest are not comprehensive. After all, complete books could be written on each one of the problem areas. Rather, these solutions are the ones we—and others—have used for solving some of the most common problems. The solutions provide general directions, places to begin.

If, on the other hand, the specifics of your problems make them seem unique, keep this in mind. The solutions presented here *all* resulted from problems that once seemed unique. Niche marketing is still evolving, and nobody said it was easy. But if others can resolve their problems and make niche marketing work, so can you. Guidelines 13 through 19 should get you started.

Recap

You can go a niche too far. Be sure to husband your resources. And be aware of possible pitfalls.

13

Dealing with Production and Operations Problems

Serving a number of niche markets means more production and operations complications.

Look at some of the major production problems that came up in our survey:

- "Demands greater flexibility" (group vice president, apparel manufacturer).
- "Reduced scale. Poor economics" (corporate director of marketing, apparel manufacturer).
- Difficult to maintain "quality assurance across larger product offerings" (manager of analysis, tire manufacturer).
- "Capacity shortages" (corporate director of marketing, apparel manufacturer).
- "Increased capital expenditures and added stress on equipment" (vice president of marketing and public affairs, servicer and rebuilder of industrial equipment).
- "Packaging differences" (vice president of corporate planning).

Nor do service companies escape operations pitfalls:

- "Additional computer programming" (director of marketing services, savings bank).

- "Required new systems" (senior vice president and manager of strategic planning, commercial bank).
- "Weak support systems" (vice president of marketing, investment firm).
- "Applications for large segments have to be reworked to service smaller target markets" (senior vice president, commercial bank).
- "More customizations and schedule changes demand more programming and better coordination (director of advertising and sales promotion, commercial airline).

So don't make the mistake that many managers do—not paying enough attention to production and operations. Here's where you may lose your competitive edge. In fact, a survey of CEOs (not restricted to niche marketers) cited manufacturing efficiencies as the very basis of Japan's competitive advantage.[1] And manufacturing and operations are even more critical for niche marketers. You don't have long runs to mask inefficiencies in start-up times, changeover times, coordination, and the like.

Management Conflict

We found that producing long, inexpensive runs is often a deeply ingrained cultural attitude among production and operations people. They've prided themselves on producing products their way—efficiently. Niche marketing asks them to change. So they balk.

One operations vice president for a large consumer products company approached the president and said that he could not change the production facility to comply with every new product some guy from the field came up with. The president agreed with him and then told him he would be replaced with someone who could!

Solution 1. Involve People More

No doubt firing people is one way to send a message throughout the organization. But we question whether fear is an effective method of fostering initiative and cooperation.

Set up planning teams where functional area managers get together and jointly decide what will be produced to serve various target markets (as opposed to "Here's what we're going to do; now let's see how you're going to do it."). The basic idea of the teams is to make the manufacturing and operations manager a better marketing person. To make the marketing manager a better manufacturing person (we must admit that sometimes marketing people do get a bit out of line). To make a better manufacturing person out of the finance manager. And so on.

Solution 2. Reallocate Resources

See that manufacturing and operations have the equipment or other resources for expanding the product or service line. Do the same with other functional areas. Lack of funds? Then settle for an evolutionary approach.

Solution 3. Change the Reward System

Many companies that move into niche marketing have been slow—too slow—to change the way people work by changing the basis on which they are compensated.

Don't judge your operations manager by how inexpensively he or she can produce and then ask him or her constantly to make line changes. Do this and you'll have one paranoid person.

No one likes to fool with the compensation package. But sometimes it must be done.

Managing Quality

Double your products and services, and you more than double your quality problems.

But don't expect sympathy from your customers. They look at just one product at a time, and if they're not happy with its quality, you're in trouble.

Of course, besides trying to keep your customers happy, you'll still have problems associated with trying to correct quality deficiencies. It's not uncommon to have 25 percent of your manufacturing or operations facilities tied up reacting to quality problems.

So you've got to get it right the first time.

Solution. Consider Strategic Quality Management

Take a look at three stages in the approach to quality shown in Table 13-1.

If you're operating at the inspection stage, can you succeed in the niche-marketing generation? No.

All that will happen is that you'll have 25 percent of your plant tied up

Table 13-1 Three Major Quality Stages

Identifying characteristics	Stage of the Quality Movement		
	Inspection	Statistical quality control	Strategic quality management
Orientation and approach	"Inspects in" quality	"Controls in" quality	"Manages in" quality
Emphasis	Product uniformity	Product uniformity with reduced inspection	The market and consumer need
Methods	Gauging and measurement	Statistical tools and techniques	Strategic planning, goal setting, and mobilizing the organization
Responsibility	The inspection department	The manufacturing or operations and engineering departments	All departments, with top management exercising strong leadership

SOURCE: Adapted with permission of The Free Press, a Division of Macmillan, Inc., from *Managing Quality: The Strategic and Competitive Edge* by David A. Garvin. Copyright © 1988 by David A. Garvin. Garvin includes an additional stage—quality assurance—between statistical quality control and strategic quality management. For simplicity, this stage was not included.

in rework—if you're lucky. Producing more varieties of products or services will increase the time required for rework.

You've got to have close to zero defects.

Can it be done?

Hewlett-Packard did it. The company used to have 25 percent of its plant tied up in rework. It then implemented statistical quality control. The results are convincing. For example, in 2 years, soldering defects in its printed circuit boards dropped from 5500 parts per million to fewer than 100 parts per million.[2]

Although necessary, aiming for zero defects through statistical quality control is not a sufficient condition for successful niche marketing. It requires strategic quality management. Key characteristics are:

1. Making quality a strategic—as well as a tactical—concern. Managing quality is more than just keeping cost down. It's also a major competitive tool. Because customers are involved, it's a way to locate and dominate niche markets.

2. Generating companywide involvement. Your whole company must be attuned to managing quality, starting with top management. If strategic quality management doesn't start there, it just won't happen.

Activities for implementing stages one and two (see Table 13-1) are usually localized within the production engineering or operations departments. So, it's possible to carry them out successfully without direct involvement of top management.

But implementing stages one and two is not in itself sufficient for achieving strategic quality management (stage three). Strategic quality management must pervade the organization. Top management must assume a major leadership role.

For example, the materials and controls group at Texas Instruments got everyone involved. First, top management took courses in quality management. Then they *taught lower level employees*. Think anyone could miss the message?

3. Defining quality as your target market does. Zero defects won't do you any good if the quality of your product or service doesn't match your target market's perception of quality.

Corning Inc. (formerly Corning Glass Works) has the right idea.

> It is the policy at Corning to achieve total quality performance in meeting the requirements of external and internal customers. Total quality performance means understanding who the customer is and what the requirements are and meeting those requirements without error, on time, every time.

4. Competitive benchmarking. How does the quality of your product or service match up with that of your competitors? This is not always an easy question to answer. (If you have doubts, review Guideline 10.)

5. Setting yearly goals for quality improvement. Make sure that these goals are both long and short range and that they're measurable.

Rigid Production and Operations

To be a nicher, you've got to produce in smaller lots and respond quickly to changes. You've got to be flexible.

Yet most production and operations are geared to running stable, unchanging systems.

Here are eight solutions.

Solution 1. Eliminate Layers
of Management

In niche marketing, it's not rote performance that you need. Rather it's
employee initiative. Employees must have the ability—and desire—to
solve problems. They should be involved.

Japanese automobile-factory transplants have shown that the United
States' productivity problems do not stem from the workers but from
management. To involve employees and improve productivity, you've
got to push decision-making authority. To get this kind of involvement,
many companies have done away with layers of management.

We talk more about short chains of command in Guideline 16.

Solution 2. Use
Employee-Management Teams

Cross-Functional Teams. Your present organizational structure is
probably too functionally compartmentalized. Take the advice of Robert
L. Callahan, president of Ingersoll Engineers Inc. "Simply put together
people who can get the job done, regardless of their function." Callahan
calls it "swarming."[3]

Employees swarm at Milacron. Faced with tough competition from
the Japanese (so tough that bankruptcy was a possibility), Milacron
formed a cross-functional team of people from manufacturing and engineering as well as from purchasing, logistics, and marketing. Their
task: to design a plastic injection machine that would be competitive
with one made by the Japanese. That meant cutting costs by 40 percent
and increasing the machine's operating efficiency by 40 percent. And
the allotted development time was one year, half the usual period.

The cross-functional team completed their assignment on time. And
the product met all specifications. In the first full year of production,
Milacron sold 2½ times more of this new model (Vista) than it had ever
sold of Vista's predecessor.[4]

Do you have people like Milacron's? Probably. And people like that
welcome challenges. Find them. Give them a task and the resources they
need.

Self-Managed Teams. Texas Instruments CEO Jerry Junkins claimed,
"No matter what your business is, these [self-managed] teams are the
wave of the future." And, they're effective for both product and service
organizations.[5]

But self-managed teams do not work in all situations. They're practical
where the job is complex and dependent on more than three people.

Typical tasks assigned to self-managed teams include working with customers, developing new products or services, ordering equipment and materials, setting production schedules, solving production and operations problems, determining schedules of team members, and helping to decide who should be on the team—all without a boss within the team.

People within the team are cross functional. Usually they have different skills and are from different parts of the company. This diverse composition enables them to break down functional bureaucratic barriers.

Members can be blue-collar or white-collar, or a combination of both. The number of team members might range from 3 to 30. The team's life depends upon the assignment—anywhere from a few months to an indefinite time period.

Self-managed? Hard to believe that such a structure could work? But it does. And according to the management guru, Peter F. Drucker, the old command-and-control management method must go.

Let's take a look at how self-managed teams have helped some companies:[6]

- At 3M a cross functional, self-managed team tripled the number of new products of one division.

- At Johnsonville Foods productivity rose by over 50 percent between the years 1986 and 1990. Much of this increase was attributed to self-managed teams.

- A self-managed team at Federal Express is credited with locating and solving a billing problem. The savings: $2.1 million per year.

- Aetna Life & Casualty was able to reduce the number of middle managers by almost 80 percent. And what about customer service? *It improved!*

The future of self-managed teams? According to a survey conducted by the American Productivity and Quality Center of 467 *Fortune* 1000 companies, about half of the companies said they plan to use self-managed teams more in the future.

Quality Circles. Want to make your individual departments more efficient? Quality circles, used in the United States, have produced only mixed results. Still, as some companies have discovered, you may find that quality circles can help. McDonnell Douglas claims that quality circles, called "Solutions Through Employee Participation," increased productivity while reducing costs. Savings: $6.5 million.[7]

Harley-Davidson also sings praises about quality circles. Over a 10-year period (1978-1988), Harley-Davidson set up 117 quality circles involving half of its employees. This emphasis on quality, plus a niche-marketing approach, eventually helped Harley-Davidson fend off the Japanese competition. In fact, Harley-Davidson is number one in its chosen niche.[8]

At Thorneburg Hosiery Company, quality circles helped the knitter's group achieve 99.3 percent first-quality production (the industry average is about 90 percent).[9]

Solution 3. Consider Extra Pay for Extra Work

Often membership in cross functional teams means more work for employees. Besides their regular job, they're also a member of a team. Is that the way it's done in your company? If so, consider extra compensation.

- Give bonuses for completing development on time and according to specs.
- If the new product or service turns a profit, say in the first 2 years, reward each team member with a percentage of the profit.
- Allow team members to buy into the new product or service—say 1 percent or 2 percent each. If the new product or service succeeds, they share in the profits. If it fails, they, like the company, lose their investment.

And how about giving members of a quality circle recognition—if not compensation—when they make a significant contribution?

Solution 4. Consider Flexible Production

Would you like to know how to vary your product configurations at minimal cost? Then take another lesson from the Japanese. Widely misunderstood in the United States, *Kanban* means something more than "just-in-time (JIT) inventory." Although it's extremely important to have inventory arrive at the moment it is needed, that's only part of the process which makes the *Kanban* system highly effective.

A major reason many companies, and perhaps your firm, cannot produce a wide range of products is the time it takes to change over production of one model to another. You need hours, maybe days, to take out the dies and jigs and replace them with different ones.

The Japanese have been able to overcome this obstacle by, among other things, having extra machine components so that tools can be left set up, by specially fabricating jigs so that they can be quickly put in and taken out of machines, and by keeping the additional jigs and tools next to the machines instead of in central tool bins.

Are these methods successful in reducing changeover times? You bet. For example:

- Toyota trimmed the setup time for a bolt maker from 8 hours to 1 minute.

- Mazda cut back setup time for a ring-gear cutter from 6.5 hours to 15 minutes.

- Mitsubishi Heavy Industries shortened the setup time for an 8-arbor boring machine from 24 hours to 3 minutes.

- Yanmar Diesel (a Japanese manufacturer of diesel engines for tractors, sailboats, and the like) compressed the setup time for a cylinder block line from 9.3 hours to 9 minutes.[10]

Such improvements have enabled the Japanese to produce, at little extra cost, many different models for diverse markets. In fact, sometimes even at lower costs.

For example, in the mid-1970s, Yanmar was facing a doubtful future. Japan was experiencing a recession, and the demand for diesel engines had plummeted.

Now, competition among Japanese firms has a ferocity that's hard for American firms to imagine—except among Japanese firms with strategic alliances. Yanmar had such an alliance with Toyota.

Toyota was into flexible production. Yanmar took a lesson from them, and the results were astonishing. Factory productivity almost doubled. At the same time, costs of some parts were reduced by as much as 72 percent. Furthermore, work-in-process inventories were cut by as much as 80 percent. Required break-even production volume dropped from 80 percent to 50 percent of capacity.

You'd think that Yanmar would reduce the number of models produced. Not so.

Rather, it increased the number of different engine models from 250 to over 900!

Yanmar's achievements are especially noteworthy since prior to these changes Yanmar was already considered to have well-run manufacturing facilities.[11]

Flexible manufacturing can work for American manufacturers as well. After losing money for 3 straight years (thanks, in part, to Komatsu) Caterpillar realized that to get back in the game it would take more than cost cutting.

For example, its transmissions plant supplies Caterpillar's total line— over 120 different types of transmissions. On the original assembly line, where transmission cases were produced, stood a long line of 35 machine tools for milling, drilling, boring, tapping, deburring, and reaming crude steel. At every machine stood an operator.

Transmission cases were run through in batches, since the machines could handle only one kind at a time. So what do you suppose happened around the machines? The work area became jammed with bins of cases waiting for the next batch run.

After one batch was run, it was knockdown and setup time, which took the operator from 4 hours to 2 days. Once set up, two or three tries might be required for the machine to be adjusted properly. With these kinds of adjustments being made at 35 stations, piles of cases worth $1000 each ended up in the scrap heap.

And that was just for starters. When the drill bits became dull or broke off, they'd make off-sized holes. More scrap.

Then Caterpillar redesigned the plant.

One operator now handles several machines, thus saving labor costs.

Using flexible cellular units that can be programmed for any transmission size, Caterpillar reduced changeover time to seconds, again saving labor costs.

With fewer bins of cases waiting for the next process, there are inventory savings.

The new system selects the right tools from a rotating belt. They're inserted into spindles. And the machine does it right. No scrap here.

The new machines electronically sense trouble. If the torque is off, the spindle stops. The operator replaces the worn drill bit before it becomes dull or breaks and before the hole gets off-sized. No scrap here.

The result is savings in labor, inventory, scrap, *and* production time. It now takes only 15 days instead of 3 months to build a transmission.[12] Small wonder that Caterpillar is converting its other plants to flexible manufacturing systems.

Think you can't afford to retool your factory? Maybe you'd better think about how much it will cost if you don't.

Solution 5. Consider Using Small, Flexible, Low-Cost Facilities or Subcontracting

Take a page from the automobile manufacturers. C&C Inc. (part of Masco Industries), Vehma International (part of Magna International), and ASL build parts and modify vehicles for Detroit's Big Three.

Our prediction: the Big Three will soon use small manufacturers—either owned by them or independents—to assemble cars for tiny niche markets.

The Big Three's present operations are based on high-volume production runs. A rule of thumb is that their plants must have yearly volumes of 150,000 new-model cars to turn a profit. So, it's not in the cards for them to think about small niche markets, at least for their existing plants.

On the other hand, it's estimated that miniplants could make money on only 10,000 cars a year. One of the reasons: they would use many vehicle parts designed and built for the Big Three auto companies' mass-produced cars. Furthermore, miniplants, because of their size, would have the ability to change designs quickly.

What about your own operation? Ask yourself, "Should I build miniplants?" If the answer is no, what about subcontracting to one?

Solution 6. Consider Using Strategic Alliances to Achieve Flexibility

Strategic alliances, such as joint ventures and consortia, are becoming more common. Strategic alliances can be either horizontal or vertical.

These alliances go beyond traditional business relationships. There's a greater sense of shared responsibility for each other's sales and profitability. Each party has a stake in the other's performance. Risks and rewards are shared.

At their best, strategic alliances allow you to concentrate on your strengths. You use your partner or partners to perform other activities necessary to make your product or service successful in the marketplace. Your competitive stance is strengthened.

And the best news yet for niche marketers is that strategic alliances may not require large amounts of capital. Because of resource pooling, costs are spread—or minimized—while still realizing economies of scale. Kirin (a Japanese brewer), for instance, reduced the risk of currency fluctuations through a horizontal strategic alliance with Molson Breweries of Canada. The Kirin beer that is sold in Canada and the United States is brewed by Molson. Molson also profits because it's using its excess capacity.

In industries with rapid changes and high costs of R&D, joint efforts may be necessary to make the project feasible. Siemens and Philips N. V. joined to develop a 4-megabyte chip. Siemens also has joined Intel in designing chips.

Small regional airlines have strategic alliances with major trunk carriers to gain access to the majors' worldwide reservation systems. The majors also benefit because the alliances allow them to provide service to smaller markets.

Merck also uses strategic alliances. Unlike many of its rivals in the pharmaceutical industry, Merck is not trying to stay on top through mergers and acquisitions. Instead, it's developing a network of strategic alliances that will give it access to new markets and new technologies. For example, Merck acquired key research (on heart drugs) from Du Pont by trading certain marketing rights. The vehicle they used was a new, jointly owned company.

In the airline industry, Alegis, former parent to United, learned the hard way that strategic alliances are less risky than mergers and acquisitions. After integration by acquisition failed, United kept its sales-generating links to hotels and Hertz with strategic alliances.

Excessive Product Development Costs

Development costs always seem high. But when you're developing products and services for niche markets, they take on astronomical proportions. For sure you've got to combat high product development costs.

Solution 1. Consider Concurrent Engineering

How is a product designed and made in the United States?

The engineering department (hopefully with input from marketing) designs the product. The blueprints are handed to manufacturing.

Manufacturing checks them out. Too expensive and/or difficult to make. Tosses them back to engineering for redesign. Engineering reworks them. Throws them back to manufacturing.

And so on.

This led MIT's H. Kent Bowen to come up with the 15-80 rule: 80 percent of the cost of product development occurs in the first 15 percent of the development cycle.

The good old American way worked wonders for a number of years until foreign competition, using concurrent engineering, came along.

In concurrent engineering, both engineering and production design the product and the manufacturing process simultaneously. This makes sense (and, it makes even more sense when marketing, finance, and human resources are also part of the process).

But does it work?

You bet. Digital Equipment Corporation claims that using concurrent engineering cut their cost of new product development by one-half![13]

But getting functional areas to work together can be tough. Here's how Caterpillar is doing it. At first the plan was to move the design engineers into the plants so they'd work more closely with production personnel. But the then incoming chairman, Donald Fites, had another thought, "Hey, wait a minute, why just manufacturing and engineering people? Why wouldn't you want the whole team involved in a family of products working together?" So marketing is also in the factory.[14]

That's a good way to build a team and to design and build products and services that make sense from engineering, manufacturing and operations, and marketing points of view.

Solution 2. Simplify Your Products and Services

Boss Kettering said, "Any third rate engineer can make a product more complicated, but it takes a real genius to make it simpler."

Simplicity in products and services pays off.

Even so, somehow that's something American manufacturers didn't really strive for. That is, until the Japanese started using simplicity—effectively—as a competitive tool. To the Japanese manufacturers it meant lower production and operations costs and higher profits. To the consumers it meant fewer breakdowns and lower prices. Win-win situations.

Also, complex products are tough to produce with automation. Just ask General Motors about its Saturn plant.

Some claim that being good at making products or services simpler is as important as being able to develop new products or services. We would agree.

Many U.S. manufacturers are now striving to simplify their designs, helped by computer-aided design (CAD) and computer-aided manufacturing (CAM). IBM developed a laser printer that has many fewer parts than one made by Hewlett-Packard. (A side benefit: originally one of the reasons IBM strove for simplification was so the printer could be assembled by robots. IBM found that, with fewer parts, assembly was so simple that they could do it more cheaply by hand.)

Giddings & Lewis redesigned its Masterline lathe (using a cross functional team), making the lathe simpler and lighter. And with a 35 percent lower price tag.

A good rule of thumb is: Use concurrent engineering. And then keep improving—and simplifying—your products and services.[15]

Solution 3. Use Common Parts or Modules

How about making identical parts or components that can fit into a number of different niche products or services? This is something that aerospace and electronics firms have been doing for years.

One of the reasons Ricoh was able to keep costs down on its digital

IMAGIO 320 and 320F copiers was because a large number of their components was also used in Ricoh's conventional copiers.[16]

It's reported that Detroit is starting to make more parts that can fit into a wider variety of cars. (We hope these stay under the hood—shudder—otherwise this could lead to even more look-alikes.)

Recap

Life gets complicated when you start thinking of more products and services for more numerous and smaller markets. Say you've targeted some lucrative niches. Now it's no longer business as usual. And so the problems start.

Production and operations people like to keep things simple and, to their way of thinking, efficient. Involve production and operations people from the start. You may have to reallocate resources or change the reward system.

You'll have to do a better job at managing quality. This will call for involvement from both the top down and the bottom up.

Production and operations must be less rigid. Eliminate layers of management. Get people's participation through employee-management teams, such as cross functional teams, self-managed teams, and quality circles. It may require extra work, so consider changing your compensation packages.

You're going to have to come up with new ways of getting the job done. Think about flexible production and operations. Or using small, flexible, low-cost facilities. Or subcontracting. Or strategic alliances. And think about how to drive down product development costs by utilizing methods such as concurrent engineering, product and service simplification, and the use of common parts.

More complicated? You bet. But it can be managed.

14

Dealing with Logistics Problems

Tell your logistics manager, "We're going to get bigger by acting smaller," and he or she is bound to mutter, "The only thing that will get bigger is my headache."

Maybe so. Niche marketing usually means that storage and transportation become more complex and costs more difficult to control.

But logistics managers should never say no to challenges because of the headaches they might cause. Logistics managers must transform these headaches into costs. Then it's up to whoever makes the overall decision to decide whether the costs are acceptable.

As one marketing executive told us, "Marketing deals with profits; sales deals with volume." Accept that logistics costs will go up. Your main focus must be on higher profits.

For example, one firm sold and delivered oxygen cylinders to hospitals by the truckload. Then along came home health care. The firm decided to capitalize on this new market.

We can imagine the distribution manager's reaction when faced with servicing homes with single tanks. He reached for an oxygen mask himself and gasped, "The costs . . . the costs . . . It's impossible."

Well, of course, his costs would go up. What he failed to realize was that the margins would be higher as well because customers were willing to pay for this service. In fact, the new home market turned out to be very profitable.

Nevertheless, focusing on margins is psychologically difficult to do. Costs are real, but profits are potential. But if you're going to be a successful niche marketer, you've got to concentrate on supplying customers' needs as your number one priority. So we want to emphasize this again: You've got to fix your attention on margins, not costs.

Please don't misunderstand us. We believe that once a specific solution to a marketing opportunity is defined, it should be implemented at the least possible cost. That is, if the decision is made to deliver one tank of oxygen to an individual home, it should be delivered at the lowest possible cost while still maintaining acceptable service standards. Expecting costs to go up does not mean accepting inefficiency.

The solutions to logistics cost problems in niche marketing are basically those that you'd apply to any logistics cost problem. But before you start worrying about how to reduce storgage and transportation costs, look at logistics from a systems approach. If you see your logistics system as a series of independent events, each with its own cost outcome, you'll never get beyond the headache stage to the opportunity stage.

Analyzing Your Logistics System

First, examine what is stocked, where it is stored, why it is being stored, and any transportation linkages. Then review how these logistics activities affect other activities, such as production, sales, and customer service. Do this analysis for your firm, your suppliers, and your customers. Your findings will probably reveal more than one way to save money. But that will be just a start. You'll also gain insights into how to turn logistics into a competitive weapon.

Value Chains

A good tool to use in analyzing logistics costs and opportunities is the value chain. Examine the value chain in Figure 14-1.

The Firm's Internal Value Chain. One of the key benefits of the value chain as an analysis tool is that it highlights the linkages between activities. The hazards of viewing activities in isolation are obvious. For example, a company may reduce operations costs by producing in large lots only to find its finished goods being warehoused (outbound logistics) and its costs skyrocketing, thus eating up all the savings (and then some).

There's another reason why value-chain analysis is useful. It helps to foster breakthrough creativity. Incremental changes in a given activity can reach a point of diminishing returns. Far greater benefits may be realized by reconfiguring the value chain. For example, one company was able to lower its overall transportation and production costs by prepro-

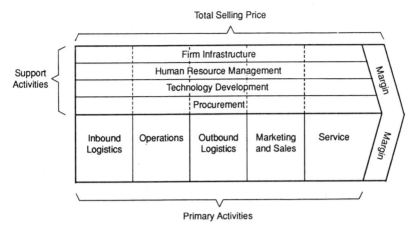

Figure 14-1. A firm's value chain. *(Adapted with permission of The Free Press, a Division of Macmillan, Inc., from* Competitive Advantage: Creating and Sustaining Superior Performance *by Michael E. Porter, p. 37. Copyright © 1985 by Michael E. Porter.)*

cessing near the points of production rather than by hauling everything to its main plant for processing. Although production costs went up, inbound logistics costs went down, more than offsetting the increased production costs.

Exploiting linkages within the value chain can be a good source of cost reductions. The Japanese excel at this. For example, they reduce inbound logistics (warehousing) and operations (manufacturing costs) through their much publicized *Kanban* system involving, among other linkages, just-in-time inventory.

The Distribution-Channel Value Chain. Besides understanding your own value chain, it's also necessary to understand the way that your firm is a part of the overall channel value chain. As Figure 14-2 points out, each channel member has its own value chain. Through an understanding of channel members' value chains, it is sometimes feasible to reconfigure the product or service so that all parties gain.

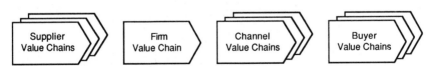

Figure 14-2. The distribution channel's value chain. *(Adapted with permission of The Free Press, a Division of Macmillan, Inc., from* Competitive Advantage: Creating and Sustaining Superior Performance *by Michael E. Porter, p. 35. Copyright © 1985 by Michael E. Porter.)*

For example, a baking company used eggs as a basic ingredient for its products, and a major activity was breaking the eggs and disposing of the shells. This had been going on for years.

Someone discovered that a significant part of the total expense was shipping "shells" in and shipping them out. This person discovered that the egg producer would be willing to break the eggs and ship the yokes and whites in tank trucks. Shipping costs were considerably less. Furthermore, this gave the egg producer an outlet for cracked eggs. In addition, the bakery's costs of egg breaking and waste disposal were eliminated. The payoffs were that the egg producer charged less and earned more, and the baking company received more and paid less. A win-win situation.

How many companies are shipping in "shells" only to ship them out again?

Henry Ford didn't. Not for long at least. He was walking through his Willow Run auto plant and noticed used, wooden shipping boxes that were about to be discarded. He went back to his office, made some sketches, and then called in his purchasing agent. He demanded that from then on the parts be shipped in wooden boxes that met his newly developed specifications.

Naturally the purchasing agent told him the supplier would charge extra to change the boxes. Ford said, "Pay it."

Somewhat bewildered, the agent did what he was told. Ford then went to the operations manager and told him the floorboards for the cars would now be arriving assembled in the shape of a box! He paid 10 percent more for the boxes and saved 50 percent on the floorboards.

Employee-Management Teams

Consider using cross functional or self-managed teams for company and channel value-chain analysis and for solving specific problems (see Guideline 13).

Plainly, the information you need to analyze includes each channel member's value chain as well as your own. Gathering this information requires insight and specialized knowledge. Pull together a team made up of managers and employees who routinely work with suppliers, distributors, and buyers to focus on all their value chains. In addition, include specialists who are extremely familiar with your own company.

For improving efficiencies within a small organizational unit, think about using quality circles. (Remember that quality circles have had mixed success in the United States.)

But can they work for logistics?

Just ask J. C. Penney.

Penney started its first quality circle in 1980. Today it has quality circles at all its distribution centers.

The payoff? Hundreds of productivity improvement projects have been implemented, ranging from better customer service to significant dollar savings. The working environment was also improved.[1]

Strategic Alliances

Gene R. Tyndall, the partner in charge of the Logistics and Transportation Consulting Group of Ernst and Young, Washington, D.C., gives an account of how a strategic alliance can work between a manufacturer and a customer to reduce supply-chain inventory costs.[2] A 2-day joint brainstorming session was held, during which four problem areas were pinpointed:

1. Shared forecasts and end-user consumption data
2. Integrated inventory-management methods
3. Transportation-freight costs
4. Integrated administrative systems (methods)

By changing their approach to these areas, both parties were able to reduce their inventories by at least 30 percent, a shared savings of several hundreds of thousands of dollars. Then, operational changes immediately brought about a 15 percent reduction in costs for both parties. A win-win situation.

After you've analyzed your firm's value chain and the distribution value chain, you'll have identified some specific storage and transportaion problems that need to be solved.

Inventory Problems

Will niche marketing increase your inventory problems?

Count on it!

Let's take a look at a sampling of some of the headaches experienced by niche marketers.

- "We're still trying to contain warehousing costs, but with the increased number of products . . ." (executive of a paper manufacturer).

- "We had a problem with inventory. We had to learn how to accommodate small levels of demand" (vice president, corporate development, paper-forms manufacturer).

- "Since many retailers return unsold products at the end of the season, increasing segmentation makes logistics planning—which is already difficult because it's a seasonal business—even more complex" (director, marketing research for a manufacturer of a health-care products company).

- "Keeping track of small case quantities is demanding. When you're dealing with a large-volume product, if you miss a case it's no big deal. There's a million of them lying around. But if you're dealing with a small production run, you need a much better method of keeping track of where the cases are and where they need to go" (vice president, food processing company).

Here are tips on how to keep your inventory costs within reason.

Solution 1. Consider Just-in-Time Inventory

How much warehouse space do you have?

If you're an American manufacturer, probably much more than you think. In fact, some factories might better be called warehouses than factories. Why? Because as much as 70 percent of factory floor area is used for warehousing inventory and related aisles.[3]

So now you're thinking about niche marketing and getting bigger by acting smaller. Be careful. Perhaps the only thing that will get bigger is your factory-warehouse.

Here's just one reason why: safety-stock inventory. Suppose that you have one product that brings in $1 million, and you need $50,000 of safety-stock inventory. Now you start going after niches, and instead of one product you have four. You may now bring in $2 million, but you also need $200,000 in safety-stock inventory.

Double your sales and quadruple your inventory. And that's just for safety stocks—just one factor used when determining your economic order quantity.

It's time to think about just-in-time (JIT) inventory systems. Have your materials, parts, and components delivered just before you need them. Japanese factories that use JIT use only one-third as much space for inventory.

Think of it! Implement JIT and you might be able to double your manufacturing floor area. And your inventory would drop dramatically. Yanmar Diesel found that JIT reduced work-in-process inventories by as much as 80 percent![4] Think of the cost savings and the freeing up of assets.

And there are labor savings. For instance, you may have more "warehouse" employees than you imagine, as one firm with 1000 employees found out. Only 40 employees were called material handlers. Yet a careful study showed that many employees spent about 30 percent of their work hours moving material in and out of their departments. So actually the force of material handlers was closer to 320 than to 40.[5] What if the firm could get it back to 40 by using JIT?

JIT, to be successful, must be closely linked with production systems. For this reason, we think that examining value chains will be of great help when implementing JIT.

Solution 2. Consider Bar Coding

Bar coding can bring order into your storage areas and save you money at the same time. Here's how some firms are using this technology:

- Picking, receiving, warehouse movement
- Return goods processing
- Returnable container controls
- Physical inventory taking

The benefits of bar coding increase when you have a large variety of products. Compared to manual systems, bar coding reduces the entry time required while greatly increasing accuracy.

At Milwaukee Electric Tool's distribution center in Olive Branch, Mississippi, a direct-contact infrared bar code identification system is used. Since inventory data are entered by scanning, there's no longer a need for skilled data-entry operators (in fact, the distribution center saved $40,000 in clerical costs the first year bar coding was used).[6]

Bar coding also improves your ability to keep track of items, for example, when taking inventory.

But bar coding's help in keeping track of your items doesn't stop in your warehouse. Bar coding can help locate products anywhere in the distribution chain. Federal Express has this down pat. Of course you'll get next-day delivery. And Federal Express can tell you, at any minute, where your parcel is.

Bar coding is impractical because of the nature of your product? Then consider voice-recognition systems. For example, at a meat warehouse an operator speaks directly into the computer, "From IBP (International Beef Packers) . . ."

Solution 3. Consider
Computerized Inventory
Control Systems

Whether you use bar coding or not, a computerized inventory-control system is a must. A computerized inventory system can reduce your inventory by as much as 15 percent to 20 percent. Perhaps even more. For example, when Special-T-Metals Co., a division of Sun Distributors LP, replaced its manual system with ProfiTool (General Data Systems), its inventory turns were increased by 15 percent. And the number of out-of-stock items decreased![7]

Solution 4. Consider
Automated Warehouses

Niche marketers can reap huge benefits from automated warehouses: greater speed and accuracy, better utilization of floor space, and reduced labor costs.

For example, Unisys Defense System automated its material management center's warehouse and reduced its inventory level by 37 percent. Inventory accuracy is now over 99.9 percent. Pick rates have doubled, and wrong-part picks have virtually been eliminated.[8]

Of course, fully automated warehouses require large capital expenditures and aren't for everyone. Yet, even partial automation can substantially improve logistics and make niche marketing more feasible. Using an automated conveyor system for part of its incoming shipments, Certified Grocers Midwest cut the order lead time by 50 percent. And productivity was increased!

Be careful you don't fall into the old suboptimization trap. If you change one part of operations, others will also be affected. A high-speed conveyor system is of little use when other parts of the system can't keep up with the pace.

Solution 5. Consider Unit
Loading Groupings

Not able to automate your warehouse? Still, you may be able to gain efficiencies by changing how you store and load inventory.

Most companies store materials by picking activities. To gain efficient picking throughput, they group fast movers together. Still you may be able to improve efficiency by family groupings, category groupings, or optimum order picking.

Family Groupings. A large distributor of drugs and beauty aids, Mc-Kesson Corp., stores and ships products by retail-drug shelf placement. McKesson uses this storage and shipping system as a marketing advantage. When retail outlets receive their orders, their shelf stocking is simplified.

Category Groupings. Amidro pharmaceutical wholesaler in Switzerland tried to reduce warehouse costs by using systems suggested by mathematical models. But these systems didn't work. There was just too small a turnover of many items, a typical problem for niche marketers.

Through a detailed study, the company found there were groups of items with similar characteristics like optimum order rhythm, correct safety margins, and seasonal trends. Products were assigned to these groups by four primary characteristics.

The result was a 30 percent reduction in warehouse stocks without sacrificing customer service.

Optimum Order Picking. A manufacturer of construction equipment, Komatsu American Corporation, uses optimum order picking. It sets up its storage areas according to the size of items and uses different materials handling equipment in each area. Komatsu's workers are cross-trained so they can stock and pick between storage areas.

Solution 6. Reconfigure Warehousing

It's hard to believe, but many methods of reconfiguration are overlooked, perhaps because it is such an obvious solution.

Hub and Spoke. Improved delivery time with less inventory. Great for niche marketers.

But does it sound improbable? Well, maybe not if you use the hub-and-spoke concept.

In hub-and-spoke warehousing, you have full stocking locations that service either stockless or reduced-stock satellite locations. Large loads are shipped to the spokes. There they are sorted out and consolidated with other products for distribution. Economies of scale are preserved for incoming and outgoing shipments and for inventory storage. The hub-and-spoke system also avoids buffer stocks at each of the spoke warehouses.

Wal-Mart has a network of eight distribution centers that fill 80 percent of its stores' needs. The result? Wal-Mart's distribution costs are less than one-half of the mass merchandising industry's costs.

Or, how about banks? They have regional full-service centers. But, to provide their customers with convenience, they also have limited-service transaction satellites, the same principle as the hub and spoke.

Or publishers? Thomas Publishing prints its *Thomas Register* in three cities. The registers are shipped to 89 spokes throughout the country. From there, the Postal Service or local delivery services take over.

Federal Express used the hub-and-spoke system to take off. Memphis is its hub. Computerized resorting, loading, and rerouting directs the overnight packages to appropriate spokes. Then the spokes make the next-day delivery as promised.

Public Warehousing.   Public warehousing is commonly used for serving markets with low sales volumes. It provides flexibility for changing needs, which is just what niche marketers with low volumes need: low capital resource requirements and flexibility.

Association Distribution Centers.   Like the idea of public warehousing but think it's too expensive? Then perhaps you can use association warehouses. For example, the Canadian Grocer Manufacturers Association has a distribution center in Vancouver, saving manufacturers at least 10 percent.[9]

Shipping from the Manufacturing Site.   Often existing channels can't, or won't, carry small units of a large number of products in inventory. And warehouses are out of the question. If this is the case, consider shipping directly from the manufacturing site. That's what Scott Paper does for some of its products. It promises emergency deliveries of its products anywhere in the country within 24 hours. For Scott, this system is cheaper than warehousing.[10]

Predistribution.   Predistribution is common practice among mass merchandisers and food chains. For example, at Pic 'n' Pay, about 70 percent of the products are sorted and put on an outbound truck without ever entering their warehouses. Their system uses in-house prepared bar-coded shipping labels to indicate store designation and to direct cartons to the proper trucks.

Freight Problems

With more products going to different target markets, freight problems—and costs—are bound to increase.

Here's a sample of what niche marketers told us:

- "We're faced with higher break-bulk costs" (director of market development, chemical manufacturer).

- "We've had a major problem in trying to get fair shipping rates for small quantities" (director of corporate planning, coal producer).

- "Now that we've got a number of different products going to a number of different niches, there's the problem of making sure that delivery is correct. Our trucking routes are far more complex" (director of marketing, newspaper chain).

- "We found that serving several new niche markets required different types of delivery vehicles" (director of marketing, livestock feed processor).

How can you cope with these very real problems?

Solution. Reconfigure Transportation Systems

Reconfiguring transportation is just as obvious as reconfiguring warehousing. And just as often overlooked.

Consider switching transportation modes. The cheapest way is not always the best. It's back to value-chain analysis.

Freight Forwarders. Niche marketers are often faced with having to deliver a large variety of products in small quantities. Yet, we found many companies believe that a private fleet eliminates the need to use public carriers. Accordingly, their trucks deliver small volumes. In some cases, the gross margin of these shipments did not even meet fuel costs.

The lesson: Consider air and truck freight forwarders, pool car operators (rail), and ocean freight forwarders. You'll find you're not alone. For example, more and more companies are using regional trucking firms that provide a host of customized less-than-truckload services. Some trucking firms are becoming niche marketers too.

Shipping Associations. Since shipping associations are nonprofit, you might find this a cheaper alternative to freight forwarders.

Auxiliary Carriers. Again, don't overlook the obvious. How about using UPS? Parcel post? Bus package service?

Intermodal Transportation. Perhaps you can increase speed (and maybe even decrease costs) by using a combination of carriers.

Contract Distribution. Perhaps, at least for some of your products, you might be better off turning over your shipments to third party alternatives. Since they know the shortcuts, they may be able to save you money at the same time. That's one of the reasons why the use of contract shippers grew at a double-digit rate during the 1980s in the United Kingdom.

Recap

Niche marketing won't work unless you can find a fast, efficient, and cost-effective way to get that product out to your special niche. Do this better than your competitors, and you have a valuable selling tool in your pocket.

As a niche marketer, you have nontraditional problems that require innovative solutions. More than ever, you must learn the logistics not only of your own firm, but also those of your suppliers, the distribution channels, and your customers. Some solutions will be costly—but worth it. Others will require new technological know-how. Still others may be quite simple.

Look at them all. Look not only at your company's value chain but also at the entire distribution channel's value chain. And get people involved. Not only yours, but also people from the distribution channel.

Count on your inventory problems increasing. Keep them within reason. Consider using just-in-time inventory, bar coding, computerized inventory systems, automated warehousing, and unit loading groupings.

How about reconfiguring your warehousing? Consider a hub-and-spoke system, public warehousing, association distribution centers, drop shipping, and predistribution.

Freight costs are also likely to increase. Look into changing your transportation mode by using freight forwarders, shipping associations, auxiliary carriers, intermodal transportation, and third party alternatives.

You'll run into blind alleys. But all of this analysis is not wasted. What you don't use to satisfy today's niches may help you with tomorrow's.

15

Dealing with Channel Problems

You probably have some distribution channel problems with your current products and services. But you've established a system that generally works.

However, what about the new niche products and services you're contemplating? Will your present channel system work equally well for them? Perhaps your distributors may not share your enthusiasm for differentiation and target niches. Or, maybe your distributors are just inappropriate.

Our survey of niche marketers spotted a number of such problems:

- "Existing channels were not suitable for niche products" (marketing executive, industrial manufacturing).

- "Multichannels cause confusing turf" (vice president for strategic marketing, telecommunications firm).

- "The use of new channels made some distributors unhappy, and now they don't give us any business" (senior vice president, insurance company).

- "The benefits of targeting are not yet fully understood. Channels have to be educated" (vice president, food processor).

- "It's a major challenge to motivate channels to champion additional and more diverse products" (vice president, insurance company).

These problems fall roughly into four categories:

1. Unsuitable existing channels
2. Unmotivated channels
3. Conflicts among channels
4. Price-cutting conflicts

Potential solutions, suitable for niche marketers, are offered in the following pages. One or more, perhaps with adaptations, will work for you.

Unsuitable Existing Channels

There are a number of reasons why your present distribution channels may not be suitable for your new niche markets.

They might, among other things, lack the specialized skills to help launch your niche product or service. Or perhaps the lines already dominating your channel would reflect the wrong image.

Maybe the mix is wrong. Selling life insurance, stocks, and bonds through financial planners makes sense. But not to people shopping for jeans at Sears. The Sears "mass-marketing mania" may work for some products and services but not for others. You can't sell all things on the basis of high traffic alone.

So a question you must ask yourself is this: "Should I use my present channels for my niche products and services?"

Sometimes the decision is not yours to make. Your customary channels may refuse to handle your niche product or service. If that happens, you'll have to switch channels. Not a happy prospect on the face of it, but one that can be resolved, sometimes with fortuitous outcomes.

If you have to switch channels, here are four possible alternatives.

Solution 1. Use Horizontal Channels

The Gap Stores were successful in creating an image for their stores: rock music, psychedelic colors, and modish salespersons. When The Gap's management decided to start selling baby clothes, they knew their present stores just wouldn't be suitable. So they created a new network of stores, GapKids, with more suitable music, colors, and salespeople.

Another example is the upscale Acura, targeted for a different market segment than Honda's other models. Honda decided against displaying its Acuras next to the other Hondas. And they decided against using regular Honda salespersons to sell it. Honda didn't want the salespersons bouncing back and forth between the two brands. Key customer buying motives for a Civic were drastically different from those for an Acura. So Honda clearly differentiated the Acura by building an independent dealer network.

On the other hand, take a look at Cadillac's Cimmaron (if you can still find one). The Cimmarons were found next to the traditional Cadillacs in the dealers' showrooms. Too bad. Not only did these models serve different segments, there was also an image conflict that hurt the upscale Cadillacs.

We're sure the same issue arose at planning meetings in Tokyo and Detroit. Both groups addressed the question, "Do you realize how much it would cost to have separate channels for our new brands?" There was no doubt that the costs were high, but only Detroit needs to ask whether these costs were higher than the cost of failure.

Think about your new niche product and service target markets. Will your existing channels be able to get the job done? Or, will you run into image problems? Will the salespersons be the right people for your new niche product and service target markets?

Solution 2. Go Direct

A regional baker wanted to start servicing a niche it had neglected: the small mom-and-pop stores. But its route drivers wanted no part of this, and with good reason. The drivers owned these routes and had exclusive distribution rights. They were making enough income just serving the larger accounts. For the route owners, serving the smaller stores wasn't worth the effort.

So the baker bought out the route owners and hired route salespeople to work directly for the company. Now in control, the baker serviced the mom-and-pop stores.

Frito Lay and L'eggs also found that going direct was a better answer. Instead of going through the traditional pipeline channel, they use employee van delivery. This ensures immediate restocking of shelves and maximum control over positioning.

Solution 3. Use Channel Specialists

Setting up horizontal channels or going direct is fine. But what if you can't afford those solutions?

As a further complication, you may be using a certain type of intermediary now, but you can plainly see that for a new niche product, service, or target market, this particular channel just won't work.

Again, don't overlook the obvious: alternative kinds of intermediaries, such as selling agents, manufacturer's representatives, brokers, and wholesalers and/or industrial distributors.

There may be an unexpected plus. These intermediaries may know the market better than you do. So you may benefit from both a targeted channel and knowledge of the market. Like killing two birds with one stone.

Solution 4. Form Strategic Alliances

Lack expertise or the financial resources to reach a market? Unable to find suitable intermediaries to handle your product or service?

Then consider a strategic alliance.

Sharing Sales Forces. Many companies do just that. For example, small West European manufacturers who want to sell abroad but lack the know-how and finances have turned to large firms with international sales networks.

Known as "piggybacking," this type of strategic alliance has become widely used, especially in France. Companies have found piggybacking particularly helpful in reaching markets in Eastern Europe and Asia.

Rhone-Poulenc Rorer, a chemical producer, and Pechiney, a metals company, are two French sources for piggybackers. Rhone-Poulenc Rorer has alliances with over 200 chemical companies. Pechiney, unlike Rhone-Poulenc Rorer, does not limit its alliances to companies with similar products.[1]

Some companies have used strategic alliances that go beyond sharing distribution facilities. Merck and Johnson & Johnson, for example, formed a joint venture company. Its purpose: to develop and market over-the-counter medicines for the U.S. market. Johnson & Johnson brings to the venture marketing expertise and sales and distribution capabilities. Merck contributes product candidates and research and manufacturing expertise.

Sharing Physical Facilities. Need more retail outlets but lack the capital? Or maybe your volume won't sustain a separate store?

Then how about opening a store within a store? For example, Flour Pot cookie stores operate inside Arby's. Car Phones Connection, Inc., has outlets in automobile dealerships and car washes. United Parcel Service (UPS) has service centers for mailing packages in hardware stores and drugstores.

Unmotivated Channels

It was probably hard enough to win niche-marketing support from management. But that may have been a cakewalk compared to getting the support of your channel.

For example, food retailers reacted negatively to the proliferation of food products. There were too many products and too little space, making it tough for manufacturers to get all their products on the shelves. Even tougher when retailers began targeting their own markets. Now they carry only those products best suited for their customers.

One of the most profitable retail food grocers, Stew Leonard, has a targeted marketing plan that calls for fewer than 1000 products. On the other hand, a traditional supermarket carries more than 20,000 items.

To avoid or overcome such channel problems, here are four possibilities.

Solution 1. Make Sure the Channel Is Appropriate

The channel may mesh with your frame of reference, but what about your distribution channel's viewpoint? How do they see themselves? As your selling agents?

No way.

They see themselves as purchasing agents for their customers. And they want to get paid by you, and paid well, for performing this service.

So a prime consideration for you is whether or not the channel members will think of your product or service as suitable for the assortment they offer their customers. Providing you with a service *you* need is not a high priority for them.

So look at your niche product or service the way your channel does. The best channel from where you sit may not be the right one if channel members aren't as convinced as you are. Save yourself some time by considering who could profit the most by selling your niche product or service.

Solution 2. Win Support Early

Obtain input from your distribution channel while you're still in the process of developing your niche products and services. Make channel members part of your team. They'll be more enthused about your niche products and services. And the more enthused they are, the more they'll sell.

Although most companies test products and services on consumers and some even include consumers in product or service development, few companies invite channel members to participate in the initial development.

Yet, we've seen cases in which thousands of dollars were spent after the fact trying to persuade channels about the great new products or services. And we've also seen the great new products and services fail because of the lack of channel acceptance.

It's almost a paradox. On the one hand, manufacturers want channel members to be partners; but, on the other hand, they treat them as obstacles to sales.

How about borrowing a concept from Du Pont? Du Pont's solution is to use a distributor marketing steering committee. Or, take a page from Cherry Electrical Products, which employs a distributor marketing manager whose job is to work with distributors to develop formal marketing plans.[2]

Solution 3. Offer Appropriate Incentives

You've got the right distribution channel, and you've won their initial support.

Now, gain their continuing support by making sure they have the right incentives.

Channel members have expectations concerning margins, turnover, and volume. If you don't meet these, you're in trouble.

As a niche marketer, you're probably on a tight budget. Even so, you feel obliged to conform to the expected discount structures. And you do.

A good move?

Maybe not.

Here's why. First of all, since your niche products and services are targeted toward relatively small markets, you're *not* likely to meet your channel's turnover and volume expectations. And that's bad.

But that's just for starters.

Your niche products and services will require a higher level of support. The channel's salespersons will have to have better-than-usual product or service knowledge because they're serving specialized needs. And you'll need a higher level of market feedback because specialized needs are seldom static.

So your incentives have to be great. But don't think of incentives only in terms of margins. Be creative. Higher margins may not be the tool you should use.

Instead of boosting, for example, the margin from 30 percent to 40 percent, how about increasing merchandising programs? Advertising allowances? Sales "spiffs"? Or contests for dealers?

How about territorial protection?

Or your incentives might be in terms of accounts payable or receivable financing. Or inventory floor plans. Or consignment selling.

Incentives might take the form of reducing operating costs such as warehousing. How about drop shipping? Or sharing a computerized inventory system? Or even providing detail persons to stock shelves?

Solution 4. Educate

Channel members usually need special education and training to successfully sell new products and services. And this is particularly true of niche products and services, which are targeted for specialized (yes, even subtle) customer needs.

Salespeople need to be aware of such differentiated needs in order to properly satisfy them. It doesn't make sense to produce a niche product or service and then use a mass-merchandising approach to sell it.

Channel members also need to be educated on the principle of getting bigger by acting smaller. Only when they understand the potential benefits will they offer their full support.

Don't confuse marketing to your channel with real education and training. Many companies, in the guise of education, put on slick marketing sales programs. But their real objective is to get distribution. Education and training should have the objective of making your channel members more knowledgeable and, therefore, more capable of dealing with your new niche products and services.

One national food company that was embracing niche marketing found its sales force was far more educated in marketing, and specifically niche marketing, than its channel members. To reduce the education gap, the manufacturer offered to pay tuition for channel members who would attend executive development seminars on target marketing at local universities.

Think through what you'll need to do in the way of channel education and training while you're developing your niche product or service. Don't wait until the product is on the wholesalers' shelves. By the time you get your education and training act together, it may be too late. You may find your products back on *your* shelves.

Conflicts among Channels

Suppose you've taken a careful look at your present channels as potential distributors for your new niche product or service. You decide to add a new channel; the ones you have are unsuitable, incapable, or unwilling to give you the kind of coverage you'd like to have.

So you add a new channel and bang! You're right in the middle of a turf war between the old and the new. Sentiments like this will be commonplace: "If they put a captive [company-owned] branch in my territory, I'm dropping their line."

Not an uncommon situation.

Nor a nice situation, either. Turf wars are disruptive to sales and profits.

In the example above, ironically, the captive branch also thought of the distributor as a threat. What they both failed to realize was that each channel served different target markets! The captives focused on the large construction market, while the independents serviced the residential market. There was no major source of real conflict. Only imaginary.

There are several things you can do to avoid such conflicts.

Solution 1. Establish Boundaries

Decide which distribution channels are going to serve which target markets, and establish clear boundaries.

But recognize there will always be some disagreements. Set up a procedure for handling these disputes.

Sounds simple, doesn't it? Yet we've found very few companies that do it.

Solution 2. Communicate Boundaries

Before your program gets under way, make sure everybody understands that different channels are not in competition with one another. If you don't, you'll have a rash of conflicts.

But when we say "make sure everybody understands," we don't mean send a memo. If that's all you do, you can expect more than a turf war. It will be more like Armageddon. And do you know something? You'll deserve it.

You don't have time to communicate properly? Then remember the axiom, you never have time to do things right the first time, but you always find time the second time.

Still don't have time?

Then make your adventure into niche marketing less ambitious. So you will have time to do things right the first time.

Price-Cutting Conflicts

Your discount structure may allow high-volume channel members to sell at a much lower price level than low-volume members. And you know what happens. Here are some ideas to prevent—or minimize—such clashes.

Solution 1. Adjust Your Quantity-Discount Structure

Perhaps your quantity-discount structure is too high. Or perhaps instead of quantity discounts, you should consider nonprice incentives. Such as merchandising programs, advertising allowances, and contests and prizes.

Solution 2. Use Different Products and Services for Different Channels

Perhaps you can further resegment your niche. If that's possible, make sure the products and services are clearly differentiated. Levi Strauss raised the hackles of department and specialty stores (where it sold its top-of-the-line jeans) by bringing out a cheaper line for K Mart.

Solution 3. Drop One Channel

Solutions 1 and 2 may not be viable. Now comes biting-the-bullet time. You'll have to choose between one channel or the other.

One candy manufacturer did this. A buyer at a large supermarket chain told the candy manufacturer, "You've got a problem. Mass merchandisers, like K Mart and the Price Club, are selling your candy cheaper than we can buy it."

The manufacturer responded, "I don't have a problem. You do. My price structure stands. Take it or leave it."

Resolving Conflicts

Regardless of how much time you spend in educating your channels, how clearly you set up and communicate territorial boundaries, or how you handle price cutting, conflicts are bound to arise.

Make the resolution of these disputes the responsibility of one person, someone with the authority as well as the ability to make tough choices. And make the person available. Unattended conflicts are bound to fester.

Recap

We've focused on *potential* channel problems for niche marketers. But potential means just that: potential, not inevitable.

Avoid many of the possible land mines with advance planning, not only in identifying your market niche and developing a product or service for it, but in selecting an appropriate delivery channel as well. Don't leave this decision until you're ready to enter the market.

Find out everything you can about your current channel or channels. Will your proposed product or service be accepted? Enhanced? Doomed? How about your target market? Is the channel likely to be accepted? Got problems? Then look into alternatives such as horizontal channels, going direct, market specialists, or strategic alliances. Be proactive rather than reactive.

Involve channel members early. Distributors of niche products and services need greater skills (and more pampering) than distributors for mass markets. Use education and training, innovative incentives, and a win-win psychology to gain their support.

You may never have a channel problem, but preparing for one should be part of your planning process. Turf wars and price cutting can erupt unexpectedly. Have one person who will be in charge of these disputes, a person with the authority and inclination to resolve conflicts quickly. Don't risk losing that lucrative niche you've worked so hard to locate.

16
Dealing with Organization and Planning Problems

Successful niche marketing requires that you look for value-added products and services. But everyone is looking in this direction. You've got to get there first, do a good job with the fundamentals, and you'll win.

We found that niche marketers ran up against two major obstacles to fast action:

1. An unwieldy organizational structure
2. An inflexible planning procedure

Here's how you can overcome these blocks to successful niche marketing.

An Unwieldy Organizational Structure

Consider these solutions.

Solution 1. Reorganize

Here's how reorganization helped Lever Brothers. The company had experienced dramatic growth during the 1980s, more than a doubling of actual tonnage volume and market shares. This growth caused the account managers to spend most of their time on the high-volume megabrands, while neglecting the smaller-volume, but more profitable, niche brands.

As Joe Tallarico, senior sales planning manager, put it:

> Not enough time was being spent for strategic planning of the smaller niche brands. We've found that these products take as much, if not more, emphasis than larger-volume brands. The target is smaller, and you must better understand all of the dynamics of why, where, and when the consumer is purchasing your products.

Lever Brothers solved this problem by modifying its organizational structure. Product lines were split into categories. A manager was put in charge of each of these categories, thus allowing for greater effort to be spent on developing effective marketing and account strategies for niche products.

The results were very positive across the full lineup of brands, but particularly for the niche products.

Solution 2. Shorten the Chain of Command

If you've got layer after layer of management delaying and filtering information from the field, how can you move quickly?

Bureaucracy must be reduced. *Having a short stem* is one way to do it.

At Weirton Steel the salespersons report to district managers. District managers to the vice president of sales. The vice president of sales to the CEO. Period. This enables Weirton to respond quickly to changes and new market needs.

At troubled Wang they're trying to accomplish the same thing. They've reduced the complexity of their field organization. There are fewer business managers. Now they can deal more crisply with local problems and opportunities.

Solution 3. Decentralize

What if you can't have a short chain of command as you're now structured?

Decentralization is exactly what many large corporations are doing. And, as a result, they're getting more authority closer to the field. Hewlett-Packard, for example, has 50 independent business units.[1]

Colgate-Palmolive also has been organized into business groups: oral care, fabric care, home care, and body care. These groups are headed by experienced general managers and staffed by people in marketing, sales, technical, finance, and market research. Each group has considerable (but not total) decision-making authority. The result: they're making better and faster decisions.

To help ensure that Colgate-Palmolive stays decentralized, the company also follows a decentralization policy with acquisitions. Companies that have been bought are *not* dismantled and integrated into the parent company. For the most part, they are left as independent operating units.

Sure, corporate headquarters exerts influence in setting objectives and establishing some common procedures. But the business units still have a great deal of independence.

Or how about Johnson & Johnson? One hundred sixty six autonomous businesses.[2]

Or take the $2.3 billion manufacturer of electromechanical and hydraulic parts and equipment, Parker Hannifin Corporation. According to its CEO, Paul G. Schloemer, its success has been based on decentralization. And he keeps business units small. "When a division gets to a point where its general manager can't know and understand the business and be close to the customer, we split it off." Usually that translates into plants of 300 to 400 employees.[3]

In Japan, it's the same way. Some of the best-run Japanese companies are also decentralized. For example, Matsushita Electric has 161 consolidated units, and Hitachi Ltd. has 660 companies.

Matsushita's and Hitachi's decentralization did not happen by chance. Their decentralization was—and is—very deliberate. It prevents upstart products and services from getting smothered by mature businesses.[4]

TW Services also has a very decentralized system. Each division sets its own targeted growth rate. Then, to meet these objectives, divisions develop new products to serve their target markets. Divisions have their own planning departments that work with the operations people in developing these plans. So TW's planning system is decentralized in a decision-making sense. But, of course, it's still controlled at the top by plan review, approval, or rejection.

For example, at TW's food service division personnel work very closely with clients on a day-to-day basis. They have to be very responsive to their customers' needs or they can lose a contract very quickly. Their structure is such that customers' information flows back through to decision makers quickly. Their food service managers have a lot of latitude in implementing new ideas and programs. They don't have to go through a bureaucracy of corporate staff (and many of the other inhibitors to change).

Solution 4. Create a New Organization

Sometimes an organization is so ossified that internal changes are impossible.

Is this your situation? Then consider setting up a new entity.

That's what General Motors did. Top management couldn't get people to buy into the organizational changes needed to launch the Saturn project. So an entirely new organization was formed.

An Inflexible Planning Procedure

Your organization's structure may push decision making close to the field. But make sure your planning system allows for rapid changes.

You've got to have a plan. But, as General Eisenhower said, "Planning is indispensable. But plans are useless." Create a plan. But be prepared for it to quickly become obsolete. You'll have shifts in the economy, government regulations, competitors' actions, pricing policies, and so on.

So you may have to change your plan. Don't make the mistake of one baking company. It developed a plan, but the plan did not take into consideration the development of low- and no-fat ingredients. While other companies jumped at the opportunity, this baker's management hopelessly looked at the plan and said, "It's not in the plan."

It seems hard to believe, but they really thought they were doing the right thing. Their reasoning, "Why else plan if you're just going to drop it as soon as a change comes along?"

On the other hand, Entenmann's moved quickly. Using the new no-fat ingredients, Entemann had a staggering increase in sales. Estimates place it as high as 45 percent to 50 percent in some markets.

How many times have you heard (or thought) this? "We put together a marketing plan every year. And what a waste. We spend 2 weeks putting it together to make management happy. Then we get back to business, and nobody ever looks at the plan again. Next year we go through the same rite of spring again."

In fact, many marketing plans do nothing more than take up shelf space. But even so, not all the effort developing the plans was wasted. Just putting plans on paper causes more rigorous thinking and greater involvement—only if it's once a year. But the value of a written marketing plan is increased tenfold if it becomes a working document, one that you refer to every day to track progress.

For example, a retailer told us that its marketing plan is one of the most used documents in the company. People at all levels refer to it regularly. Why? Because it is written and formatted to help solve problems and make decisions.

Take another case, a regional dairy council that puts on nutrition seminars for various groups. Naturally some groups have greater value than others to the accomplishment of the council's objectives. The executive director found that the seminar leaders, when requested to make a presentation, would look first at their calendars to see if they were available to give seminars on that specific date.

The executive director railed at this practice. She insisted that the seminar leaders first look at the marketing plan to check the importance of groups.

For the groups that had the highest priority, the seminar leaders should make sure that they were available. It almost didn't matter what their calendars said.

But if the marketing plan is to be a working document, you've got to be able to change the plan—and quite often. Now we know—and you know—that lengthy plans don't get changed. It's too cumbersome. This means plans have to be short.

Solution 1. Use a Fact Book

A short plan doesn't mean that you shouldn't spend time assembling and analyzing facts concerning past performance and future projections. You must. If you don't, forget about formal planning.

But you don't want most of this fact-finding information located in the plan itself. There's another place for it. In a fact book.

Here is the place to keep such data as performance profiles of your product or service target market.

The performance profiles should include such information as

- The target market's size, as well as its potential and key buying motives
- Distribution channels' key buying motives, sales to the target market by each distribution channel, and your market share of each distributor channel's sales
- Sales, market share, and competitive benchmarking of direct competitors
- Other external forces, including indirect competition, technological trends, and economic and governmental conditions
- Internal facts, such as past sales, profitability, availability of resources, and successes (and failures) of past marketing programs
- The rationale for selecting your strategy

Don't underestimate the value of this type of information. For example, a drug company's management did a market research study and discovered that doctors associated the company's drug with a side effect—one that the drug actually didn't have.

Strange. They looked at all their promotional materials and this side effect wasn't even mentioned. However, a study of their competitors' ads revealed the answer. All competitors' advertisements claimed that their drugs did not have this side effect. Because this company did not mention the absence of this side effect, the doctors assumed that it was present. Having competitors' ads readily available in a fact book made this analysis quick and feasible.

Ask yourself, "Do I have basic market data at my fingertips? Such as the number of customers in my target market? The names of my direct competitors? Samples of their advertising (print, radio and/or TV)?"

Now look at the questions again.

You asked, "Do I have it at my fingertips," not "Could I get it?"

We've talked with so many people who say, "We can get this information in no time." But if you don't have a regular procedure, just see how long it takes you to get it together.

Try it.

We asked a director of marketing to do this. He called in his assistant and asked him, "Get me a copy of all our competitors' advertising." One hour later the assistant returned. The director of marketing gave us a big smile and asked the assistant for the results. The assistant responded with a question, "Which competitors?"

Don't kid yourself. You need backup material—a fact book. Keep it neat, orderly, up to date, and indexed. However, since it's back up material, parts can be copies of printed materials. Some can be typed. Some can be in pencil. Whatever form it takes, just make sure you have a fact book.[5]

Solution 2. Use a Working Plan

This plan is exactly what it purports to be: a working plan. It's not meant to sell management. If that's your primary goal, then consider another format. Your working plan should be formatted so it will give you day-to-day guidance.

Now, let's see what a short—and flexible—marketing plan might contain.

First, you will have a plan for each product or service target market. This plan includes the following:

1. Summary strategy statement

2. Sales and profit objectives, by total and by appropriate time periods
3. Action plans (what will be done when, by whom, and at what cost)
4. Budget

For items 2, 3, and 4 you'll have planned targets and blank spaces for what is actually achieved and the variances. In this way, it's a working document. One that you'll refer to daily. And the plan will be short. It might consist of only 5 to 10 pages. A product or service target market plan outline is shown in the Appendix.

Since you'll probably have more than one product or service target market plan, you'll need a summary plan. It will make it easier for you to monitor total sales, profits, and expenses. The summary plan will help you coordinate with other functional areas, such as production-operations, human resources, and finance. It also will give you a better sense of overall operations. And finally, management also will want to see a summary plan so they too can get the big picture.

Although there are many variations, the simplest (and easiest) way to handle such planning situations is to prepare individual product and service target market plans separately and then to consolidate them into a summary plan.

A sample format (with explanations) for a summary marketing plan is shown in the Appendix.

Put your marketing plans on your computer. Changes can be made quickly, and changes in the product or service target market plan will also change the summary plan.

Recap

Organization and planning is the foundation for the implementation of your niche-marketing strategy. This foundation is largely invisible unless cracks appear. And when they do, they're almost impossible to repair.

Immediately make sure that your niche products and services are receiving enough management attention. Larger-volume products and services will have a higher priority if management is spread too thin. Reorganization could be the solution.

And you've got to react quickly to changes in the market. Decision making must be made at the lower levels. Make sure your organizational structure is not unwieldy. Shorten your chain of command. Can't do this with your present organizational structure? Then decentralize.

Make your marketing plans flexible. Keep facts and documentation in a separate place—in a fact book—so you can keep your working plans uncluttered and short. Create a summary plan to provide an overall perspective.

And put your marketing plans on your computer.

Follow these suggestions and your marketing plan will be a living document. It will specify exactly what you want to achieve. You'll be able to use the plan to monitor and record results. If the results significantly deviate from the plan, then your plan will signal that it's time for a revision. And your plan will be easy to change.

17

Dealing with Personnel Problems

You expect to have problems with the sales force when you begin niche marketing. (We talk about these problems and their solutions in Guideline 19.) But you're bound to have personnel problems in other areas as well. When other firms started serving smaller market segments, they encountered these trouble spots:

1. Management resistance
2. Personnel shortages
3. Resistance to organizational change
4. The big bang approach

Management Resistance

Don't expect your typical mass-market manager automatically to become a niche marketer. Niche marketing, especially if initiated under the big bang approach, may differ too much from management's past practices.

With niche marketing you're focusing your energy on smaller target markets as opposed to larger, more visible segments. That makes a lot of people nervous. They think you're giving up a larger market. They don't realize that the sum of the smaller markets might be bigger than the mass market.

Any time you start talking niche marketing, some executives will still insist on going after the entire market. Typically this problem will arise in larger companies, where people are more accustomed to a mass-marketing mentality.

Aside from this, niche-marketing plans need to be developed for each product and service target market served. Planning becomes more complicated. When you deal with many more products, services, and markets, you can expect major problems in coordinating strategies and tactics.

So niche marketing requires more teamwork, which may not be easy to get. Conflicts are always daily fare. It's small wonder that they'll intensify when you start niche marketing.

There is also the problem of planning for implementation and control. Consider communications. When you begin to increase the number of products, services, and target markets, how do you keep everyone informed?

You may also have problems in measuring performance within niches. Your accounting system may not be equipped to provide this information.

So, niche marketing means change coupled with increased complexity. And change and complexity increases the possibility of chaos. Management's attitude and philosophy must be in reasonable harmony with your niche strategy.

Unfortunately, convincing top management—or subordinates—of the value of niche marketing may not be easy. Strange as it may seem, sometimes that's one of the toughest parts of niche marketing. Let's face it. It's hard for people who have been in the industry for 20 to 30 years to reorient their thinking. This is especially true of managers who have become "rich and famous" by being mass marketers.

You've got two groups to convert: (1) top management and (2) middle management.

Top Management's Resistance

We've found that talking about the logic of niche marketing *usually* won't make converts out of top management. Unless, of course, top management is desperate because sales and profits are dropping. If you're not in this unfortunate situation, what else should you do?

Well, you can *try* to explain the soundness of niche marketing. You can point out what is happening in other industries, perhaps even in your own. Give them copies of this book.

But mass-marketing strategies got top management where they are today. So it usually requires more than just logic or pointing out what is happening (or has happened) to other companies to alter their attitudes.

What can you do? Here are two solutions.

Solution 1. Become Numbers-Oriented. Numbers-oriented means something more than just looking at bottom-line sales and profit or loss. It's knowing what percentage of sales and profits are coming from which customers, which customers are expanding their purchases, which customers are decreasing their purchases, and so on. If you don't have the data, start collecting it.

Solution 2. Establish a Track Record. A bank in Florida started with one niche-marketing program. It worked. So the bank tried another. And another. Gradually niche marketing became diffused throughout the bank.

Put together a successful track record, and you've got top management almost to the altar.

Middle Management's Resistance

So you've got top management enthused (or maybe you *are* top management). A necessary start, but not sufficient.

In his book, *Corporation Man*, Antony Jay reports an incident that we have heard over and over again in various guises. A new (brought in from the outside) headmaster of an English boarding school was determined to initiate major changes. Unfortunately (for him), his proposed reforms encountered resistance from the old guard staff who were entrenched with their old ways of doing things. He couldn't get them to change. And he couldn't fire them all.

The result was that the headmaster accomplished only a little of what he wanted to do. The school continued as it had for generations.[1]

Business situations can be just as touchy—in fact, touchier. Ruben Gutoff went to Standard Brands (now part of RJR Nabisco) and was charged with putting life into a lethargic organization. He lasted less than 2 years as president.

On the other hand, Lee Iacocca, coming into Chrysler, succeeded in turning Chrysler around. Of course he had a number of things going for him that Gutoff didn't, among them the executives he had brought with him from Ford and placed in key management positions. It's reported that Gutoff went to Standard Brands almost as a lone ranger (although it's also reported that his autocratic style of management was a major factor in causing him to step down).[2]

Switching to niche marketing can bring out all kinds of foot dragging. For example, behind many apparent production and operations problems are, in reality, personnel problems. As a marketing and planning executive for an insurance company told us, "Internal operations still have the one-size-fits-all culture."

To get middle management behind niche marketing, you can, as with top management, explain the benefits of niche marketing. Hold seminars. Point out what is happening in other industries and perhaps your own. Give them copies of our book too. Become numbers-oriented. Establish a track record.

Solution 1. Get Top Management's Support. You're not likely to embark on a widespread use of niche marketing without top management's approval. But if you want to reduce middle management's resistance, make sure you have top management's *support* as well as its approval. And by support we mean something more than giving you enough rope to hang yourself.

Middle management knows who top managment is. And they're going to hang on every word from the top. After all, they're the people whose pictures are in the annual report. A casual opinion from top management will be accepted much more readily than may have been intended.

Of course, top management's support is not sufficient to ensure the success of niche marketing (ask Ruben Gutoff!). But without it, don't count on getting much support from middle management.

Get top management to be champions of the cause.

Solution 2. Involve Middle Managers in Planning. Involvement is the key to successful planning.

Nothing flatters people more than being taken seriously, and there is no better way to take managers seriously than to bring them into the planning process. Experience shows that managers are more likely to implement a plan that they are involved in. After all, people who have participated in drafting plans want to see those plans succeed. They're owners.

For example, the director of marketing for a bank hired a consultant to develop a procedural model for locating branch banks. The finished model was shown to the president. He thought it was excellent and told the director of marketing to implement it. The director of marketing then explained the new procedure to the other departments (real estate, branch banking, and so on) so that all understood their roles.

A year later the model was junked. It failed because most of the bank's executives really didn't care whether or not it succeeded. In fact, because of rivalries, some managers were more interested in seeing it fail. After all, it wasn't their plan.

Only people who are involved in drafting plans are going to try their best to make the plans succeed. As an executive of an oil company said,

"The biggest benefit of our planning process is not so much the plan as it is the involvement of all levels of management who contributed to the plans."

With niche marketing you've got a real plus: it's easier to get people involved. Niche marketing allows more people to have a piece of the action. As Steve Neumann, director of marketing research for Schering-Plough health-care products, said:

> Everybody was pretty receptive to this within the sales group and the marketing organization . . . I think the reason for this is that with niche marketing you have an opportunity to have more autonomy and control. Instead of managing a small piece of a large business, you're managing something that's very visible, and you can see the results and show other people the results very quickly. You get credit for that if the results are good . . . So people like to get involved with this.

To get managers involved, form teams to gather information and develop strategies. That's the way it works at Armstrong World Industries. Management teams have a much stronger sense of confidence in the strategies that they put together because they've been involved in developing the foundation information.

Make sure that involvement is not limited to senior functional area managers. Get input from the field, and get them involved.

The plan must permeate the organization all the way down to the sales force. And there has to be a 100 percent commitment to the plan, or it's not going to work. It's as simple as that.

Solution 3. Decentralize.   Perhaps you can't get this kind of involvement because you're too big. That's a good reason to consider decentralization. At B. F. Goodrich, for example, each business unit has some very broad objectives, such as, "to seek out lower-volume, higher-profit businesses." But beyond that it's up to the business units to decide how to meet their objectives. In other words, the organizational structure encourages managers to act like managers.

Personnel Shortages

Niche marketing probably will require more people, and not just in sales.

To support each product or service, you'll need more plans. So you'll need more people to develop them. And you just may not be able to get people. Even if you can, they may be inexperienced. Slipups are more likely.

When Campbell Soup first moved into niche (regional) marketing, the Sacramento office planned a V8 juice program for Hispanics in Sacramento. The campaign called for an offer of free ice chests. But the promotion had to be dropped because the chests didn't arrive on time. The inexperienced regional staff misjudged how long it would take to implement the program.[3]

For its Ready-to-Roll game, a regional promotion held in Chicago, Kraft planned a top prize, a 1990 Dodge Caravan LE valued at $17,000. The odds of winning were 1 out of 15,160,000.

But because of a printing error, thousands of customers wound up with the "winning" ticket.[4] Such an error would have been less likely to occur if the national promotion had been guided by more experienced people and subjected to more rigorous control.

Not having enough staff to provide adequate service is another potential pitfall. For example, banks that target niche markets usually fall short on service. One survey revealed that 38 percent of queried executives claimed they were unhappy with the level of service their banks offered (conversely, only 3 percent were dissatisfied with their law firms).[5]

But where do you get the people? Aside from the obvious—hire more—what can you do?

Solution 1. Look within Your Company

You may be surprised—you may need fewer additional personnel than you think.

That's what they found out at a bank in Florida. According to its administrative vice president for marketing, since the bank started targeting smaller segments, *it now has less staff.* The bank is more focused and making the most out of its human resources. As the vice president put it, "We're only working with priorities, where we'll get the best use of our dollars."

Jeffery L. Leininger, senior vice president, Mellon Bank N.A., was another who said they found personnel resources within their company (at least for one niche—serving smaller companies):

> People who had been dealing with smaller companies simply were extracted from different parts of the organization and put into a unit to serve this niche. They had the requisite experience. It was just a matter of getting them all in one place.

Lever Brothers needed more personnel when it reorganized to category management. The company found the needed people in its retail sales force. Through mergers, acquisitions, and shutdowns, supermarkets had undergone a major consolidation of stores. Also, many chain store customers had become headquarters-controlled and required less coverage. Lever Brothers recognized that it was overrepresented at the field level, so many of these personnel were reallocated to headquarter accounts as category managers.

In fact, placing personnel in charge of niche markets may be a way to help motivate people. For executives in many companies, it's "Farewell, fact track. Hello, slow track." Making managers responsible for given niche product(s) or service(s) may be a way to help energize them in lieu of rapid promotions and raises.[6]

But there is one caveat. Others have tried to switch executives from other areas into niche marketing. And not without difficulties. One executive of an insurance company said, "We've moved administrative people into niche marketing. These executives have a real lack of sophisticated marketing knowledge. And our results show it."

Even moving sales executives into marketing planning can be risky. For example, in one company that implemented regional marketing, many of the responsibilities of the marketing department fell to the sales department. Such responsibilities included developing advertising copy and buying media—things that sales executives had no expertise in. The results were disastrous. The company's market shares of several of its major brands dropped, as well as its profits.

Solution 2. Develop Staff Specialists

You may need to change the traditional brand manager organization to make niche marketing work. The typical brand manager is a generalist dealing with most of the marketing activities for the brand. Serving a few mass markets requires only a few brand managers. Experienced people can usually be found.

But niche marketing will require more managers. You probably won't have enough seasoned ones to go around. You may be able to get more mileage out of less experienced people (that is, handle more niches) if specialists are on tap. Specialists, for example, in the areas of market research, data analysis, planning methodology, advertising, sales promotion, and sales force management who can assist when needed.

Solution 3. Use Mentors

Borrow a page from sales management. Assign the most experienced person to the least time-consuming account. Then he or she can assume the role of a mentor and spend considerable time tutoring others. The mentor must understand the purpose of this role (structure the mentor's compensation package accordingly—that should do it). The less experienced should feel comfortable seeking the mentor's help. Make sure that it's a mentor relationship, not a competitive one.

Or how about using retired executives as mentors? So many corporations send managers with rich storehouses of experience out to pasture. Instead, assign them to work with new managers. Since the retirees no longer have line responsibilities, they may be far less competitive and more oriented to "help the kids."

Solution 4. Use Part-Time Employees

Many women who entered the work force in the 1980s are discovering that 12-hour days aren't what they want. Yet many are highly qualified and would like to continue working on a reduced schedule or part-time basis. Why not utilize their know-how for niche-marketing activities?

Solution 5. Be Creative

Still short of people?

Then seek out unconventional sources. That's what a regional convenience store chain did. Try as it might, it couldn't locate enough personnel for store management. So the company put together a management trainee program for graduates from Ireland's business schools. Ireland has excellent business schools. But employment opportunities for graduates are scarce.

Here's the way the program works. The company brings over graduates of Irish business schools' undergraduate programs. They're enrolled in a fully paid MBA program at a local U.S. college of business. While working on their MBAs, students also work in the convenience stores. They become store managers after 18 months.

Students stay an average of 3 years. This company feels that 3 years of high-quality help from these students is better than other marketplace alternatives. And the company gets an unexpected benefit: some of the students stay on as permanent employees.

Solution 6. Hire Consultants

Sometimes using consultants may be a logical choice. Get a consultant who's a specialist in the niche that you've targeted.

But a warning.

It may be that a well-qualified consultant will be hard to find. For example, a lot of firms want to go after the Hispanic niche. Yet, there are only a few advertising agencies competent enough to serve this market. So some firms go with the best they can find, and sometimes the results can be embarrassing.

For example, Coors' ad jingle, "Turn It Loose," when translated by one Hispanic subgroup meant, "Drink Coors and get diarrhea."

Solution 7. Make a
Gradual Transition

OK. So looking within the company doesn't solve the problem. You're still short of people. Staff specialists can't do it. And hiring consultants or more people is not in the cards.

In this case, start slowly with just one, two, or several—whatever you can comfortably handle—niche markets. Having a number of niche marketing programs developed and managed by inexperienced people is like having a number of loose cannons aboard.

A vice president of marketing at a major bank ruefully told us of his experience. His bank had over 80 branches located in different neighborhoods and commercial areas, such as Hispanic, blue collar, affluent, black, and commuting stations. He uncovered seven niches.

Since each of these markets was different, why not develop marketing programs for each of these seven segments? He didn't have experienced personnel. So he hired seven recent college graduates to be branch marketing specialists. After all, they would be in charge of only small marketing programs.

The result?

A disaster.

For example, the person in charge of the branches located in the affluent areas got a good buy on radio spots for the Harvard-Princeton game. Since the game was not to be televised, what better way to reach the wealthy stay-at-homes?

The commercials were prepared by the branch marketing specialist. The vice president, in between meetings, scanned them. They seemed OK.

But he missed one critical element: the commercials exceeded the 1-minute time limit for the spots, and the commercials were cut off before the complete messages had been aired.

"Strictly bush league! Destroying the image of the bank!" according to the president.

The vice president of this bank told us some other incidents that happened in relatively short periods of time. Very funny (to us).

The bank soon dropped the niche-marketing program. It had gone a niche too far.

Realize that switching from mass marketing to niche marketing is not a simple process. It will take longer than you think. We've found that it may take as few as 3 or as many as 5 years to fully implement niche marketing.

Resistance to Organizational Change

Niche marketing will require organizational changes. And don't underestimate personnel's fear of change. It will be greater than you think.

They'll be worried about their jobs being wiped out. If they're not worried about that, they'll wonder how the organizational changes will affect their careers and their job status. If they aren't worried about their jobs, then they'll probably be questioning the practice of niche marketing itself.

Solution 1. Presell the Need for Change

Presell and make sure you cover all the bases, starting at the top.

Some people will not be happy with their new jobs. Preselling won't solve all the problems, but it will help. As Jeffery L. Leininger, senior vice president, Mellon Bank N.A., said, "Not everyone was satisfied with the job they ended up with . . . Frankly, the organizational response was positive because I think a lot of people felt we had to segment the market more finely."

In spite of potential problems, selling the need to switch to niche marketing—and subsequent organizational changes—might be easier than you think. Niche marketing is getting good press. People have become more familiar with it than they were, say 5 years ago.

Solution 2. Use the Evolutionary Approach

You know your markets, how soon you need to make changes. And you know your organization.

What if you feel there will be considerable resistance to niche marketing?

We've recommended an evolutionary approach as a solution to other problems, such as personnel shortages. Evolution can also prepare your people for organizational changes.

The Big Bang Approach

Let's assume you're following the big bang approach. Organizational changes need to be made. Yet, because job titles and reporting relationships will be changed, you can't notify personnel in advance. What can you do?

Solution. Have Your Infrastructure in Place

Campbell Soup switched from 9 sales territories to 22 regional markets overnight. Because of planned changes in reporting relationships, there could be no phasing in.

Although the switch was successful, it was not without problems. One executive mentioned to us that if they had it to do over again, they'd have more of the infrastructure in place to make the transition smoother. For example, he said the speed and secrecy with which the changeover had to take place left the corporation without adequate job descriptions and training manuals. Even the sites for the new regional offices had not been selected.

If you have to move fast, then expect associated expenses.

Recap

Because getting started in niche marketing means change and increased complexity, mangement's attitudes are critical. They must be in tune to niche marketing if it is to succeed.

Use facts and figures when you talk to top management. Use the same for middle managers, but don't let it stop there. These people need to be in on the ground floor—drafting plans, spotting problems, gathering information, and developing strategies.

Everyone will start yelling for more people. What to do? Take a fresh look at what you've got. Perhaps it will only be a matter of reorganization. Perhaps some of your own people can be used as specialists, mentors, maybe even consultants. Don't be limited by what they now do—focus on what they *can* do.

If you *have* to go outside, don't be limited to conventional sources.

Sudden change can demoralize personnel. You'll deflect lots of resistance by preselling your people on niche marketing's potential and by using an evolutionary approach.

But what if your firm has opted for the big bang approach? Learn a lesson from others who have taken this path: Transition will be smoother if you have a solid infrastructure in place.

Preparation is the key. Whatever you can do to eliminate resistance, people shortages, and confusion will pay off in a smoother entry into niche markets.

18

Dealing with Advertising Problems

In niche marketing, the target market is usually pretty well defined. So tailoring advertising for a specific audience ought to be easier than appealing to a mass market. In many ways it is. But what makes advertising niche products or services tough, as so many companies told us, are these problem areas:

1. High cost of media
2. High cost of promotional material
3. Blurred images
4. Insufficient time and resources

High Cost of Media

Mass advertising to niche markets would be like a farmer throwing 90 percent of his seed on stone. You simply can't afford to squander your media budget on infertile ground.

Here are four ways to keep costs down.

Solution 1. Seek Focused Media

For instance, the *Farm Journal*, through a computerized process, prints hundreds of versions of the magazine in a single run. Using selective binding, *Farm Journal* has printed as many as 8,896 different versions of one issue.

Although the cover and main feature stories are the same, special articles and advertisements vary according to the type of farm, size of farm, geographic location, and so on. By matching the special material with its extensive subscriber data files, the *Farm Journal* targets thousands of niches with each issue. This journal is a great medium for a manufacturer selling implements, herbicides, fertilizer, and such to farm operators and owners.[1]

Don't be afraid to use something as simple as an insert. If you're in the consumer market, how about using inserts to be used in special advertising sections of your target markets' newspapers or to be inserted in their mailboxes? Target geographic areas, from zip codes to regions. And it's easy to test market inserts' effectiveness by mailing to just one zip code.

Solution 2. Form Strategic Alliances

You know and we know that you won't always be able to find media targeted specifically toward your niche. And even when you can, advertising gets expensive, perhaps too expensive.

Bill Brooks, supervisor of commercial marketing for Gulf States Utilities Company, explains how they were faced with prohibitive media costs and how they overcame them:

> We wanted to reach decision makers and influencers for heating and/or air-conditioning systems for hotels, motels, restaurants, health facilities—places with high thermal loads . . . But we operate regionally, and a lot of people who make decisions for our target market are outside our service area. For example, restaurants may be part of chains with their home offices . . . located outside our area . . . National media for this target market was too expensive. And we can't afford to call person-to-person . . . So we found a number of other utilities—located in various parts of the country—who have a similar problem.
>
> We formed an association, The Electric Energy Ad Council, and now share advertising costs.

Strategic alliances might stretch your promotion dollars when going after niche minority markets.

A good way to do this is to highlight cultural contributions, aspirations, and recreation with product advertising. That's what Dewar's White Label scotch, Coca-Cola, and Coors beer did to increase sales among blacks. Their promotions included tie-ins with a black artists' workshop program, the United Negro College Fund, and a black rodeo.

Solution 3. Get the Trade to
Cosponsor Promotions

Sounds unlikely? It's not if you go a step beyond regional marketing and work directly with specific distributors and retailers.

For example, set up a traffic generator, like an in-store sweepstakes at a supermarket. The retailer will participate if the promotion has good business-building potential. It can be a win-win situation: the retailer gets a traffic builder and more sales; you get more sales. Plus another benefit. Retailers' support for your product is guaranteed up front.

Cut down your costs by developing several generic programs. Then, for a given account, make adaptations, if necessary, to the most suitable program.

Still seems unaffordable? Look over your pricing practices. Use account-specific programs in place of display allowances, feature pricing, and the like.

For cosponsored promotions to work, they must be win-win situations. Be sure to set up objectives for the trade participant as well as for yourself, and then help make sure the cosponsor's objectives are reached.

Solution 4. Go Direct

You're going after smaller market segments, so you've got to shake off your ties to the traditional way of doing things.

It always pays to advertise.

Right?

Well, most of the time. But not always.

An international division of a regional bank wanted to increase prospect awareness of its services. Its advertising agency recommended advertising in regional editions of selected business publications. The results were extremely disappointing and expensive.

A marketing consultant was called in. After looking at the prospect list—fewer than 100 clients—the solution was obvious. Go direct.

The bank used direct mail, sending a letter and specialty gift, a travel alarm with an international time dial. A very successful promotion.

At HomeFed Bank they found that, for their home equity credit lines, the market had become too saturated for mass media. A shotgun approach just wasn't paying off anymore. So HomeFed switched to direct mail, using their own client base as well as external mailing lists. The payout? Good.

Toyota, going after a more narrow niche with its upscale Lexus, supplemented its mass advertising with direct mail to give a boost to showroom sales.

How about using videocals for highly selective markets? A hybrid between a video and a periodical, videocals follow the same format as a monthly magazine: regular features and special-interest stories on a specific subject, interlaced with commercials. Home Broadcast Network's videocals are targeted toward affluent special-interest groups. Some of its theme videos include "Golfer," "Driver," and "Hunting and Fishing."

Spiegel targeted 20,000 of its most valued customers by sending a free 7-minute videocassette showing its fall collection. With background music, "It's Back to School Again" (Fats Domino), the film featured the latest from Spiegel's own Design Studio Collection as well as apparel from Flora Kung, Escada, and Anne Klein.[2]

Consider making your direct mail *real* relationship marketing. Get chummy with your target market. Instead of the occasional coupons or brochure, set up a lasting relationship. For example, General Foods sends out a quarterly *What's Hot* magazine. Targeted toward children, it has articles on topical items such as current TV shows and dinosaurs (who says they're extinct?). Of course, *What's Hot* is mostly a number of ads camouflaged as games and puzzles. And to no surprise, it's also laced with cents-off coupons for many of its brands.

Too brash for your target market? Then you can take a softer approach. Mercedes' quarterly magazine is sent to a highly selective list, for the most part to purchasers of new Mercedes cars. Containing absolutely no hard sell, its articles are about legends of the Mercedes' greats. The magazine is slick and beautiful. The recipients in the target market like to display it on their coffee tables in case their guests didn't see the Mercedes in their driveways. And they can't help seeing it themselves every day—Mercedes in the home as well as on the road.

High Cost of Promotional Material

Production costs are high. Still, you've got to develop materials for a number of niches.

Here are four ways to cut costs.

Solution 1. Use a Modular Approach

Your niches will require different promotional materials, depending upon age, income, or whatever segmenting criteria you use. You don't need to provide the same—or the same amount of—materials to your whole population. Yet some of the niches will probably require at least some of the same promotional materials.

You can save money by building modules.

First, decide on the core materials you'll use for all segments—the general population.

Then, identify what other promotional materials each niche needs. You may find that you come up with, say, 10 different promotional materials. But some of the niches will need some of the same 10.

Here's an idea from A&P markets. A&P has multiple districts, and each district advertises somewhat differently from the others. A&P developed a center in Landover, Maryland, to coordinate the printing of in-store circulars and freestanding inserts. District offices send, by modem, product information they want included in their districts' versions of the ads. The entire composition and printing operation is handled by computer in the central office using as much duplicate material as possible. Then the completed mats are sent back to the districts, again by modem, to be printed there.

Solution 2. Be Selective about Frequency

Some niches need promotional materials more frequently than others. Why cover all niches the same number of times? Develop media plans that are niche-specific.

Solution 3. Use Standardized Formats

American Airlines gets mileage out of ads that appeal to different segments yet remain low in cost because of economical standardized formats. (See Figure 18-1 on the next two pages.)

Some companies have commercials designed around athletic stars. They use standard formats, but, to appeal to regional preferences, they use West Coast athletic stars out West, East Coast athletic stars in the East, and so on.

For example, the Middle Atlantic Milk Marketing Association advertises in the Philadelphia and Baltimore-Washington areas. The association developed 30-second TV spots for each area, but the first 15 seconds was identical in both ads. Both ads began with a young boy on the baseball field yelling at the outfielders, "Move back!" The local homeowners began shuttering their windows. The scene was set for the young batter to smash a home run. But then it dissolved into a current professional game. In the Philadelphia version the hitter was Mike Schmidt and ended with appropriate Schmidt copy. In the Baltimore area it was Cal Ripkin. Very effective. Two ads targeted to specific regions with marginal increases in cost over one generic ad.

Solution 4. Find Multiple Uses

Suppose you need a photograph or an illustration for an advertisement. Don't be foolish and cut back on the quality of the photograph or artwork.

Reduce the cost of commissioning new artwork by paying for the right to use the photograph or artwork in a number of places, such as brochures, posters, trade-show displays, catalog sheets, calendars, or press kits. Not only does further using the same photograph or artwork save money, it also reinforces the campaign's effectiveness.

The same goes for the advertisements themselves. Find multiple uses. Include reprints of your magazine ads in your direct mail, and so on.

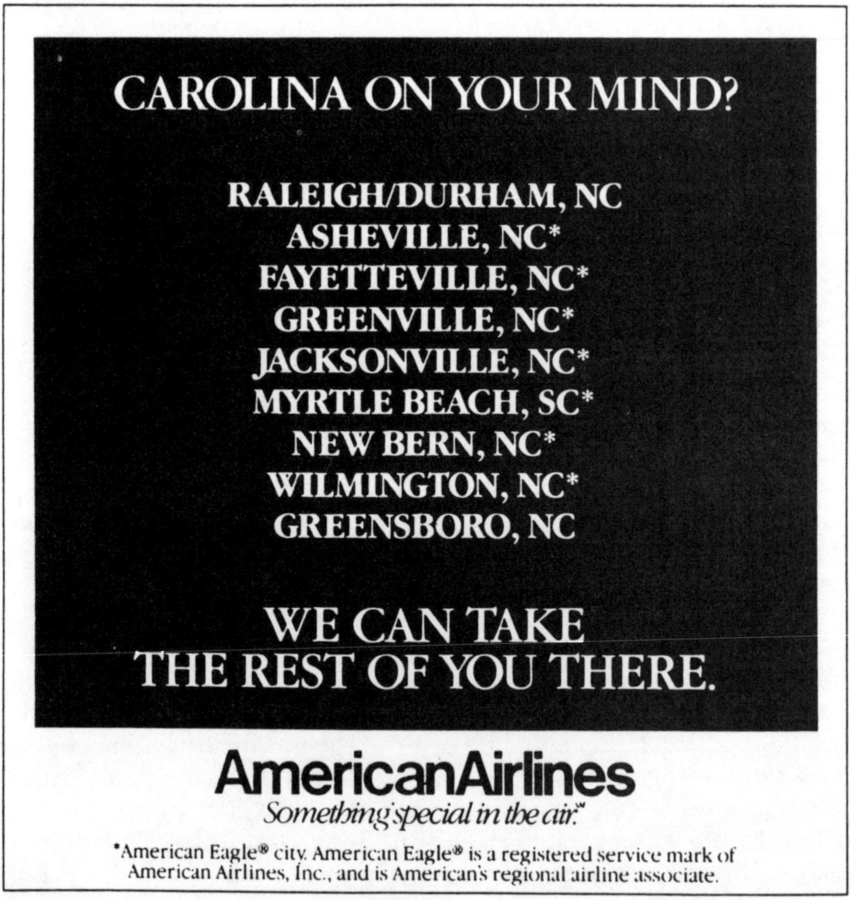

CAROLINA ON YOUR MIND?

RALEIGH/DURHAM, NC
ASHEVILLE, NC*
FAYETTEVILLE, NC*
GREENVILLE, NC*
JACKSONVILLE, NC*
MYRTLE BEACH, SC*
NEW BERN, NC*
WILMINGTON, NC*
GREENSBORO, NC

WE CAN TAKE
THE REST OF YOU THERE.

AmericanAirlines
Something special in the air.

*American Eagle® city. American Eagle® is a registered service mark of American Airlines, Inc., and is American's regional airline associate.

Figure 18-1. Standardized ad format for regional markets. *(Courtesy of American Airlines)*

Blurred Images

Promoting different products and services to different target markets can blur the image of your company or product. This can be a real problem for niche marketers. As an executive of a drugstore chain said, "If a company is marketing in a number of different niches, what does the company stand for?"

A blurred image may be costly. It's believed that Noxell Corporation's Clarion Cosmetic brand lost sales as a result of a blurred product image that included both hypoallergenic and fashion positioning.

In addition, some niches may feel left out. A marketing director of a bank claimed that a major public relations effort was required because certain segments felt they were being discriminated against in favor of more upscale niches.

Here are two things you can do to avoid this problem.

Solution 1. Use a Targeted Approach

If you can't find targeted ways to reach the niche, think again about serving this niche. Possibly you'd be better off not segmenting your market so finely.

Solution 2. Use Mass Marketing Selectively

Perhaps you can't figure out how to talk with one segment without talking down to another and offending them. If so, use mass media *only* for broad-based communications programs, such as umbrella corporate-image ads.

Insufficient Time and Resources

First of all, don't squander your limited resources by unnecessarily changing your advertising campaign. We've found that most campaigns are changed because management—not the customers—is bored with the campaign.

Aside from that, you're going to have to be a better manager. At one company we talked to, all regular programs—consumer events and deals for the trade—pass through a centralized group. The vice president of marketing said, "We handle it like a logistical program."

But even such scheduling may not solve the time and resource shortages.

And you know the easiest way to get in trouble. Just overextend yourself.

You, like all marketers, operate in a fishbowl. Everything you do has high visibility.

And that's twice as true when it comes to advertising. After all, it just takes those five people to call the CEO and complain about an ad.

With niche marketing you'll be running more ads than you'd do as a mass marketer.

Be careful you don't lose control.

We've heard a number of horror stories about marketers who did (as with the ads for the Harvard-Princeton game). And we're sure that you have too.

Our advice: If you can't execute all your advertising properly, scale back. Do what you can with excellence. If necessary, let go of some niches.

Don't go a niche too far.

Recap

Advertising to niche markets requires a different approach than advertising to mass markets.

You know that media costs which would be acceptable for a mass-marketing campaign would be totally unacceptable for a niche-marketing campaign. So look to focused media. Or strategic alliances. Or get the trade to cosponsor promotions. Or go direct.

Costs of promotional materials must also be pared. How about modular approaches, media plans that are niche-specific, standardized formats, and multiple uses for promotional materials?

Keeping costs down is not the only problem. You also run the risk that multiple promotions might cause blurred images. Selling more products and more services to more target markets may make it difficult for your customers to identify what it is that your company represents. If you can't find media for a targeted approach and you still feel that you must advertise, use mass advertising selectively.

Niche marketing will tax your management skills. No longer will you have the luxury of going all out with one major campaign bash. Instead, you'll have to juggle one small campaign after another, coordinating copy, budgets, and people.

Be realistic about what you can do. Don't go a niche too far.

19
Dealing with Sales-Force Problems

More products. More services. More target markets. More work. It's plain to see that you, like others we talked to, will have some hurdles to overcome with your sales force.

Be on the lookout for these problem areas:

1. Entrenched sales culture
2. Insufficient sales coverage
3. Highly specialized customer needs
4. Lack of cross-selling
5. Lack of sales orientation by customer-contact personnel

Entrenched Sales Culture

There is a near certainty that niche marketing will require a major change in your sales-force culture.

Look at some obstacles that other companies have faced:

- "Sales-force reorientation was needed since the sales force was used to a broad-brush approach" (insurance company).
- "Sales personnel equate targeting with giving up on other prospects" (insurance company).

- "You've got to get the salespersons to focus on profit instead of volume" (aluminum manufacturer).

Possible ways to effect change:

Solution 1. Educate as Well as Train

Companies invest heavily in training: showing their salespersons how to do specific tasks better. And that's essential. Unfortunately, very little attention is devoted to education: giving a better understanding of the tasks, the relationship between the tasks, and the relationship between the tasks and the company's objectives.

Salespersons have a natural bias against niche marketing (they're volume oriented). So you've got to explain the *why* as well as the *how.*

Some of the whys you should cover are:

- Splintering of markets
- Advances in technology enabling companies to profitably serve niche markets
- How companies have been outniched
- Your industry trends

And besides using education to gain acceptance, educate to get assistance in locating new niches. Salespeople probably know more about your markets than anyone else in the company.

How to do this? Give them copies of this book. Hold freewheeling seminars on niche marketing.

However it's not only your salespersons that need to be educated. When one company decided to take a regional marketing approach, many of the sales managers were promoted to regional marketing managers. But a survey done by an independent group indicated that the former sales managers knew virtually nothing about marketing and how it differed from sales. To many former sales managers, marketing was synonomous with advertising.

Solution 2. Change the Compensation Package

Niche marketing may change your sales force's responsibilities. For example, Ted Stover, director of marketing research for Carolina Freight, describes a problem they faced:

> One of our niche-marketing programs called for our sales people to
> call on manufacturers' representatives. Now manufacturers' repre-
> sentatives are salespersons themselves. A lot of them don't even have
> an office—they just have an answering service. For our people to con-
> tact them, they have to call at night, after work, or on weekends.

People tend to do things they're rewarded for. Unless your salespersons
are compensated for performing their new tasks, your new niche-marketing plan is likely to fail.

Here are several approaches to changing your compensation plan.

Base Compensation on Accountability.   Avoid having all of the compensation package based on the level of performance of the business
unit. Of course some compensation can be based on sales and profits
generated at the business-unit level, but the bulk should be tied to individual performance.

Base Compensation on Desired Performance.   You may have been
compensating your salespersons for volume sold. But, for example, your
new program may require cross-selling. Then why not consider a plan
followed by INB Financial?

To encourage salespersons to service new niches, INB Financial
changed incentives. Branch personnel formerly got credit for every account they sold. But no longer. If a branch employee just sells checking
accounts and not other services, he or she doesn't receive credit. This
motivates bank salespersons to sell the full line of products.

Consider Self-Liquidating Compensation Programs.   Is it too expensive to compensate salespersons for selling niche products or services?
Then why not make the compensation program self-liquidating? Set it
up so it's completely incremental. Then, basically it costs you nothing.
Every dollar you pay out means that you made more money than you
had budgeted.

Insufficient Sales Coverage

You may find that your niche-marketing strategy will overtax your sales
force. For example, some large-company niche marketers mentioned
these problems:

- "Too many diverse segments to serve" (newspaper).
- "Program overload" (food processor).
- "Sales force could not follow up on generated leads" (bank).

- "Too many small customers" (trucking firm).

- "Increased risk of missing big sales [because of fragmentation]" (insurance company).

- "Allocating sales-force time between targeted and national accounts" (cigarette manufacturer).

With niche marketing, there is just not enough salespersons' time to go around.

Here are four solutions.

Solution 1. Improve Coordination

The vice president of a major food company put the problem this way:

> We have a single sales force that's selling 4000 SKUs. They've got plenty to do with existing product lines . . . Now, with niche marketing you start to add additional complexity to their lines with new items. Furthermore, these products are low volume . . . But yet we need more than their fair share of time to introduce these new items and keep track of them. It's a disproportionate higher demand of time vis-a-vis the amount of sales that they're going to make on it . . .

To solve this problem, the company has concentrated on spacing new introductions. By doing so, it has made the task of assimilating new products more manageable for the sales force.

Solution 2. Look for Hidden Resources

First, closely examine what your sales force is now doing. For example, Transcon Lines found that its salespersons were responsible for very few accounts. Transcon's policy was that if a sales representative had a territory bringing in $100,000, it was good enough—even though the $100,000 came only from one or two accounts. Its sales force was definitely comfortable.

But then Transcon decided it wanted to go after smaller niches with a two-pronged approach: indoctrinating and refocusing. First, computer analysis showed the small number of accounts salespersons were calling on. Management told the sales force that one or two accounts that produce $100,000 was not enough. They also had to have 10 or 15 accounts to go along with that basic account of $100,000. Transcon then had its sales force go out and prospect—under company guidance.

What about administrative personnel? Can they be used as salespersons?

Weirton Steel found out they could. David M. Gould, vice president of sales and marketing, said that all district managers have accounts that they call on in addition to their sales-management duties. This way Weirton can cover more territory with fewer people. Gould mentioned that he did, however, cut back on district managers' administrative work loads.

At IBM and AT&T, they put all available administrative personnel into the field for a month. Not only did this increase sales, but the sales calls had the added benefit of making the administrative people more market-oriented.

Solution 3. Change Channels of Distribution

In its refrigeration gases division, Du Pont found that once it started serving smaller market segments, personal sales visits became too costly. So now it uses telemarketing to reach customers.

Solution 4. Seek Strategic Alliances

Use sales forces of firms like Rhone-Poulenc Rorer or Pechiney. Or a strategic alliance such as Merck's and Johnson & Johnson's. (At least at first the joint venture used the sales force of Johnson & Johnson's Mc-Neil Consumer Products Company.)

Gulf States Utilities, a regional firm, had this problem: a number of decision makers and influencers who affected power usage in Gulf States' areas were scattered throughout the United States. Personal sales calls needed to be made to these individuals, yet the cost would have been prohibitive for Gulf States. The solution: Gulf States and other regional utilities with like needs formed a group whose purpose it was to make necessary direct contacts.

Highly Specialized Customer Needs

Serving narrowly targeted markets with specialized products and services requires greater knowledge, both of customers and of products and services. And this means using different selling techniques.

Scott E. Kuechle, manager of analysis for B. F. Goodrich, describes how their selling approach changed:

> We were a heavy commodity-oriented company. Our salesmen were selling primarily to large distributors. It was a technical selling situa-

tion, essentially between two chemists. The distributors were the ones who had to worry about selling to the users. Now our salesmen call on the users. Instead of talking about the chemical attributes of a product, they've got to translate what the product does for the user. That's a big change.

Salespeople have to go from being technically competent to understanding the needs of the market.

Most companies find that such a transition takes time. It's something that has to evolve. For example, you can't take existing staff and say, "Beginning tomorrow we're going to have a sales culture in this retail environment. No more waiting for business to walk in and merely taking orders." It won't work.

You just can't say "sell" and expect it to work any more than you can say, "we're now going to start improving quality," and expect that statement, by itself, to improve quality.

Here are four things you can do to help overcome this problem.

Solution 1. Make Sure Your Salespersons Are Properly Trained and Equipped

Train your people. An obvious solution.

And, since niche markets are more fragmented and more specialized than mass markets, your salespersons are going to have to be equipped with better data and increased sales technology. Many manufacturers now give their sales staff hand-held computers, allowing them to capture up-to-date information on individual wholesale-retail outlets.

Solution 2. Make Organizational Changes

What if your products or services are so complex that your salespersons can't develop expertise in all areas? No amount of training will work. For example, a bank's commercial lending officer can't become an expert in trust banking *and* construction *and* international lending. And so forth.

At Illinois Power Company, they used to consider their business as providing electricity and natural gas to customers. Now they see themselves as providers of quality energy services valued by customers.

This new mission required salespersons to thoroughly understand customers' needs. But needs vary from niche to niche.

Many niches required the salespersons to have in-depth knowledge of their customers' businesses. For example, some niches required long-term, complex selling, such as a major capital investment decision that might take 5 years.

The solution? Illinois Power aligned its marketing and sales function according to the U.S. Standard Industrial Codes (SIC). Salespersons are no longer jacks-of-all-trades to a whole range of customers. Now a salesperson is specialized in technologies that apply to his or her specific area of responsibility.

Solution 3. Develop Relationship Marketing

Perhaps your customers' needs are so specialized that relationship marketing might be the way to go. For example, INB Financial offers special financial services for lawyers belonging to major law firms. The bank assigns an account executive to each major law firm. The assigned banker becomes the private banker for attorneys within a given firm.

The bank has done the same thing at large corporate headquarters. For example, the private banker goes in and makes presentations to executives in small group settings and then may work with some executives individually. Do the executives like this service? You bet. There is one large corporation that the private banker visits almost every day.

Solution 4. Hire Product Specialists

Sometimes hiring specialized help gives the sales force needed support.

Service Bureau, a time-sharing subsidiary of Control Data Corporation, sold database management and accounting software programs. Then the company developed a new time-series forecasting program and asked its sales force to sell it.

It failed. The sales force didn't know anything about time series.

The solution was to hire forecasting consultants who met with Service Bureau's customers who expressed an interest in this product.

Lack of Cross-Selling

Suppose that you do have highly specialized customer needs and your sales force is organized by products or services. You have a number of lines of products or services. How do you ensure that cross-selling will take place?

Solution 1. Compensate

Make it worth your salespersons' time to cross-sell. At a trucking firm, should one of their office-moving representatives turn in a lead that results in business for its management services, the salesperson gets $250. But it doesn't always take money. A packaging corporation has found that personal recognition is incentive enough.[1]

The important point is that both companies make sure their salespersons are rewarded in some way.

Solution 2. Communicate

Some companies conduct regular meetings so salespersons can get to know each other and each other's products or services. Others use employee publications for this purpose.

However it's done, salespersons must have an understanding of the company's other products and services. Getting to know other salespersons helps build confidence in them. After all, salespersons value their accounts and don't want someone messing up these relationships.

Solution 3. Have a Point Person

That is the way it's done at Mellon Bank N.A. Commercial lenders are in charge of account relationships. One of their primary responsibilities is to cross-sell all the other products and services of the bank. The commercial lenders use their basic product knowledge to prequalify what various accounts will need. Then they bring in experts to help close the sales.

Lack of Sales Orientation by Customer-Contact Personnel

The critical 3 feet is when the prospect comes face-to-face with the salesperson.

Sometimes niche-marketing plans call for nonsales personnel to assume partial sales duties. And what if these people are really not salespersons? Step up the training? Increase the compensation package?

Even these solutions may not work.

Listen to the laments of a vice president of marketing of a major bank:

> We have done extensive sales training. But we still have problems . . .
> I don't know what the answer is. It's almost endemic within the bank-

ing industry. You can preach, teach sales training until the cows come home. You can build skills and everything else, but . . .

We did a rather comprehensive mystery shop of some 800 visits over the last couple of months. I've seen video tapes of focus groups . . . Our people are still doing a pretty poor job.

Of course, compared with other financial institutions, we're no worse. But it's no great comfort that they do a pretty lousy job too. It's like having the best state room on the Titanic . . . I don't know what the answer is . . . It obviously isn't sales training by itself. It isn't management by itself. It isn't compensation by itself . . .

Yet another bank vice president pointed out where additional problems arise:

We offer a great range of products . . . How can marginally paid people, like people in branches, know all of the attributes of various products and how to communicate them to various segments? It's very difficult to get them to switch their whole mind-set from product to product, from segment to segment, to know what drives the segment that they're selling to.

Solution 1. Make the Program Fail-Safe

Faced with some—but not all—of the above problems, the NBD, N.A. developed a highly sophisticated database for the retail market. These data were then integrated into action-oriented programs. For example, they developed a graphic representation of the niches, including the services used by people in those niches.

Each branch platform person has a PC on his or her desk linked to the database. If a customer comes in wearing grubbies and asking for a gold Master Card, the platform person would ask this person where he or she lives and then enter this information into the computer. If this person lived in an affluent neighborhood, displayed on the terminal screen would be information indicating to the platform person that this person is an upscale customer. The screen would also indicate appropriate cross-selling opportunities based on the products other people of like characteristics have.

Solution 2. Make the Program Idiot-Proof

A division vice president for marketing of another major bank pointed out how they avoided sales problems at the branch level. It was simple. They did not count on branch personnel for sales efforts.

For example, for their equity credit line, they use direct mail. They buy screened lists that give them homeowners by income ranges and geographic areas.

The division vice president went on to say that the direct mail piece presells the customer. At the office, then, platform people are order takers, not order getters. This is a function that platform personnel can—and will—do.

Recap

Try to head off problems with the sales force before you put your niching strategy to the test.

Your salespeople are used to a mass-marketing approach. Instinctively they'll feel they're not doing their jobs when they're following a niche strategy. Overcome this tendency with education and training. Revamp the compensation package.

Niche marketing will demand more selling time, not less. You can help here. Coordinate new introductions and promotions so they don't all take place at once. But that probably won't be enough. You're going to need more people. Look inside the company for hidden resources. Changing distribution channels might help. And don't overlook strategic alliances.

Once in the field, your sales force will be faced with highly specialized customer needs. They'll need training and more sophisticated equipment. Organizational change may be an answer. You may have to develop some of your salespeople to become product or industry specialists responsible for fewer but more in-depth customer contacts. You may even need to consider relationship marketing, providing valued targeted customers with exclusive, personalized service from one or more of your people.

More products, services, and target markets will demand more cross-selling. Look for ways to motivate your people to make this extra effort. Innovative compensation packages can help. Try to keep communications flowing. Cultivate point persons.

And sometimes your new niche product or service will have to be sold by personnel who just are not sales-oriented. Then don't expect them to be order getters. Make your marketing program fail-safe (or even idiot-proof) by requiring them only to be order takers.

Weaning your sales force from their old mass-marketing tactics will take perseverance on your part. But stay with it. You need their commitment if you hope to grow bigger by acting smaller.

PART 5

Putting It All Together

20

Developing a Niche-Marketing Network

Serve a hodge-podge of niche markets, and you may be acting small. But you'll never grow bigger. Your company must be more than a collection of stand-alone niche products and services.

There are two reasons why. First, you don't want your firm to amount to a number of stand-alone niche businesses. Stand-alone businesses are burdened by corporate overhead costs. They're vulnerable to competitors who don't have to bear such corporate deadweight. These competitors can invest more in R&D. Or in quality. Or in marketing. Or they can offer lower prices to the target market. Sooner or later these competitors will zap you.

Your business must be focused. Niche products and services must be linked together to make the network cost-efficient. Or to give sister products and services competitive advantages. For instance, today Thompson Medical's original Slim-Fast is by no means a smashing sales success. Yet, this niche product receives continuing sales support. Why? Because it's a defensive flanker whose purpose is to raise the cost of market entry for a potential low-price competitor to its flagship Ultra Slim-Fast.

The second reason your niche products and services must be tied into an overall strategy is to help avoid funding problems.

Suppose you're with a billion-dollar company. Imagine going to corporate headquarters, hat in hand, requesting a budget for a product or service that promises half a million dollars in sales. Is that going to turn on the CEO? Not unless you can show that the product or service is an integral part of a strategic network.

But strategic networks don't just happen; they must be planned. Here are seven steps to lead the way:

1. Classify market positions.
2. Identify resource linkages.
3. Look for additional niche markets.
4. Set priorities.
5. Build a hierarchy of networks.
6. Make it work.
7. Evaluate misfits, then develop them or drop them.

If you have multiple product and service groupings, then follow Steps 1 through 4 for each product and service group.

On the other hand, if you have a limited product and service line, you'll need to do Steps 1 through 4 only once. And you can skip Step 5. Steps 6 and 7 apply to all.

These steps just provide a starting point. It's inevitable that you will modify them to suit your purposes.

For example, you may find that for your purposes just reading through the steps will be all that you'll need to do. You'll pick up a few ideas on how to build the network and you can do so without paper and pencil. You'll never need to construct a chart.

On the other hand, you may wish to follow these steps in a more formal written manner.

Step 1. Classify Market Positions

One thing you know for sure: you're not going to drop everything you're doing today and start from scratch. You're going to continue, at least in the short run, serving target markets with your present products and services. So take a look at what you've got to work with, both niche and mass-marketed products and services.[1]

Start with the lowest level of product and service planning. Match each product and service to a specific target market (product or service target market). For each product or service target market, rate its growth potential and competitive position. Use a chart similar to the one shown in Figure 20-1.

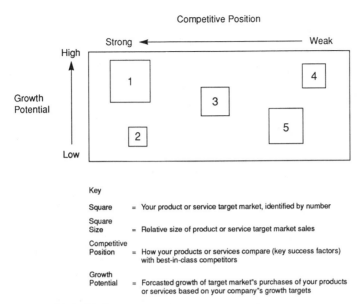

Figure 20-1. Market position chart—present product or service target markets.

Step 2. Identify Resource Linkages

Some of your product and service target markets will be linked together by the use of common resources.

Two common linkages are production or operations and promotion. Other possible sources of sharing include brand name, technology, transportation, warehousing, channels of distribution, human resources, purchasing, and service facilities.

But it's not enough that various resources are shared. Real benefits must be achieved. For example, two products might use the same production facilities, but are there significant savings as a result of this sharing? Economies of scale? Leveling off of production cycles? Or could these products or services be produced independently at or about the same cost?

At this stage, only concern yourself with real drivers—linkages that provide significant cost benefits or, in some other way, offer substantial competitive advantages.

Using the same chart (Figure 20-1), map out significant activity and resource linkages between product and service target markets. The example in Figure 20-2 shows the relationships among five product or service target markets.

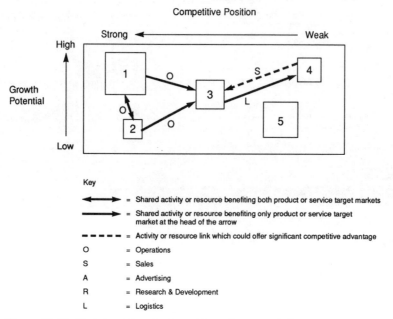

Figure 20-2. Market position chart—activity and resource linkages among present product or service target markets.

In this case:

- Product or Service Target Market No. 1 is sharing operations with No. 2 (both benefit).

- No. 3 is benefiting from No. 1's and 2's operations (but No. 1 and 2 are not benefiting from No. 3's operations).

- No. 4 is sharing logistics with No. 3 (but No. 3 is not receiving any logistics benefits from No. 4).

- No. 4 *could* aid No. 3 by sharing its sales force (but No. 4 would not benefit by sharing its sales force with No. 3).

- No. 5 stands alone—not sharing any major activity or resource with any other product or service target market.

Step 3. Look for Additional Niche Markets

You've identified the product or service target markets that share resources, which resources they share, and potential resource-sharing possibilities. But before you decide how to allocate your resources (devise a strategy), examine other opportunities.

- Examine your present product or service target markets for new niche markets. Consider each of the product and service target markets on your chart. Maybe linkages can be created (or enhanced) by further subdividing one or more of your present product or service target markets. Or perhaps subdividing a product or service target market will better capitalize on its potential. (Review Guideline 3 for suggestions on finding niches in your present markets.)
- Look for new product and service target markets. (Review Guideline 4 for suggestions on finding niches in new markets.)
- Identify resource linkages of potential product and service niche markets. You'll probably come up with a a number of good prospects for inclusion in your niche-marketing strategy. Select the best candidates. Number them and then position them in the chart. (See Figure 20-3.)

In this case:

- No. 6 can share operations and R&D with No. 5, and both would benefit.
- No. 7 can share advertising with No. 1, and both would benefit.
- No. 8 stands alone.

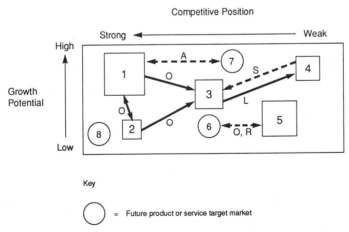

Figure 20-3. Market position chart—activity and resource linkages among present and future product or service target markets.

Step 4. Set Priorities

Your diagram now includes those product and service target markets that are part of your present strategy as well as new product and service target markets (those that passed the initial assay). Now put each of these product and service target markets through an eight-question screening.

Why not follow a mini-midi-maxi approach? First, the mini-method. Just get cursory answers for all of the questions. If the product or service target market is an obvious misfit, eliminate it from further consideration. But if it seems feasible, then do a midi-analysis. If your product or service target market passes this test, then proceed with a detailed maxi-approach.

1. Will Top Management Be Comfortable with the New Niche Product or Service?

Consider top management's predisposition toward certain product and service lines. You know your management's inclinations. If not, find them out.

Then consider if top management will stick to the plan. Some niche product and service target market strategies require long-term funding to give them a chance to develop. Others do not. If your company suffers from "quarteritis," consider the short-term payoff markets.

Here is why. Let's say that your company does suffer from "quarteritis." Further suppose that you've got two alternative product or service target markets under consideration. One has a very promising long-range payout, but it's going to require considerable funding in the short run. The other product or service target market is just the opposite. Short-term results are likely to be very good, but in the long term—not so good.

Under these conditions, you'll probably decide on the short-term alternative. (A sad commentary on U.S. business decision making. But sometimes it makes no sense to tilt at windmills.)

There's another reason you want to make sure payouts are compatible with management's thinking. "No manager who has a longer time horizon than his or her superiors can expect to survive." Of course, there's a corollary that states, "But neither can the business survive if the time horizon is inadequate to encompass the actions required today in order to protect the business in the future."[2] But that's another story.

2. Will the Niche Product or Service Target Market Help the Growth of Existing Business?

A new niche might support a major component of your overall strategy. For example, a bank wanted to increase business in the upscale market. Because these kinds of customers in this market begin using banking services at a young age, it's next to impossible to get them to switch once they've become upscale. So the bank went after a new, though unprofitable, niche—college students. When they become upscale and very profitable, they'll already be the bank's customers.

3. Will the Niche Product or Service Lower Overall Costs?

Don't lose sight of the big picture. If a product or service target market shares costs with other product or service target markets, you stand to improve your overall competitive posture.

When cost-sharing benefits are very high, it may be possible to enter a niche that appears unattractive when it is viewed in isolation. For example, management may have know-how that would give the firm a competitive advantage in new markets. Philip Morris was able to transfer its knowledge of consumer-goods marketing, especially cigarettes and beer, to other packaged goods like yogurt, coffee, and ice cream. Philip Morris has been very successful in these markets.

Procter & Gamble's Attends (adult incontinence-protection pads) are made with similar production technologies as its baby diapers, Luvs and Pampers. Also, Attends uses the same distribution channels as the diapers. As a result, Attends is a profitable niche product. And, by sharing production and distribution costs, Attends helps increase the profitability of Luvs and Pampers.

A trucking firm had freight going in one direction and nothing in the other. Management looked to niche markets (and found them) as a way to utilize this unused capacity.

However, be careful of just "filling holes in the factory." We found too many instances of companies being so mesmerized by using up excess capacity that they didn't properly evaluate the needs of the market.

Always ask yourself, "Does the cost of linkages outweigh the benefits?" Sometimes the answer is "No."

Often the costs of linkages are not obvious. With combined purchasing, for example, increased bargaining power may be a benefit. However, overall costs may be higher because of different ordering cycles or geographic distances between the processing units.

The point is not to get too caught up with cost savings unless they're significant. Otherwise you'll just be adding complexity to your business.

4. Will the Niche Product or Service Improve Sales Stability?

A parts manufacturer for military jet engines was concerned about decreases in defense spending. Its solution: to seek niche markets to achieve sales stability. One of its finds was selling reconditioned parts to commercial airlines. Airlines, like everybody, are *always* interested in saving money.

5. Will the Niche Product or Service Improve Your Competitive Position?

Perhaps a new niche can serve as a flanker to keep out competition or check competitive inroads. Seiko, for example, produces different brands of watches, such as Lauris, Citizen, Pulsar, and Seiko. Heublin markets different brands of vodka, such as Smirnoff, Relska, and Popov. Good strategic networks.

In some businesses, related products and services offer a powerful advantage. The U.S. semiconductor industry is a case in point. Throughout the 1970s and early 1980s, it pursued smaller and smaller market segments. The cost of entry was low, competition was minimal, and only small capital additions were required.

Meanwhile, the U.S. semiconductor industry gave the "junk"—the large-volume, low-price business—to the Japanese. After all, the profits were in the high end.

But then the ante was upped. The market began to demand more and more specialized chips, requiring large R&D and capital investments for continued technological growth. By 1988 it took more than one dollar of capital investment to generate a dollar of sales, even in high-volume markets.

The relatively small U.S. firms, unable to meet these funding requirements, fell behind. Far behind.

The U.S. semiconductor industry was a victim not of nimble nichers, but of hugh Japanese firms that had large-volume bases (as well as strategic alliances).

Perhaps you need to take a careful look at your competition—both existing and potential—to see if you can find new ways to improve your competitive position. Figure 20-4 is a framework for thinking through this process.

Suppose that this chart represents your position.

Competitors	Product or Service Target Market			
	1	2	3	4
Your Firm	✓			✓
ABC Company	✓	✓	✓	
DEF Company	✓			
GHI Company				✓
XYZ Company	✓	✓		✓

Figure 20-4. Competitive analysis chart.

You are competing with ABC Company, DEF Company, and XYZ Company in Product or Service Target Market 1 and with GHI Company and XYZ Company in Product or Service Target Market 4. Note that you have possibilities for cost sharing in two product or service target markets, 1 and 4. This may put you in a better cost position than DEF Company or GHI Company. On the other hand, ABC Company and XYZ Company may have cost advantages over you.

Your job, then, is to carefully assess the linkages that ABC and XYZ Companies possess. Do they offer enough cost savings to warrant your thinking about expanding into related markets, such as product or service target markets 2 and 3?

Competitive analysis is a critical step in building a strategic network of product and service target markets.

6. Is the Niche Market Structurally Attractive?

An approach used for industry analysis can help niche marketers.[3]

Key determinants of a niche market's desirability are the size of the niche, competition, bargaining power of the customers, bargaining power of the suppliers, threat of substitute products and services, and governmental control.

Size of the Niche. The niche market must be big enough to make it worthwhile. As an executive of a trucking firm put it, "We look at the size of the niche market. We don't want to have our salespeople chasing something not that great."

But don't dismiss low-volume new niche products and services too quickly. New markets are not easily forecasted (as can be seen in the Gatorade example).

Competition.   What about competitive intensity? Who will be your competitors? Small firms with limited resources? Or companies with deep pockets and commitment to the market? Is there a threat of new competitors? If so, what are their characteristics?

Can you be the market leader? Better think twice if you're only going to play second fiddle. In many niche markets there's only room for number one.

Bargaining Power of Customers.   Some niche markets aren't attractive because buyers have too much control over price. Or, when there are only a few buyers, the loss of one or two of them can change the balance.

Niche markets can also be unattractive when the product or service represents a significant portion of the buyers' overall costs, and the buyers' products and services are in highly price-competitive markets. These buyers will be willing to spend time looking for the best price, making you vulnerable to competition.

Bargaining Power of Suppliers.   Is the product or service dependent on specific technology, materials, or parts from suppliers? If so, will the suppliers exact a toll and keep you from reaching your profit objectives?

Threat of Substitute Products and Services.   How unique is your product or service? Do you need to worry about substitutes? If not now, how about in the future?

Governmental Control.   Is this niche market in a highly regulated industry where the government will specify your profit level? For example, a pharmaceutical company found that it couldn't do business in Brazil. High inflation rates demanded frequent price increases. Yet the government refused to let the company make the necessary price increases. The reason: people needed the drugs and couldn't afford higher prices. A company executive told us, "We couldn't make a profit, so we shut down the plant." And then he gave us this bit of advice, "Avoid sob sister industries in countries with high inflation."

Value Added.   As a rule, target those industries with high potential value added. There should be a relatively large spread between what you pay for raw materials, semifabricated materials, and parts and what you sell your product for.

For example, see Table 20-1, which shows the value added for two imaginary companies. In Company A there is $0.65 value added, and in Company B only $0.20.

If the price of materials increased by 10 percent, Company B would like to pass these costs on to the purchaser. Yet, what if competitors can offer substitute products that are unaffected by the cost increases?

Company A is in a safer position. Because of the high value added, the firm, through increased efficiency, has a shot at absorbing the cost increases. A great advantage, especially in inflationary times.

7. Is the Niche Accessible?

Identifying a market segment is useless unless you can reach it. For example, you may wish to serve a segment consisting of men who have the psychographic personality traits of high achievers. What media would you use to tap this segment? What channel of distribution? You need attributes that point to specific people by occupation, education, or high income zip codes.

8. Is the Niche Measurable?

You should be able to determine the overall potential of the niche in quantitative terms. What is the market's potential?

Or if you're selling the same product or service to several niches, can you measure the purchases of each niche? If you can't, you'll never know if your marketing efforts are paying off.

A tip-off on measurability: the clearer the answer is to the question of

Table 20-1 High and Low Value Added

	Company A	Company B
Selling price	$1.00	$1.00
Cost of raw materials, semifabricated materials, parts	0.35	0.80
Value added		
Expenses (selling, administrative, labor)	0.60	0.15
Profit	0.05	0.05

whether the niche is accessible, the more likely it is that you can measure the niche.

Expect Backtracking, Hammering, and Fitting

If you followed the mini-mid-maxi approach, you probably found that some questions could be answered definitively on the first sweep through the eight-question screen. Others, when considered in the context of subsequent questions, may have required reconsideration.

But you have your existing and potential product and service target markets prioritized. You've set aside those that don't fit.

Step 5. Build a Hierarchy of Networks

Examine potential places for sharing between product and service groups. See Figure 20-5. (Your organizational structure will probably vary from the one shown in Figure 20-5, but the principles for developing a hierarchy of strategic networks are the same.[4])

Let's look at Business Unit A. Suppose you've developed a strategic network for each product or service group, i through j. Now consider where sharing could be beneficial between these product and service groups. Constructing a diagram similar to that shown in Figure 20-2 (Steps 1 and 2) might help you visualize actual and potential linkages.

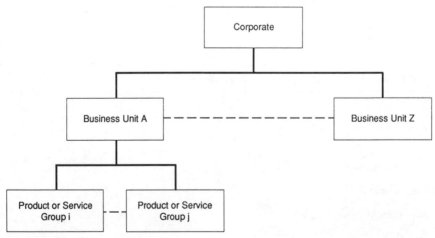

Figure 20-5. Organization chart.

(If you have a large number of product or service target markets, show linkages between product or service groups rather than between product or service target markets.)

Then, to help you understand how best to exploit sharing among Product and Service Groups i through j, go through Steps 3 and 4 again, only this time strive to optimize sharing possibilities between product and service groups.

The payoffs can be substantial. For example, two of Procter & Gamble's product groups (soap and toothpaste) each had a number of target markets. Some target markets were the same for both product groups.

Hotel buyers were one of these target markets. To capitalize on this linkage, Procter & Gamble created a hospitality marketing unit to handle all sales to hotel buyers. Overall costs went down. Result: a competitive advantage.

After you've looked for possible linkages between product and service groups, do the same for the business unit level.

Step 6. Make It Work

Four ingredients are key:

- Bottom up and top down
- Management teamwork
- Variable planning targets
- Management commitment

Bottom Up and Top Down

It's usually top down. Right?

You're right.

But that's wrong.

Find out what works in the marketplace. Start from there. And then integrate what works into a strategy. That's bottom up.

Avoid basing your strategy's linchpin on an idea that hasn't been proven to be successful in the field. Suppose you say, "Computers. Now that's an area we should be in. It would complement our present products and services quite nicely because we've got the technical capability to carry it off. Yes, that's where we should be." So this idea becomes the strategy for a business unit. Then it's up to middle management to find a way to make it work in the marketplace. Unfortunately, too often such a strategy is not implementable. It's just an idea.

If your strategy is like that, you'll probably join ranks with Xerox and computers, GE and computers, Exxon and office automation, and so on.[5]

An executive from a major Midwest electric company told us why their planning works. The company requires input from the field—the people who know what works and what doesn't. The role of corporate top management is to prioritize the company's efforts. But not without strong—and, as he emphasized, *strong*—input from lower echelons. The company's planning process is both bottom up and top down. And that's why it works.

Of course, perfecting such a comprehensive planning process doesn't happen overnight. Some companies claim it takes at least 3 years. But you can also count on some dividends immediately.

Management Teamwork

Horizontal strategies don't just develop. There are just too many barriers:

1. Unequal sharing. For example, see Figure 20-5. Product or Service Group i might benefit greatly by sharing the sales force with Product or Service Group j, but Product or Service Group j may actually be hindered by this relationship. Not an easy hurdle to overcome.

A consumer product company realized that distributing a variety of sample products to newlyweds would be an excellent way to introduce newly formed households to its brands.

That's when the trouble began.

Some product managers didn't want to repackage for this target market. "Too costly." Another product manager of a very upscale product didn't want his product to be associated with its "commonplace cousins." And still other product managers were concerned about how the costs would be shared.

While no one questioned the merits and long-term overall profitability of this program, the internal obstacles were never overcome.

2. Loss of control. Through sharing, a manager is less able to direct the destiny of his or her organization.

3. Performance evaluation and compensation. Managers are rewarded by the success of their fiefdoms. So why expect them to volunteer to hand over their resources?

Sharing between product or service lines can be managed, and often is, by business unit managers. However, in most companies business units are seen as stand-alone businesses. Consequently, the barriers to sharing are great. (But don't blame this on niche marketing. It's a common situation, regardless of the size of targeted segments.)

To get managers to work together:

1. Make sure that products, services, and target markets are grouped where linkages are most important.
2. Formalize committees and task forces that cut across your organizational structures. Use these to coordinate product and service, channel, and customer policies.
3. Use job rotations, training, and management get-togethers.
4. Base compensation packages on participation and cooperation in the three ways described above.

Variable Planning Targets

The third key ingredient for successful strategic networks is to avoid blanket planning targets. Set specific objectives for each niche product or service target market.

Suppose you have a target of 30 percent gross margin for your products and services.

Does that mean you should get a 30 percent gross margin across the board?

Of course not. Price sensitivities will vary. So each product and service should seek its optimum margin. The best margin for some may be over 30 percent. This allows the option for setting gross margins under 30 percent for others.

Surprisingly, many of the companies we talked with felt that the target gross margin was a mandate for each product or service. Only a few saw this as an opportunity for pricing flexibility.

Then there's another reason you shouldn't set blanket planning targets. Your niche product and service roles will be different. Some may be geared toward long-term growth. Some toward profitability. And so on.

Management Commitment

Finally, recognize that for some niche markets—those that you're developing—you must be realistic about short-range expectations. We found that this is where a lot of companies make big mistakes. They always expect immediate paybacks.

Set up, from the start, a minimum of time and funding required for support. Then get a commitment from management. This won't guarantee that funds will be available, but having a prior commitment will help.

Step 7. Evaluate Misfits, Then Develop Them or Drop Them

No doubt you found some product or service target markets that just didn't fit into your strategic network.

Suppose that research has told you the misfit is too valuable to let go. Further suppose that you have the resources to develop that niche. Here's what you should do: set it up as a stand-alone business.

Make it an entrepreneurial unit or "skunk works" (as it's called by some), with one person responsible for its success.

Don't—we repeat, don't—attach it to an existing business unit. Experience has shown that it just won't work. The new business will be trifling in comparison with existing business. Both will require time. And where will management put its efforts? The same place that you would.

For example, an architectural hardware wholesaler's main market was contractors who bought solely on a bid basis. For these contractors, price was their key buying motive. For the wholesaler, key success factors were low-cost blueprint takeoffs, proficiency in bidding, and large-volume purchases of hardware.

The wholesaler was considering a niche market of contractors who bought architectural hardware on a negotiated bid basis. However, these contractors differed from the bid-basis contractors. The primary concern of the former was that the hardware be exactly right, and they wanted plenty of service to see that it was. Although price was a factor, as long as it was in a reasonable range, it was OK. Clearly the key success factors for this niche were considerably different from those in the bid-basis market.

Wrap these businesses together and guess what would happen? (We've been through this before but it's worth repeating.) Management would spend its efforts on the large-volume, established bid-basis business. This elephant would sooner or later roll over and smother the fledgling negotiated bid-basis business.

As with managing niche products, running an entrepreneural unit may be a way to motivate and retain managers in slow-growth companies. For example, Hyatt had a large number of promising young managers. But its expansion rate of new hotels had slowed, meaning it would take years for these managers to get a chance to run a hotel. So Hyatt encouraged these managers to start new businesses under Hyatt's umbrella, such as a new waste-consulting company.[6]

But be careful not to overextend your resources. It will take more time and effort than you imagined to establish new businesses. Unless you give them the required time and resources, they will just become product and service target markets that didn't quite make it.

Recap

Building a strategic network will take time, resources, and effort. Probably far more than you imagine.

But the payoffs will be substantial.

You'll develop a second-to-none knowledge about your present and potential product and service target markets. By the time you've worked through the seven steps to building a strategic network, you'll be an expert on your company's operations, sales, advertising, R&D, and logistics. And if you really did your job, so will a lot of other people.

Maintaining your company's focus will become second nature. Niche products and services will be linked into a strategic network that will yield measurable benefits.

The addition of new niche product or service target markets will be based how they tie in with your overall strategy, helping you to avoid funding problems.

And here's something else to look forward to: the process will be easier next time. Once you've set up a network, periodic fine-tuning may be all that's required. At least for a while.

Epilogue

Focus, focus, focus.

We're back to where we started.

But we want to make sure you don't miss out on the passing parade.

So you've resegmented the market. You've out-niched your competitors and you're successful.

But it's a passing parade.

U.S. Shoe found out the hard way.

Demographic data revealed that more women were entering the workplace. U.S. Shoe acquired Casual Corner and concentrated on this niche. A good move. They out-niched their competitors. The 20-store chain expanded to 737 outlets by 1988.

But it's a passing parade.

New competitors, such as The Gap and The Limited, targeted customers even more narrowly. And Casual Corner, now out-niched, ran into trouble.[1] Casual Corner just forgot what made them famous.

Focus, focus, focus must be continual.

It's not like winning the big prize; it's a never ending search.

Steve Neumann, director of marketing research for Shering-Plough Health care products, claims:

> Segmentation has been one of the most critical strategies to our sun-care strategic business unit. We conducted a comprehensive attitudinal segmentation study among consumers in 1984 and again in 1987. This study has allowed us to keep in touch with the wants and needs of a niche-oriented market which is incredibly volatile.

However, every 3 years—especially in some industries—may not be often enough. You really need to establish a dialogue with your niche on an ongoing basis so you can test ideas. You've got to keep in touch!

But don't rely solely on formal surveys, regardless of how often they're conducted.

The former speaker of the U.S. House of Representatives, Tip O'Neill, used to say, "All politics is local."

The same is true of marketing. All marketing is local. Back to what Ervin Shames, president of Kraft USA, says, "Talk to consumers individually, not as a group."

Marketers should spend perhaps 50 percent of their time in the field. But your whole firm must become market-oriented. See to it that everyone in your company has occasional contacts with customers.

Make your focus on customers continuous.

And this is right where you should begin.

Appendix

KEY BUYING MOTIVES: INDUSTRIAL PRODUCT

Referral   _____

Performance (Primary, measurable operating characteristics
of a product. Examples: a lift truck's load capacity, acceleration,
and handling).

_____

Features (Measurable characteristics of a product that
supplements performance. Examples: air conditioning on a
lift truck, technical advice, training, and adaptability for
technical upgrade).

_____

Reliability (The probability of a product's not failing within a
specified period of time).

_____

Conformance (The degree to which a product meets established
standards).

_____

Durability (Use one gets from a product before it breaks down
and replacement is preferable to continued repair; also
trade-in/resale value).

_____

Serviceability (Maintenance costs, availability of replacement
parts and service, cost of service, ease of servicing, extent of
downtime required for servicing, and certainty of continuity
of service).

_____

Aesthetics (Users' tastes, such as preference of design and
appearance).

_____

Perceived Quality (Users' impression of the product stemming
from, for example, general reputation of the firm; exclusivity;
customer list; quality of advertising and salespersons; and loyalty
toward brand, salespersons, dealers, distributors).

_____

Reciprocity   _____

Awareness   _____

Availability (hours, location)   _____

Tradition (habitual behavior)   _____

Low Price (including deals)   _____

Trial Offer   _____

Billing Procedure/Credit Terms   _____

Delivery   _____

KEY BUYING MOTIVES: PROFESSIONAL SERVICES

Performance (Primary, measurable characteristics of a service. Examples: prompt service and absence of waiting time).

_____   _____
_____

Features (Measurable characteristics of a service that supplement performance. Examples: location and hours).

_____   _____
_____

Conformance (The degree to which a service meets established standards).

_____   _____
_____

Serviceability (Certainty of continuity of service).

_____   _____
_____

Aesthetics (Users' tastes, such as appearance of report).

_____   _____
_____

Perceived Quality (Users' impression of the service stemming from, for example, general reputation of the firm, exclusivity, customer list, quality of advertising and salespersons, and loyalty toward salespersons).

_____   _____
_____

Reciprocity   _____

Awareness   _____

Tradition (habitual behavior)   _____

Low Price (including deals)   _____

Trial Offer   _____

Billing Procedure/Credit Terms   _____

Referral   _____

KEY BUYING MOTIVES:
PACKAGED FOODS, BEVERAGES, AND DRUGS

Performance (Primary, measurable characteristics of a product. Examples: Flavor, essence, nutrition/healthfulness, freshness, and shelflife).

_____ _____

Features (Measurable characteristics of a product that supplement performance. Examples: convenience of use and packaging).

_____ _____

Conformance (The degree to which a product meets established standards).

_____ _____

Aesthetics (Users' tastes, such as preference of design and appearance).

_____ _____

Perceived Quality (Users' impression of the product stemming from, for example, general reputation of firm; exclusivity; customer list; quality of advertising and salespersons; and loyalty toward brand, salespersons, dealers, distributors).

_____ _____

Reciprocity   _____

Awareness   _____

Availability (hours, location)   _____

Tradition (habitual behavior)   _____

Low Price (including deals)   _____

Trial Offer   _____

Billing Procedure/Credit Terms   _____

Delivery   _____

*Adapted from Ronald R. Gist, *The Executive Course in Marketing Management*, Denver, 1987, and David A. Garvin, *Managing Quality*, (New York: The Free Press, 1988), Chapter 4.

The charts on pages 239–241 are from Robert E. Linneman, *How to Prepare and Use the Annual Marketing Plan*, New York: Penton Learning Systems, 1989, p. 3.88–3.89. Reprinted with permission.

COMPETITIVE BENCHMARKING CHART				
	Your Firm	Competitor	Competitor	Competitor
Key Success Factors	(Ratings of Comparative Key Success Factor Strengths: High=3, Average=2, and Low=1; Trend by ↑, —, or ↓)			
1.				
2.				
3.				
4.				
5.				
Target Market's Ratings of Augmented Product/Services	(Superior, Above Average, Average, Below Average, Inferior)			
Relative Financial Strength	(Very Strong=3, Average=2, Weak=1; Trend by ↑, —, ↓)			
Company Commitment	(Aggressive=3, Holding=2, Divestment=1)			

Adapted from Robert E. Linneman, *How to Prepare and Use the Annual Marketing Plan*, New York: Penton Learning Systems, 1989, p. 3.27. Reprinted with permission.

PRODUCT OR SERVICE
TARGET MARKET PLAN

Product or Service _____
_____

Target Market _____
_____

Key Buying Motives   Key Success Factors

_____   _____
_____   _____
_____   _____
_____   _____
_____   _____

i

TABLE OF CONTENTS

ii

ACTION PLANS

ACTION PLAN	Start Date	Completion Date	Formal Review	Responsibility

Action Plans: Describe each major program to be carried to. Use as many pages as necessary. Then, for each program, specify what steps need to. Describe what steps needed to. Specify the persons responsible and the timetables as necessary.

2

STRATEGY

SALES AND PROFIT OBJECTIVES

Month	Sales			Profit		
	Planned	Actual	Variance	Planned	Actual	Variance
Jan.						
Feb.						
Mar.						
Apr.						
May						
June						
July						
Aug.						
Sept.						
Oct.						
Nov.						
Dec.						

Sales and Profit Objectives: The profit criterion used here is gross profit, such as merchandising profit. You may wish to use some other criterion, such as profit.

1

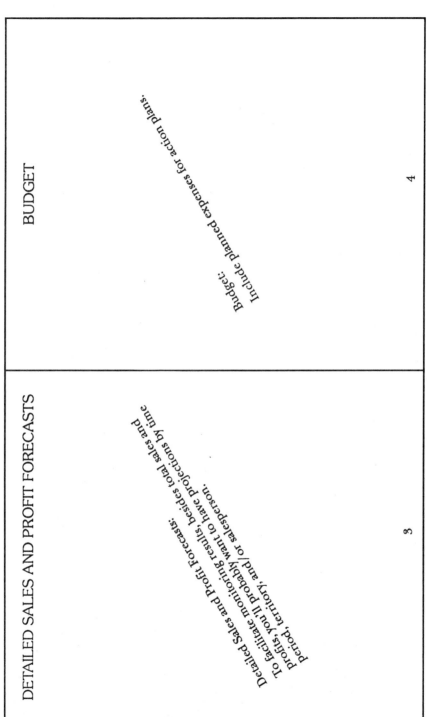

DETAILED SALES AND PROFIT FORECASTS	BUDGET
Detailed Sales and Profit Forecasts: To facilitate monitoring results, besides total sales and profits, you'll probably want to have projections by time period, territory, and/or salesperson. 3	Budget: Include planned expenses for action plans. 4

The product or service target market plan is adapted from Robert E. Linneman, *How to Prepare and Use the Annual Marketing Plan*, New York: Penton Learning Systems, 1989, pp. 3.162–3.164. Reprinted with permission.

SUMMARY MARKETING PLAN

TABLE OF CONTENTS

i

OVERALL STRATEGY

CONSOLIDATED SALES AND PROFIT OBJECTIVES

Month	Sales Planned	Sales Actual	Sales Variance	Profit Planned	Profit Actual	Profit Variance
Jan.						
Feb.						
Mar.						
Apr.						
May						
June						
July						
Aug.						
Sept.						
Oct.						
Nov.						
Dec.						

— Consolidated Sales and Profit Objectives or service
— Consolidated Sales of individual product or service
— Consolidated totals Copy
— Consolidated totals of individual plans, p. 2.
— Consolidated will be totals plans, p. 2.
— Figures market plans, p. 2.
— target market plans,

1

GENERAL PROGRAM ACTION PLANS

ACTION PLAN	Start Date	Completion Date	Formal Review	Responsibility

General Program Action Plans:

General Program Action some following new programs.
You may need to perform to any of plans, some more than one
are not related to market; it may will apply programs need to
or service. Also, advertising target of these major steps persons
research, advertising target each, specify the persons.
as blanket or service each, specify, and necessary.
product and describe program, timetables, as necessary.
List and major the timetables many pages as one
For each out. Use as many pages as
be carried.
responsible.

4

PRODUCT OR SERVICE TARGET MARKET PLANS

Product or Service _____

Target Market _____

Strategy _____

SALES AND PROFIT OBJECTIV..., p.

		Sales		Variance	
Month	Planned	Actual			
Jan.					
Feb.					
Mar.					
Apr.					
May					
June					
Sep					
Oct					
Nov.					
Dec.					

Target Market Market market plan, p.
Target Target market plan, p.
Target Service service target market plan, p.
Product or Service service target market plan, p.
For each Product or service target market plan, p.
Description appropriate product or service target market plan
Copy from appropriate product product
Copy (Major appropriate Objectives
Strategy from appropriate product
Copy and Profit appropriate
Sales from appropriate
Copy

2

GENERAL PROGRAM BUDGET

General Program Budget: from general program in and any product or service market plans.
Include planned overhead costs not included in individual product or service target market plans.

7

CONSOLIDATED BUDGET

Consolidated Budget: Summary for each product or service target market plan.
Summary of the general program budget and market plan.

8

The summary marketing plan is adapted from Robert E. Linneman, *How to Prepare and Use the Annual Marketing Plan*, New York: Penton Learning Systems, 1989, pp. 3.166–3.168. Reprinted with permission.

Notes

Introduction

1. Laurel Cutler, vice president of FCB/Leber Katz, a New York advertising agency and vice president for consumer affairs for Chrysler, quoted in "Stars of the 1980's Cast Their Light," *Fortune,* July 3, 1989, p. 76.
2. Robert D. Buzzell and Bradley T. Gale, *The PIMS Principles: Linking Strategy to Performance,* The Free Press, New York, 1987, p. 3.
3. J. A. Cookson, "British Machine Tools Fill a Niche in U.S. Market," *Manufacturing Engineering,* August 1988, pp. 81–83.
4. Peter Savage and Alice Agoos, "Higher Returns Attract Resins to Niches," *Chemical Week,* May 6, 1987, pp. 24, 26.
5. Andrew A. Boccone, "Specialty Chemicals: In Pursuit of Fast-Growth Niche Markets," *Chemical Week,* April 12, 1989, pp. 32–34.
6. Christine Dugas, Mark N. Vamos, and Jonathan B. Levine, "Marketing's New Look," *Business Week,* January 26, 1987, pp. 64–69.

1 Focus, Focus, Focus

1. Alex Taylor, III, "Here Come Japan's New Luxury Cars," *Fortune,* August 14, 1989, p. 62.
2. Thomas V. Bonoma, "What We Teach Is What We Get—Unfortunately," *Marketing News,* May 8, 1989, p. 17.
3. Ervin R. Shames, "Growing Big by Acting Small," *The 1988 Marketing Conference,* The Conference Board, New York, November 1, 1988.
4. Kenichi Ohmae, "Getting Back to Strategy," *Harvard Business Review,* November–December 1988, p. 154.
5. "Soup Researcher Defends Ad Claims by Citing Federal Data," *Marketing News,* February 2, 1984, p. 30.

2 Building a Niche-Marketing Database

1. Vince Gennaro, "The Future of Regional Marketing," *Lucrative Regional Marketing Strategies Conference,* The Marketing Institute, April 12, 1989.
2. Teri Agins, *The Wall Street Journal,* November 20, 1990, p. B6.
3. Stan Rapp, "Cigaret Giants Pioneer Data-Base Marketing in Packaged-Goods," *Marketing News,* December 5, 1988, p. 17.

4. Elliot Zwiebach, "Vons Has High Hopes for High Tech," *Supermarket News,* July 16, 1990, p. 45.
5. Janet Nesman, "Reach Out and Call Someone at Gerber," *Adweek's Marketing Week,* May 22, 1989, p. 23.
6. Elizabeth White Ludlow, "Developing, Designing and Distinguishing New Products for Specific Consumer Segments," *Innovative Niche Marketing Strategies Conference,* The Marketing Institute, April 4, 1989.

3 Mining for Niches: Where to Look First

1. Arch G. Woodside, Victor J. Cook, Jr., and William A. Mindak, "Profiling the Heavy Traveler Segment," *Journal of Travel Research,* Spring 1987, pp. 9–14.
2. Jeffrey Trachtenberg, "Firms Seek to Ring in New Customers," *The Wall Street Journal,* March 23, 1989, p. Bl.
3. Lynn W. Adkins, "Today, Airstream Is Looking Younger," *Adweek's Marketing Week,* November 20, 1989, p. 22.
4. Adapted from David A. Garvin, "Competing on the Eight Dimensions of Quality," *Harvard Business Review,* November–December 1987, pp. 101–109.
5. Michael E. Porter, *Competitive Advantage: Creating and Sustaining Superior Performance,* The Free Press, New York, 1985, pp. 144–146. For a more complete description, see this source.
6. Gary J. Coles and James D. Culley, "Not all Prospects Are Created Equal," *Business Marketing,* May 1986, p. 56.
7. "Business Bulletin," *The Wall Street Journal,* February 16, 1989, p. A1.
8. Joe G. Thomas and J. M. Koonce, "Differentiating a Commodity: Lessons from Tyson Foods," *Planning Review,* September/October 1989, pp. 24–29.
9. Coles and Culley, pp. 52–58.

4 Mining for Niches: Where to Look Next

1. Cheryl Russell, "25 Particle Markets." Reprinted with permission © American Demographics, 1990, Ithaca, N.Y.

5 The Basic Differentiation Strategies

1. Alex F. Osborn, *Applied Imagination,* 3d rev. ed., Scribner's, New York, 1963, pp. 286–287.
2. "Timex Springs into Action and Winds Up with a New Audience," *Adweek's Marketing Week,* December 12, 1988, pp. 62–63.
3. Clare Ansberry, "Kodak Stakes Out the High End of Market With New Color Film," *The Wall Street Journal,* October 5, 1988, p. B6.
4. Thomas Gross and John L. Neuman, "Picking the Best Strategists' Brains," *Marketing News,* October 10, 1988, p. 16.
5. Jacob M. Schlesinger, "Back to the Future. After Era of Blandness, Big and

Glitzy Autos Are Making Comeback," *The Wall Street Journal,* December 7, 1988, pp. A1, A8.

6. Elizabeth White Ludlow, "Developing, Designing and Distinguishing New Products for Specific Consumer Segments," *Innovative Niche Marketing Strategies Conference,* The Marketing Institute, April 4, 1989.

7. Cynthia Crossen, "Waldenbooks Peddles Books a Bit Like Soap, Transforming Market," *The Wall Street Journal,* October 10, 1988, pp. A1, A6.

8. John Motavalli, "Toward an Age of Customized Magazines," *Adweek Special Report, Magazine World 1989,* February 13, 1989, pp. 36–37.

9. Ron Jackson, "Message to the Media: Innovate or Stagnate," *Marketing News,* July 3, 1989, p. 9.

10. Dennis Kneale, "CBS Predicts Networks' Audience Will Decline Up to 10% This Fall," *The Wall Street Journal,* August 3, 1988, p. 24.

11. Lawrence Hooper, "'Segment' is New Buzzword for PC Sellers," *The Wall Street Journal,* June 21, 1990, pp. B1, B4.

12. Ronald Alsop, "Direct Marketing for Packaged Goods," *The Wall Street Journal,* May 26, 1988, p. 29.

13. Tracy A. La Flamme, "Audi's Lifestyle Marketing Plan Targets Athletes of Upscale Sports," *Marketing News,* August 15, 1988, pp. 1–2.

14. Jonathan Clements, "On the Ad for Burial Plots, Guess Whose Name Is on the Tombstone," *The Wall Street Journal,* November 1, 1990, p. B1.

6 Six Commonsense Rules for Differentiation

1. For an interesting—and very readable—discussion of line extensions, see Al Reis and Jack Trout, *Positioning: The Battle For Your Mind,* Warner Books, New York, 1986, pp. 99, 124–125.

2. Robert D. Hof, "A Washout for Clorox?" *Business Week,* July 9, 1990, pp. 32–33.

3. Douglas C. McGill, "7-Up Gold: The Failure Of a Can't Lose Plan," *The New York Times,* February 11, 1989, pp.35, 44.

7 Avoiding Cannibalization

1. Elizabeth White Ludlow, "Developing, Designing and Distinguishing New Products for Specific Consumer Segments," *Innovative Niche Marketing Strategies Conference,* The Marketing Institute, April 4, 1989.

2. Kyle Chadwick, "Coke Gives Tab a Second Chance," *Adweek's Marketing Week,* July 17, 1989, p. 1.

3. Patrick McGeehan, "Eastman Kodak and Fugi's Zoom in on Advanced Amateurs," *Adweek's Marketing Week,* April 17, 1989, p. 24.

4. John A. Lacy, "New Uses, New Users," *The 1988 Marketing Conference,* The Conference Board, New York, November 1-2, 1988.

5. George Lazarus, "Lazarus at Large," *Adweek's Marketing Week,* March 13, 1989, p. 61.

6. Amy Dunkin, Michael O'Neal, and Kevin Kelly, "The Globe-Trotter Who Took Philip Morris Global," *Business Week*, August 8, 1988, p. 58.

8 Making Regional Marketing Work

1. Lori Kesler, "A-B Benefits from Regional Approach," *Advertising Age*, February 27, 1986, pp. 48–49.
2. Alix M. Freedman, "National Firms Find that Selling to Local Tastes is Costly, Complex," *The Wall Street Journal*, February 9, 1987, p. 21.
3. Judith D. Schwartz, "Pitching the Big Top in 90 Different Markets," *Adweek's Marketing Week*, May 8, 1989, pp. 58–59.
4. Adapted from a speech given by Paul Masaracchio, general manager, Campbell Soup Company, 1989.

9 Test, Test, Test

1. Bob Kukla, "Meeting Customer Needs," *Quality Progress*, June 1986, pp. 15–18.

10 Competing in a Favorable Weight Class

1. Stephen Phillips, Amy Dunkin, James B. Treece, and Keith H. Hammonds, "King Customer," *Business Week*, March 12, 1990, cover.
2. This example, as well as some other examples in Guidelines 10 and 11, come from Al Ries and Jack Trout, *Marketing Warfare*, McGraw-Hill, New York, 1986. Readers who would like a more complete—and very entertaining—coverage of marketing warfare are urged to read this book.
3. For a comprehensive treatment on attacking an industry leader, see Michael E. Porter, *Competitive Advantage: Creating and Sustaining Superior Performance*, The Free Press, New York, 1985, pp. 513–536.

11 How to Keep From Being Outniched

1. Philip Kotler, *Marketing Management: Analysis, Planning and Control*, 5th ed., Prentice-Hall, Englewood Cliffs, N.J., 1984, p. 392.
2. Alix M. Freedman, "Mars Struggles to Reclaim Candy Crown," *The Wall Street Journal*, March 29, 1989, p. 31.
3. Most of these tactics on raising barriers come from Michael E. Porter, *Competitive Advantage: Creating and Sustaining Superior Performance*, The Free Press, New York, 1985, pp. 489–492.
4. "Japanese Heat on the Watch Industry," *Business Week*, May 5, 1980, pp. 92–103.
5. James C. Abegglen and George Stalk, Jr., *Kaisha: The Japanese Corporation*, Basic Books, New York, 1985, pp. 48–51.

13 Dealing with Production and Operations Problems

1. Jeremy Main, "Manufacturing the Right Way," *Fortune*, May 21, 1990, p. 54.
2. David A. Garvin, *Managing Quality*, The Free Press, New York, 1988, p. 30.
3. Otis Port, "Back to Basics," *Business Week*, Special Issue, "Innovation in America," 1989, p. 18.
4. Peter Nulty, "The Soul of An Old Machine," *Fortune*, May 21, 1990, pp. 67-72.
5. Brian Dumaine, "Who Needs a Boss?" *Fortune*, May 7, 1990, pp. 52–60.
6. Ibid.
7. Al Senia, "How McDonnell Douglas is Making Productivity Pay," *Production*, April 1986, pp. 77–79.
8. Vaughn Beals, "Harley-Davidson: An American Success Story," *Journal for Quality Participation*, June 1988, pp. A19–A23.
9. Sharon Nelton, "Socking It to the Old Style," *Nation's Business*, May 1985, p. 63.
10. James C. Abegglen and George Stalk, Jr., *Kaisha: The Japanese Corporation*, Basic Books, New York, 1985, p. 97.
11. Ibid., pp. 91–92, 103.
12. Jeremy Main, pp. 54–64.
13. Ibid., p. 56.
14. Ibid., p. 54.
15. Ibid., p. 56.
16. Tamotsu Harada, *Office Equipment & Products* (Japan), December 1987, pp. 51–53.

14 Dealing with Logistics Problems

1. Edward H. Frazelle, "Soko Circles in Action," *Handling & Shipping Management*, November 1986, pp. 79–82.
2. Gene R. Tyndall, "Strategic Alliances Must Be True Partnerships, " *Marketing News*, April 30, 1990, p. 8.
3. James C. Abegglen and George Stalk, Jr., *Kaisha: The Japanese Corporation*, Basic Books, New York, 1985, p. 98.
4. Ibid., p. 91.
5. Ibid., p. 97.
6. "Bar Codes Speed Shipping, Achieve 99.7% Accuracy," *Modern Materials Handling*, September 1985, pp. 88–89.
7. George M. Floor, "Hands-On Inventory Management," *Industrial Distribution*, June 1988, pp. 39–41.
8. Gary Forger, "Our AS/RS Delivers Parts 1,500 Miles Away Daily," *Modern Materials Handling*, March 1989, pp. 85–87.
9. James C. Johnson and Donald F. Wood, *Contemporary Physical Distribution and Logistics*, PennWell Books, Tulsa, Okla., 1982, pp. 619–20.
10. Denis J. Davis and Cathy Coffman, "Reshaping Warehouse Strategies," *Distribution*, December 1985, pp. 10–17.

15   Dealing with Channel Problems

1. Sean Milmo, "Europeans 'Piggyback' to Boost Sales Abroad," *Business Marketing,* July 1986, p. 20.
2. James A. Narus and James C. Anderson, "Turn Your Industrial Distributors into Partners," *Harvard Business Review,* March-April 1986, pp. 66–71.

16   Dealing with Organization and Planning Problems

1. John A. Byrne, "Is Your Company Too Big," *Business Week,* March 27, 1989, p. 92.
2. Ibid.
3. Ibid.
4. Ibid., p. 94.
5. For a detailed description, including sample forms, of how to set up a fact book, product or service target market plan, and summary plan, see Robert E. Linneman, *How to Prepare and Use the Annual Marketing Plan,* Penton Learning Systems, New York, 1988.

17   Dealing with Personnel Problems

1. Anthony Jay, *Corporation Man,* Random House, New York, 1971, p. 175.
2. "Gutoff's Rough Ride at Standard Brands," *Business Week,* October 16, 1978, p. 54.
3. Christine Dugas, Mark N. Vamos, and Jonathan B. Levine, "Marketing's New Look," *Business Week,* January 26, 1987, p. 69.
4. Richard Gibson, "Now If Only This Would Happen Over at Publishers Clearing House," *The Wall Street Journal,* June 14, 1989, Section B, p. 1.
5. "Banks Woo Small Firms, But Service Is Lacking," *The Wall Street Journal,* June 29, 1989, p. B1.
6. Joseph Weber, Lisa Driscoll, Richard Brandt, "Farewell, Fast Track," *Business Week,* December 10, 1990, pp. 192–200.

18   Dealing with Advertising Problems

1. Jon Berry, "Crossover Dreams," *Business Marketing 1989, Adweek,* May 22, 1989, p. B.M.4.
2. Cyndee Miller, "Video Makes Fashion Statement, Sets the Mood for Catalogue Sales," *Marketing News,* October 10, 1988, p. 23.

19 Dealing with Sales-Force Problems

1. Tom Eisenhart, "Cross Selling Spells Sales Success," *Business Marketing*, November 1988, p. 60.

20 Developing a Niche-Marketing Network

1. Adapted in part from Michael E. Porter, *Competitive Advantage: Creating and Sustaining Superior Performance*, The Free Press, New York, 1985, Ch. 10.
2. Bruce D. Henderson, *Henderson on Corporate Strategy*, ABT Books, Cambridge, Mass., 1979, p. 38.
3. For a more complete description, see Michael E. Porter, *Competitive Strategy: Techniques for Analyzing Industries and Competitors*, The Free Press, New York, 1980, pp. 3–29.
4. For a more complete description, see Michael E. Porter, *Competitive Advantage: Creating and Sustaining Superior Performance*, The Free Press, New York, 1985, pp. 317–415.
5. For more information on this subject, see Al Ries and Jack Trout, *Bottom Up Marketing*, McGraw-Hill, New York, 1989.
6. Joseph Weber, Lisa Driscoll, Richard Brandt, "Farewell, Fast Track," *Business Week*, December 10, 1990, pp. 192–200.

Epilogue

1. Steven Phillips, "Why U.S. Shoe Is Looking Down at the Heel," *Business Week*, July 4, 1988, pp. 60–61.

Index